Window on the West

the

COLLECTOR'S
EL PALACIO

MUSEUM OF NEW MEXICO FOUNDATION
SANTA FE

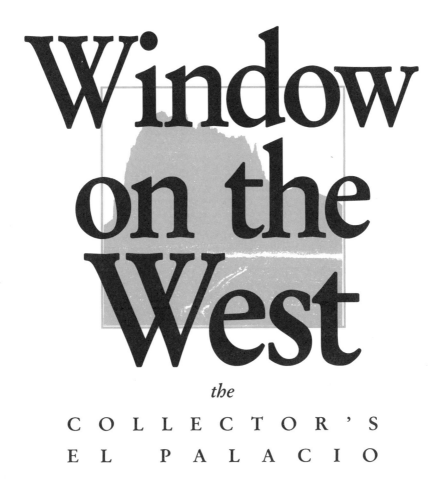

FIRST EDITION

Copyright © 1989 by the Museum of New Mexico Foundation

ISBN 0-9623304-0-X

Library of Congress Catalog Card Number 89-062009

Published by the Museum of New Mexico Foundation
Post Office Box 2065, Santa Fe, New Mexico 87504

Typeset in CG Times by Copygraphics, Inc., Santa Fe, New Mexico
Printed by McNaughton & Gunn, Inc., Ann Arbor, Michigan
Designed by Christopher Beisel

CONTENTS

ILLUSTRATIONS

PREFACE

W*indow on the West.* A fitting title for a collection of articles from *El Palacio*, the country's oldest continuously published museum magazine, which for 76 years has represented in print the collections, scholarship, and mission of the Museum of New Mexico—itself a window on the American West.

For longtime friends of the Museum, this anthology will be a mirror, reflecting as it does the endeavors and personalities of the past. For the new reader, we hope it will begin a relationship with a museum which celebrates its 80th birthday simultaneous with our publication.

Above all, we hope "The Collector's *El Palacio*" will be an eminently readable and enjoyable reminder of the vigorous role played by the Museum of New Mexico and its magazine—now published for the Museum by the Museum of New Mexico Foundation—in the rich intellectual history of a uniquely rich region.

SANDRA PREWITT EDELMAN
Publisher, *El Palacio*
Executive Director,
Museum of New Mexico Foundation

INTRODUCTION

From the appearance of its first issue in November 1913, coincident with the opening of the Museum of New Mexico in the newly renovated Palace of the Governors in Santa Fe, the Museum's magazine, *El Palacio*, was ambitious in its scope. In the first issue, editor Paul A.F. Walter explained the structure and origins of the Museum, discussed the initiation of excavations at Quarai, and reported enthusiastically on the renovation of the Palace, whose "structure inside and out appears like a cyclopean monolith and is admired by hosts of visitors." Also included in the issue were poems, book reviews, notices of upcoming meetings and other events at the Palace, and news concerning the artistic and literary community. But Walter promised more than that to come.

El Palacio lived up to this promise, through the years providing news of scholarly achievement in anthropology, history, fine art, and folk art, chiefly within the West but at times ranging further afield. In the early years it also supplied notices of social and cultural events in Santa Fe and featured lists of gifts to the Museum of New Mexico—sometimes rather pointedly juxtaposed with notices of generous gifts to other museums.

The driving force behind *El Palacio* for its first forty-five years was Paul A.F. Walter, a modest, dedicated man of seemingly endless talents and energies who also edited and ultimately owned Santa Fe's newspaper, *The New Mexican*; founded the *New Mexico Historical Review*; wrote *The Cities That Died of Fear*, a book on the Saline Pueblos; was president of the First National Bank of Santa Fe; and served as a regent of the Museum of New Mexico and a president of the School of American Research. In a 1982 tribute to him in *El Palacio*, Beatrice Chauvenet wrote of Walter: "Privy to the secrets of politicians, scientists and bankers, he kept them to himself. . . . An unobtrusive power behind the scenes, he lived and wrote history."

Walter was followed by a number of talented and hard-working editors, some more visible as personalities in the pages of *El Palacio* than he had been, and all with shorter tenure. *El Palacio*'s editors have included:

Paul A.F. Walter 1913-1958
Bruce T. Ellis 1958-1960
Wayne L. Mauzy 1960-1962
Richard Wormser 1962
Fred Wendorf/
Eastburn Smith 1963

Carol Scott Alley 1966-1968
John C. MacGregor IV 1968
Carl E. Rosnek/
Phyllis Hughes 1968-1976
Richard Polese 1976-1982
Malinda Elliott 1982-1983
Jane Rosenfelt 1983
Malinda Elliott 1984
John Sherman 1984-1985
Malinda Elliott 1986
Sarah Nestor 1987-1989

El Palacio has changed size, format, and schedule numerous times through the years, has varied its approach from the scholarly to the popular to something in between, and has worried about these things. Editor Bruce Ellis, writing in 1958, explained that:

We wish to forestall any misguided attempts of our readers to draw an analogy between this modest mention of *El Palacio*'s new, larger size and different appearance and current publicity on the 1958 American automobiles, by stating firmly that ours is a purely practical measure—to give our heretofore cramped contributors more space per page and at the same time to hold down costs by slightly reducing the number of pages. The new page size, we believe, should meet with the approval of both authors and readers. We do not place much stock in the argument that the smaller size of the old *E P* made it convenient for carrying in a pocket and was therefore of cultural value. A nationwide survey of our readers turned up but one instance of an *E P* being carried, and that was a fat 1956 issue which was habitually worn by an Upper Pecos subscriber in his left jacket-pocket —not for casual reading, but to counterbalance, by its weight, his tendency to wander in clockwise circles when he was lost in the woods. Needless to say, we do not publish a magazine for such purposes.

Despite the slings of outrageous fortune, *El Palacio* has survived and prospered to the present day, supplying informative, lively, and sometimes provocative articles in the areas of interest to the Museum of New Mexico. The oldest continuously published museum magazine in the country, the award-winning *El Palacio* is a mature seventy-six this year.

In tribute to this fact we have assembled the present volume. Our goal has been to select articles that span the years and demonstrate a breadth of subjects and approaches. We have looked always for substantial content and good writing. Punctuation has been updated, typographical errors corrected, and digressive sections deleted, but the articles are otherwise printed as they originally appeared.

The sections are introduced by people long associated with the Museum of New Mexico and greatly respected in their fields. George Ewing was director of the Laboratory of Anthropology from 1967 to 1973, director of the Museum of New Mexico from 1973 to 1981, and Cultural Affairs Officer from 1981 to 1983. Michael Weber worked in the History Division of the Museum of New Mexico from 1964 to 1947 and served as director of that division from 1970 to 1982. Edna Robertson worked at the Museum of New Mexico from 1959 to 1979, chiefly as curator of collections at the Museum of Fine Arts. Yvonne Lange was director of the Museum of International Folk Art from 1971 to 1983. And John Sinclair was the first curator at Lincoln State Monument, from 1940 to 1942, and then curator at Coronado State Monument from 1944 to 1946 and from 1947 to 1963.

Finally, we have appended a "nostalgia" section to the book. Although, with the growth of Santa Fe, *El Palacio* is no longer able to supply news of local residents and events, we think these excerpts capture the exuberant mood of the era in which the magazine had its start.

SARAH NESTOR
Editor, *El Palacio*

ANTHROPOLOGY

The Southwestern United States has had strong attraction for members of the anthropological profession for many years. Perhaps not the least reason for this is the fact that it is an attractive and accessible place in which to do fieldwork. Beyond that, of course, is the existence here of a variety of interesting and colorful indigenous cultures which have survived long beyond the time when their counterparts elsewhere in the country have deteriorated or disappeared altogether. Additionally, the Southwest has been occupied for many thousands of years, with the result that it is literally seeded with archeological sites under conditions very nearly ideal for preservation. Small wonder, then, that anthropologists of all shades of interest—archeologists, ethnographers, ethnologists, linguists— and others have elected to get their training and conduct their field research in the Southwest.

Over the years, the Museum of New Mexico and the School of American Research, plus the University of New Mexico and the Laboratory of Anthropology, Inc., provided the primary institutional support for anthropological research in New Mexico. And during that time, the journal *El Palacio* was a major publication resource for preliminary reports on archeological excavations as well as for ethnographic accounts of a general nature. In consequence, *El Palacio* itself has become an important resource for research as well as a historical record of activities and trends in Southwestern anthropology. In this section are presented the works of four individuals, each of whom made a lasting contribution to their individual areas of anthropological concern.

Clyde Kluckhohn, who went on to a distinguished career at Harvard University and who received wide acclaim for his landmark book, *Mirror for Man*, is represented in an article from a 1923 issue of *El Palacio*. "The Dance of Hasjelti" describes a nine-day Navajo ceremony held at Thoreau, New Mexico, for the dual purposes of curing a tribal member of a serious affliction and adopting another individual into a major Navajo clan. Subsequent to the period of this article, Native Americans began assuming more protective control over their ceremonial rituals, which are now less subject to study and publication. For this reason alone, ethnographic accounts such as this, by one of the country's preeminent anthropologists, is of considerable historic as well as anthropological interest.

Interestingly, the field of anthropology attracted and accepted a number of women at a time when many academic disciplines were the almost exclusive province of men. And many of these, who entered the field in their youth, attained senior status in their respective specializations and made significant contributions to anthropological studies in the Southwest. Marjorie Ferguson Tichy, better known to many of us by her later married name, Marjorie Lambert, is representative of those women who entered the strenuous and demanding field of archeology. Her *El Palacio* article, "The Archaeology of Puaray," is an excellent example of a careful but comprehensive report of excavation of an important and controversial Pueblo site along the Rio Grande. (To clarify a matter confusing to many, it should be noted that some years subsequent to the publication of this 1939 article, American anthropologists elected to simplify the spelling of its grubbiest sub-discipline by dropping the "ae" diphthong, although their British colleagues retain the Latinized spelling to the present time.) Marjorie Lambert pursued a long and successful career in archeology with the Museum of New Mexico, and after retirement, continued her professional endeavors in affiliation with the School of American Research.

Gertrude Kurath exemplifies an increasing trend in ethnographic studies toward a closely circumscribed specialization of interest. Taking dance and ceremonial movement as her particular concern, she achieved unique status in the field of anthropology. The colorful ceremonies of the Pueblo people have attracted and excited virtually all who have come into contact with them, but Kurath alone, employing a system of notation largely of her own devising, has been able to record the form and movement. Her 1958 article reproduced here, "Plaza Circuits of Tewa Indian Dancers," was prelude to her major work on the pre-Conquest dances of Meso-America.

Dr. Florence Hawley Ellis scarcely needs introduction to any with even a cursory knowledge of the Southwest. Respected scholar, prolific author, revered teacher, Ellis has made salient contributions to almost every area of Southwestern anthropology. As professor of anthropology at the University of New Mexico, she introduced countless numbers of students to the peoples and cultures of the Southwest and started not a few on the way to becoming professional colleagues. Her 1967 article, "Where Did the Pueblo People Come From?," clearly reflects years of study and experience and a remarkable breadth of knowledge. She draws upon archeological, ethnographic, and linguistic information in postulating answers to the origin, or origins, of the modern Pueblos—a very complex consideration thoughtfully presented by a senior Southwestern anthropologist.

— GEORGE EWING

THE DANCE OF HASJELTI

BEING AN ACCOUNT OF THE YEIBITCHAI
HELD AT THOREAU, N.M.

NOVEMBER 9th to 18th

BY CLYDE E. KLUCKHOHN

VOLUME 15, NUMBER 12
December 15, 1923

The Navajo ceremonial of Hasjelti Dailijs is a nine-day "medicine sing" held to cure some important member of the tribe from illness. It is always held "when the thunder sleeps." In this case the object of the ceremony was twofold: Firstly—to heal the mastoid infection of Nas Ta Ji Ya Ye (the Zuni's step son); secondly, formally to adopt Chissee Nez (the tall Apache), better known as Mr. B.I. Staples, of Thoreau, into the Tsinajini clan of the Navajo nation.

Hasjelti Dailijs is more commonly known among both "Dinne" and "Bilakana" as Yeibitchai. The literal meaning of the word is "the maternal grandfathers of the giants." The name rather summarizes the various deities who take part in the ceremony.

The medicine hogan was erected near the summer home of Mr. Staples, about two miles north of Thoreau. The timbers were from a medicine hogan which had been used in a fire dance some years before. At the same time the large shelter which was to serve as a communal cooking house was constructed.

FIRST DAY OF THE CEREMONY

The chief medicine man—Hosteen Latsanith Begay (the son of Mr. Blond Man)—arrived the morning of November 9th. The remainder of the day was spent in the instruction of the youths who were to assist in the proceedings.

After dark the first ceremony began. The bright fire in the center of the hogan showed the chief medicine man, or song priest, seated on the west side of the lodge facing east. An imposing figure, tall and well proportioned. He wore his black and white blanket with an air of great dignity. His purple shirt was secured with a beautiful belt, across his shoulder was hung his medicine pouch. The sick man entered the hogan and was placed on a blanket in front of the song priest. Then the men representing two of the Yeibitchai—the deities Hasjelti and Hostjoghon—entered. The face of the man personating Hasjelti was concealed with a mask of deerskin, on his head an elaborate arrangement of turkey and eagle feathers. He wore a deerskin mantle; from this was hung a fox hide medicine pouch, from the waist down he was habited in ordinary clothing. Hostjoghon wore a mask of deerskin colored blue, a less elaborate headdress; he was naked to the waist, around his loins a kilt of red velvet secured with a silver belt, hanging from this various sashes of silk and fur. It was explained to me that the deerskin used in the masks and mantle had to be secured from deer which had been smothered to death. It seemed that deer were run down, then secured with ropes, corn pollen placed in the nostrils, and then smothered by placing the bands over the deer's mouth and nostrils. Hasjelti placed a sort of square over the invalid's head, while Hostjoghon shook two eagle wands over him. Then entered Hostoboken, the water spirit, he was masked and in rather clownlike costume and was much bedecked with cedar spray. The goddess Host-joboard followed the water spirit. These personages entered alternately until each had placed six gaming rings on different parts of the sick man's body. Over his mouth for strength, for speech and to have good courage. Other parts of his body were touched to expel evil and for physical benefit. After the twelve rings had been used, three rings were taken to each of the four points of the compass and deposited at the base of pinion trees. This was that the evil and disease taken from the ill man's body might not remain to contaminate the hogan. These ceremonies at an end, Hasjelti re-entered the lodge followed by Hostjoghon. Much of the weird hooting peculiar to Hasjelti and one day of the Yeibitchai was over.

SECOND, THIRD AND FOURTH DAYS

The ceremonies attending these days were extremely secret and it was most difficult to learn what was going on. It seemed that the four Yeibitchai went forth each morning, one in each direction to collect food and other articles. Then the patient was taken a given distance from the hogan (in a different direction on each successive day). At this place a pit was dug and a fire built in it. The sick man was placed over the pit and allowed to inhale the fumes from certain herbs which the medicine man placed in the fire. Other ceremonies, such as a bath in Yucca suds, were performed on the invalid. In these ceremonies the demi-gods Naiyenesgony and Tobaidischini had a part in addition to the four deities before named. The nights of the second, third and fourth days were devoted to songs and prayers blessing the masks worn by the personators of the gods and consecrating the prayer plumes and medicine tubes. Toward evening of the fourth day a feast was held in the medicine lodge, participated in by the song priest and his assistant, the men representing the gods and Has Ta Ji Ya Ye and his immediate family.

FIFTH DAY

The ceremonies attendant to the inhaling of fumes were continued. In addition there was a long ceremony to secure the attendance of Hasjelti at the sand paintings, which were to begin on the following day. Other preparations were made for the sand paintings.

SIXTH DAY

At daylight preparations for the sand picture began. First, all the ashes from the fire which had been burning in the hogan were removed. Then enough common yellowish sand was carried in blankets to form a square about three inches deep and perhaps five feet in diameter.

Exactly at sunrise the work on the painting began, eight students did the actual work, the chief medicine man, from his permanent seat at the west end of the lodge facing east, corrected them when some detail did not suit him, his assistant at the other end of the structure did likewise. Some of the students were quite young, others were middle aged. One man had been studying twenty-five years and had not yet satisfied his teachers of his ability to do the work unaided. I was told that rarely does a man qualify as a full-fledged medicine man with less than twenty years of study. And no wonder. For this one "medicine sing" alone more than three hundred prayers, chants and songs must be committed to memory verbatim and also the intricate sand painting must be learned perfectly. It was most wonderful to watch the painting. The sand was dropped from between the fingers with marvelous accuracy. Each student had five colors of sand in bark receptacles: Gray blue, black, red, yellow and white. The picture represents one of the Navajo myths. A young school boy told me that the purpose of the painting was to remind the gods of how they had helped the Navajo in ancient times and to thus secure their attendance on the ceremonies of the present time.

The work was finished about 3 p.m. The song priest then sprinkled sacred meal over the figures of the picture, and the curtains at the door were drawn back to admit the invalid. At his entrance the medicine man burst into a weird chant with the rattle for accompaniment. The invalid was handed an Apache basket containing meal and, too, sprinkled the painting. A fire was built, incense put on it and the invalid allowed to inhale the fumes. He was then stripped of his clothing. Mr. Staples now entered the hogan. He was clad in a purple shirt and white trousers, wore a handkerchief around his head, "kehs," also a profusion of jewelry. All save full-fledged Navajos were then excluded from the building. Hasjelti and Hostjoghon entered the lodge. Within the hogan I understand that both the invalid and Mr. Staples were placed on the painting and prayers were said by them and for them. It seems that the ceremony was the same for both—a process of purification—the evil to be driven out of Nas Ta Ji Ya Ye to cure his sickness, the evil to be driven from Mr. Staples to fit him for membership in the tribe. At the conclusion of the ceremonies all the Navajos present who had aches or pains of any sort took sand from the painting and rubbed it upon the affected parts. The painting was then

erased and the sand carried some distance from the hogan in blankets. The sun
must never set upon a Navajo sand painting: no woman of the tribe is allowed to
look upon one. The setting sun was laid to rest with a strange chant.

SEVENTH DAY

A more elaborate sand painting depicting an important myth was the order of
the day. Considerable difficulty was experienced in protecting the picture from the
ashes which the high wind blew in through the door. When this occurred the ashes
were carefully removed with a turkey feather brush by the song priest. Finally two
more rugs were placed over the door and this helped matters, although it rendered
entrance to the hogan something in the nature of a puzzle. When the painting was
almost completed six young men entered the medicine lodge, there they removed
all their clothing and plastered their bodies with a white sticky material. Then they
went forth to beg food from the assembled multitudes.

When the painting was completed ceremonies very similar to those of the
preceding day were celebrated. Again the sand was carried out of the hogan.

At night teams of dancers from various sections of the reservation practiced the
dances which have places on the last night of the Yeibitchai.

EIGHTH DAY

On this day a very large painting occupying almost the whole of the interior of
the hogan was completed. The center of the painting was a cornstalk, this signi-
fied the main subsistence of the Navajos. The most important figures of the picture were four Zenichi (people of the rocks) and their wives.

When the painting was almost completed men began to go through the various
camps announcing that the children should be brought to a certain spot for the initiation ceremony. Then Hasjelti in his usual costume and Hostjoboard, her nude
body painted white, left the medicine hogan and went to the scene of the initiation
some 200 yards east.

Probably fifty or sixty children were initiated at that time. The boys stripped
of their clothing, wrapped in blankets and sat down, covering their heads. Together
with the girls who were also wrapped in blankets they formed a semi-circle. They
were arranged according to age, the oldest boy being at the extreme left (facing
east) and so on down to the youngest boy, then the oldest girl and down to the youngest girl who was at the extreme right of the semi-circle. In many cases the mother
stood behind her child.

When the children were finally in position Hasjelti passed down the line dropping sacred meal on them. Then he and Hostjoboard took position in front of the
line and one at a time the boys were brought forward. I have often wondered how
one would act if he believed himself in the awful presence of his gods. I now had

the opportunity to see, for these children believed that the masked figures were deities, not simply impersonators. (Until after this initiation ceremony children are not permitted any knowledge of the inner mysteries of their religion.) Most of these boys shook—partly from the cold, but also, I am sure, from sheer terror. They stood head downward while Hasjelti framed a cross upon their breasts with the sacred meal. Then Hostjoboard struck them upon the breast with her yucca swords. Hasjelti would then turn them toward the right until they faced the east, and make another cross upon their backs. Hostjoboard would strike them twice upon the back with her swords. Again they were brought to face east. Arms extended and then brought together. Hasjelti made crosses upon their arms and then their knees. Each time Hostjoboard followed with blows with her swords, first with the sword in her right hand then with the sword in the left. (It is said that the crosses symbolize the scalp knot.) As soon as a boy had gone through the chastisement he returned to his seat, recovered, and the next boy in line went forward. The boys initiated, the girls received the attention of the gods. The maidens were not forced to leave their seats, but when Hasjelti and Hostjoboard approached them their heads were uncovered and they sat motionless. Hasjelti marked a line of meal on each foot of the girl, Hostjoboard then placed two ears of yellow corn decorated with pinion sprays against the soles of their feet. In like manner five other parts of their bodies were first sprinkled with the meal, then touched with the corn. After all the girls had been thus treated Hasjelti and Hostjoboard again took places in front of the center of the line. The children were ordered to uncover and raise their heads. The deities then unmasked. It was indeed strange to note the varying expressions on the faces of the children when they discovered the deception. Generally amazement, but on some faces one noticed just a little hint of indignation at having been thus imposed upon. Then Hostjoboard placed her mask upon the faces of all in the line. Great care was taken for a slight misplacement would surely result in blindness. This done she placed the mask of Hasjelti. The man who had personated this god first sprinkled his mask and then Hostjoboard's with pollen. Hostjoboard then reversed the process. Then the first boy at the left end of the line came forth and sprinkled the masks. This was repeated until all those in the line had done so. Great care was observed in this ceremony for the slightest error on the the part of the children would cause dire calamities.

An hour after the close of the initiation ceremony, an interesting ceremony took place in front of the medicine hogan. The theurgist and the sick man were seated a little to the right of the entrance. Two new deities together with Hasjelti had a part in this ceremony. They were Taadojaii and the goddess Yebahdi. Hasjelti was dressed as before. Taadojaii was nude save a G-string, he was elaborately painted in red and white. In his right hand a gourd rattle, in his left a bow. The goddess wore ordinary squaw's dress. After many antics outside, Mr. Staples entered the lodge followed by the theurgist and the impersonators of the gods who first removed their masks. Within Mr. Staples and Na Ta Ji Ya Ye were placed upon the painting. In this case the picture was surrounded with twelve turkey wands. I could obtain no exact account of what went on within, but the loud cries and hooting issuing from the lodge suggested something rather unusual.

It was on this day that I finally obtained Kodak pictures of the painting. With considerable difficulty, however, as the song priest still insisted that if I took a picture the painting must lose something of itself thereby, and therefore be not so pleasing to the gods. Again when I proposed taking a picture through the smoke vent above the medicine man was horrified. He explained that my taking a picture would close the opening so that the evil which was to be driven out of the invalid and Mr. Staples could not escape and would remain to contaminate the hogan.

After dark the various teams of dancers again rehearsed the great dance to be held on the following evening.

NINTH DAY

The gathering was an interesting one. For the previous twenty-four hours Navajos had been pouring in from all parts of the reservation to join the not inconsiderable crowd which had already collected. Some came in wagons, more on horseback and some few on foot, so that by noon of the 17th there were between 1200 and 1500 of them present. Camps were scattered over an extensive radius and the communal cook house was quite overcrowded. An avenue of covered wagons lined the space directly in front of the medicine hogan. Everywhere a riot of color—the squaws in velvet waists and skirts of gay muslin colors outshone the male portion of the scene who had to depend on their blankets and jewelry for color.

The principal business of the morning was the final decoration of the masks, costumes, et cetera. This process was carried on in a large open shelter of cedar boughs which had been built 100 yards from the lodge. Later this structure served as a sort of dressing room. At the same time ceremonies were being carried on in the lodge to which only medicine men were admitted. The refrain of many low pitched chants could be heard.

In the afternoon a ceremony was held the purpose of which was to draw from the lodge the accumulated disease which had exuded from the body of the invalid. Three men personated the deities Naiyenesgony, Tobaidischinni and the hermaphrodite Ahsonnutli. Naiyenesgony was blackened save for white bows painted on parts of his body. Tobaidischinni had white scalp knots where Naiyenesgony had the bows. Ahsonnutli wore the conventional squaw dress. The sick man sat on a blanket in front of the lodge. Naiyenesgony approached him until they were literally face to face, then pointed his knife of lava stone directly at his face. In the same fashion Tobaidischinni pointed sticks at him, and Ahsonnutli her bow and arrow. This was repeated on the south, west and north sides of the sick man. Nas Ta Ji Ya Ye then entered the lodge while the deities performed the same ceremony on the east, south, west and north sides of the lodge. Then they also entered the lodge. There they were sprinkled with pollen by the song priest and the invalid. The song priest then gave a black tube to Naiyenesgony, a red tube to Tobaidischinni, and a blue tube to Ahsonnutli. The medicine man then knelt in front of Naiyenesgony and repeated a long prayer to which the invalid responded. The deities now left the lodge and deposited their medicine tubes at various places.

In the afternoon the Indians gathered to be addressed by Chee Dodge, the most influential and richest among them. He discussed the extension of the reservation and other matters pertaining to the general welfare. It was a good example of primitive democracy, very much like the New England town meeting.

A more brilliant setting for a dance could hardly be imagined than the one that night. The space reserved was that directly in front of the hogan. Bright fires whose flames rose seven or eight feet high burned on either side. Around them sat the multitude of gayly dressed spectators happily singing snatches of their favorite songs.

Shortly after dark the ceremonies began with the processional from the dressing room led by the chief medicine man. He was a truly impressive figure as he moved with slow dignified steps, chanting a prayer the while. The spectacle rather suggested "Holy, Holy, Holy, Lord God Almighty." He was followed by Hasjelti and four Etsethle (the first ones) who represented corn, rain, vegetation and corn pollen. Their blue masks were topped by a feather head dress, loin skirts from which hung fox skins. Bodies were painted white. In their right hands gourd rattles. When twenty feet from the hogan the procession halted. The song priest turned to face Hasjelti and repeated a short prayer. The Etsethle chanted a reminder to the people that corn is their food, that for rain Hasjelti must be prayed to, that for vegetation to grow the sun must warm the earth, and that corn pollen is necessary for all religious ceremonies. The song priest and the invalid then chanted a prayer to the Etsethle. The invalid then sat down on a chair in front of the lodge. The song priest remained standing while the Etsethle indulged in a short weird dance. Hasjelti ran up and down hooting. (He never speaks save signs.) Soon it was over and Hasjelti led them back to the dressing room.

A short while thereafter another procession came forth consisting of the assistant song priest, Hasjelti, twelve dancers who represented the old man and old woman of the original world six times duplicated, and Hostjoghon. Once in the enclosure the dance began. Singing in a falsetto and patently barbarian yet haunting, the quick movements of the dance are almost impossible of description. The whole thing was sufficiently ghostly. All night long various teams continued the dance. While dancing the dancers must not speak or cough. If they do they are sent away for eleven days to do penance. To the superficial observer there was little variation in the dance save in the number of dancers, the occasional appearance of a woman in the dance, and the appearance of Hostjoghon and Hostjobokon. As the night wore on the dancers seemed to gain more vigor, although the cold caused many of them to cover their nakedness.

Just as the sun was rising the dance terminated in the exquisite Bluebird Song. The last group of dancers proceeded from the dancing space to the dressing room. There they removed their masks and holding them in their hands they sang this beautiful lyric which is so named because the Bluebird Clan originated it. It seems to be an early myth told in story form by a man to his sister. It is totally different from any other Navajo song I have ever heard, most melodious and sung softly in a very low key. The song over, the masks had to be sprinkled with pollen and the ceremony of Hasjelti Dailjis was at an end.

Three hours later it all seemed as a dream. The host had vanished as if by magic. Nothing left to conjure with save the ashes of the fire.

THE ARCHAEOLOGY OF PUARAY

BY MARJORIE FERGUSON TICHY

VOLUME 46, NUMBER 7
JULY, 1939

Archaeology of Bandelier's Puaray, a ruin situated on the west side of the Rio Grande, and almost opposite the present village of Bernalillo, New Mexico, is important to historians and anthropologists alike. The question of the locality of certain Tiguex villages visited by Coronado in 1540, and subsequent Spanish explorers, has never been satisfactorily settled. Puaray and Sandia seem to have given students of the problem more difficulty than any of the others. Puaray existed in 1540, we are sure, but when historians have tried to place it and Sandia on the same site, or identify two or more ruins as Puaray, real confusion has arisen. It was with the hope of simplifying the question at hand, to some extent, that the excavation of this ruin was undertaken by the Museum of New Mexico, School of American Research and University of New Mexico, in 1934.

There are well over thirty known pueblo sites within the range of the Tiguex Province, which is situated in the Rio Grande Valley, and is roughly bounded on the south by Isleta Pueblo and on the north by Bernalillo, with many ruins to be found near the river and on both sides of it. Many of these sites were abandoned in pre-Spanish times, some twelve to sixteen were inhabited in 1540, four in 1680, and two, Sandia and Isleta, are existing today in almost the same localities [where] they were in ancient times. Bandelier believed the site under consideration to be the Puaray of 1680,[1] existing then with Isleta, Alameda and Sandia. It was destroyed by Otermin's army in December, 1681.

Puaray[2] of Bandelier was not chosen for excavation because it was necessarily believed to be the Puaray of 1680, in fact certain members of the staff felt reasonably sure that it was not. However, as will be seen, some of the material coming from its excavation might well substantiate Bandelier's deduction. One thing seems clear: the site was almost certainly occupied between 1540 and 1630, call it what you may. Excavation also revealed that the village was in a cultural decline during its entire occupancy and while the writer does not say it was in existence in 1680, certain objects found in it are similar to objects found in other Indian villages of 1680.

The site lies at an altitude of approximately 5,500 feet, and lies in the Upper Sonoran Zone. It rests on a barren, windswept bluff which is burning hot all summer and exceedingly cold in the winter. The Sandia Mountains loom several miles to the east, and to the west one sees only vast stretches of waste land and the far off lava flow. Farming was probably carried on below the ruin to the southeast where there is an abundance of good soil.

There are no springs near the ruin, and water must have been carried from the river below. Clay beds for ceramic purposes are to be found nearby. All up and down the valley cottonwood trees are abundant, and other timber could have been secured with some difficulty from the mountains. It is next to impossible to find a stone of any building size on, or near, the ruin, in spite of large sections of the village resting on stratified beds of river rock. However, adobe is plentiful everywhere. . . .

The ruin is made up of remnants of four compactly constructed buildings which surround a small plaza, containing a single kiva in the northwest corner. Each building extended well over three hundred feet in length. They were separated by small passageways which led to the exterior of the village as well as into the plaza. At the time of occupancy parts of the West and South Houses, at least, ascended to two stories or more. However, no actual second or third story rooms were encountered. Because of the open, and now almost desert-like, country on which the ruin rests, wall erosion has taken place more through wind action than any other factor. With the exception of a few rooms in the South Wing, and three beams in the kiva, there was little evidence of burning in the town, although mention will be made later of a building which was almost certainly deliberately destroyed.

Approximately four hundred and fifty ground floor rooms were uncovered during excavation, the majority of which were rectangular, but a few were almost square. The best preserved rooms were found in the South House with some of the wall heights well over three feet, but in most of the ruin, wall heights averaged little over one foot, and many were less. Several rooms were uncovered whose lengths exceeded fifteen feet but the average room length was nearer nine or ten feet, with widths of five to seven feet. Wall widths ranged between nine inches and a little over one foot. No architectural sequence was found on the site. The largest rooms on the ruin, however, were at the south end of the West House.

Two methods of building were used, though in one medium only, namely, adobe. Several rooms built of puddled adobe were uncovered, but much more common was the practice of laying large thick blocks of adobe together with mud in even courses, one row set up on another, probably while still slightly pliable. In no room in the ruin was an example of *corner* interlocking found. Building was by accretion; the walls of each room becoming walls of surrounding rooms in such a way that the honeycomb structure was supported by the labyrinth of rooms.

Almost invariably room walls were plastered, and floors were always of adobe.

Built-in room features were scanty, but fairly uniform in type. Fire boxes occurred in numerous rooms, and consisted of rectangular box-like structures sunk in the floors. Sometimes worn-out manos or flat river rocks were used to cap the edges or to line the interiors, but often they were plastered with adobe. A capping of adobe, or rock, usually about an inch or two above the floor was placed about each one. Occasionally two elongated rocks were set in on one edge of a fire box at about a 45-degree angle, probably to be used as pot supports. The fireboxes were usually sunk into the floors near a wall. Numerous adobe bins set in at right angles in room corners appeared. Sometimes two bins occurred within a room, and one example was had with three bins in one room taking up one entire side. There were one or two instances of benches being built within rooms. These were made of adobe, and plastered over. They averaged more than a foot and a half in height, and were long enough to hold a reclining human body. An interesting floor feature was that contained in two or three rooms where approximately two thirds of the floor was laid in at a gradual slope, ending in a slight ridge. The same situation has also been found in ruins of the Pajarito Plateau and they are said to have been used as sleeping places, the ridge making a fairly comfortable head rest . . . . [3]

Doorways occurred frequently between rooms, but since the tops of the rooms were gone, nothing is known about the upper part of these openings. With the exception of one doorway, all had rectangular bases, some of which had sills formed of flat stones. Some were built so that the opening was from the floor up, and others were set in from eight inches to a foot or more above the floor levels. All were narrow and measured less than two feet across in most cases. Numerous small circular depressions were found in the floors of many of the dwellings, and were probably used as "pot rests," for pots were found in some.

One of the most important pieces of work on the ruin was that of uncovering the kiva, the only one found on the site. It was located in the northwest corner of the plaza, and proved to be extremely interesting not only from a structural point of view, but also because of the rich stratified layers of cultural debris contained within its walls. The kiva was badly weathered, and its walls were followed with difficulty. It was built in a roughly circular fashion, puddled adobe having been placed against the sides of a large opening dug in the ground. The adobe courses were from two to two-and-one-half feet in height. The walls had been plastered, for in the fill and on several portions of the walls small patches of it were encountered.

The diameter of the kiva was thirty-two feet, and the average depth was between eight and nine feet. Some evidence of a former, and slightly larger wall on the exterior was noted, but could not be traced without seriously undermining the already badly damaged structure. The floor was of blackened adobe plaster, quite worn in places.

The slightly off-center firebox and altar-deflector were on the east side of the kiva. The rectangular firebox, set into the adobe floor, was 3 feet long 2 feet 2 inches wide and 10-½ inches deep. A rim three inches wide surrounded the top of the firebox. The firebox, lined with adobe, was reddened by long firing. Three altar stones, flush with the floor, were laid to the south of the firebox. The altar-deflector was built just east of the firebox and originally measured about 4 ft. 8 in. by 1 ft. 6 in., and the west height was 2 ft. Behind the altar was an irregular pit one to six inches deep, and slightly narrower than the altar. It extended almost six feet east, ending at the kiva wall and ventilator shaft. It was covered by six juniper beams plastered over with adobe. The ventilator shaft had been built six inches below the kiva floor, and was 4 ft. high and 1 ft. 1 in. wide. Inside, impressions of twelve former upright beams were found—six on each side. Two small cross beams and several smaller poles laid crosswise over these were also found. The rectangular opening into the shaft measured 3 ft. 6 in. high, by 1 ft. 8 in. wide and 1 ft. 1 in. deep. Nothing could be determined about its appearance above ground.

Along the north wall was found a well preserved set of loom holes which averaged slightly over two inches in diameter. The roof of the kiva had at one time been supported by four, or possibly six, beams. In two of the beam holes remnants of rotted cottonwood supports about ten to eleven inches in diameter were found, and an outline of a third beam still remained. All four holes contained ash, charcoal and *glaze E and F* pottery and culinary shards. . . .

The most interesting kiva feature was the entrance, which was located in the west wall, almost directly opposite the firebox. It was carved in the wall, and entrance was made from the outside on the west through an ante-chamber. It was situated 3 ft. 6 in. above the kiva floor, was 3 ft. 10 in. wide and 3 ft. 2 in. high. The passage was roofed with five beams with flattened tops, set in with adobe mud, and plastered neatly over. The beams averaged three and one-half inches in diameter. The rounded back of the passageway sloped outward toward the exterior. The passageway measured 2 ft. 9 in. wide and 3 ft. 11 in. long. Entrance had formerly been facilitated by a ladder of two rungs whose sockets still remained. How the top of the entrance formerly appeared we have no way of knowing, but it was obvious that it had been much wider at the top. The *sipapu,* curiously enough, was situated just below this entrance. It was a well plastered circular hole nine inches deep, and eight inches in diameter.

The structure to be described here is the most puzzling, and yet the most important of any on the ruin. At the completion of its excavation, and for some time thereafter I was pretty well convinced it was a small mission,[4] or chapel, but since then I have tempered my thought to the extent of saying it could have been. At any rate it is definitely post-Spanish in style and type of building, and all cultural debris associated with it was Spanish, or Indian copies of Spanish patterns. It showed every likelihood of having been purposely destroyed, for only the bare outline of its former foundation remained, and it seems unlikely that so large a building (judging by [the] foundation) would disintegrate so rapidly when the other older and less substantially built sections of the ruin still retained wall heights of three and a half feet, or more. This building was situated on a rocky bluff some distance southeast of the ruin. Below there is an immense grove of cottonwood trees, and from where the structure is located one enjoys one of the best views of the Rio Grande Valley, the river, and Sandia Mountains.

To quote one of the many authorities,[5] there was founded in New Mexico in 1581 the first mission at Puaray, on a high bluff overlooking the Rio Grande in front of the present Bernalillo. Founders of this mission were Friars Rodriguez and Juan de Santa Maria, who were members of the Chamuscado expedition. The mission, San Bartolomé was short lived, for its founders were soon murdered after the departure of Chamuscado, and in 1711, or thereabouts, the mission was totally destroyed and Puaray was evacuated forever.

In 1598 Oñate and his army spent a night at Puaray, during which time he reported seeing the murder of the two friars clearly depicted on the walls of a chamber, although the Indians had been careful to cover this painting with white-wash. As soon as the wash dried the scene showed through in all its bloody horror. However, nowhere on the Puaray site were there any remnants of fresco[6] art, nor were there any ceremonial rooms found, other than the kiva, where such paintings could have appeared. Remains of frescoes found at Kuaua were executed in kivas only, so far as we know, and it is possible that Puaray's kiva once contained the same. It and the Spanish structure are the only buildings on the ruin large enough for a number of soldiers to have stayed in, if this is the site.

If Indians worked on the construction of this building they did it under Spanish supervision. One has only to study its ground plan to decide this. Adobe used was of the small brick-like, Spanish type. The great thickness of foundation walls, and the more or less generous use of lava blocks and other large stones, found nowhere else on the ruin, are also important features to be considered. The main part of the building is over fifty-two feet long, the width thirty-eight feet, with the two wall lengths and widths varying but a few inches. Thus in comparing this structure with the haphazard room lengths and widths found elsewhere on the ruin it is readily seen that it was engineered by non-Indian minds. The main wall widths were three feet or more. At no point did foundations stand more than a few inches in height. The building had been completely leveled. It is also rather curious that the structure stands at such a marked angle to the main ruin.

A general summing up of the building would be to describe it as being enclosed entirely on three sides by thick walls of stone and adobe, and partially enclosed on the southeastern side, by a somewhat narrower adobe wall of a later date, for most of the original wall on this side had disappeared. The southeastern side may have had some sort of a portal at one time, and this side most likely contained the main entrance. If one will note the ground plan it will also be seen that additional walls, or possibly parts of old buttresses appear at various exterior points. Note that the interior of the building is divided into several smaller rooms. However these dividing walls, of inferior construction, appeared to have been set in after the main building was finished, or perhaps after its main period of usefulness had passed. That this structure is definitely Spanish is undeniable from archaeological remains, and that it was occupied for some time by Spanish people will also be conceded when the description of its material remains are given. It would appear to have been a building containing originally one, and then two inner rooms and might possibly have been a small chapel,[7] though not a true church in the orthodox sense of the word, which was later turned into living quarters, possibly by Spanish farmers, or the like. Even if all agree that this structure was once ecclesiastical it still does not prove this site is the Puaray of 1681. I believe the question of the location of Sandia and Puaray should remain open until more excavation is done, at least some, on the old mounds just north of Sandia pueblo, and on the ruin (Site 13),[8] which is two and one-half miles northeast of Alameda,[9] or until some new light is shed on the documentary hodge-podge of the Tiguex.

Two of the oddest structures found during our excavation were two small circular pit-houses (?) to the southeast of the main ruin. They probably have no bearing on the ruin proper, for culturally they are much older than any part of the ruin. The first one is located but a short distance from the main east wall of the church. . . . The second pit structure was approximately thirty-six feet northeast of the first one. , . .These structures should be considered significant, for they indicate a much earlier occupation of this part of the Rio Grande valley. They were in all probability only temporary dwellings.

The inhabitants of Bandelier's Puaray were prolific potters. The bulk of the pottery consisted of two distinct types. The first was a roughly smoothed, culinary ware made in forms of ollas and storage vessels. Numerous vessels of the "bird-form" were also made in this ware. Some attempt had been made to smooth and polish the interiors of these vessels which were usually a slightly lustrous black. Surfaces were almost uniformly striated in varying degrees, and many of them contained bold scratches running in sweeping and somewhat oblique lines. The rim forms of this group were generally flared to some degree. Heights ranged from well over one foot to miniatures of only a few inches. Vessel walls were one-fourth of an inch or greater in thickness. Lugs and handles were almost non-existent. This ware made up approximately one half of the pottery found in the ruin during excavation.

The second important class of pottery was glazed decorated ware. Bowls, ollas and small jars were executed in this style, as well as numerous *eccentric* forms. This ware is extremely brilliant and attractive on the whole, and occurred in innumerable bright polychrome combinations as well as in two-toned effects. The glazed decorated wares told a graphic story of the town's cultural trend. Designs were executed in glaze and paint, and consisted of numerous conventionalized geometrical symbols and many life forms. The most important date gleaned from the glazes showed that Puaray was occupied during a relatively short period of time, mainly the latter part of the *Regressive Pueblo Period*. The glazes were almost uniformly of the same type throughout the ruin, and there was little showing of early glaze types. Pottery studied came from rooms, refuse areas adjoining rooms, and refuse heaps. Dumping went on everywhere, but the most common practice would seem to have been that of throwing refuse into abandoned rooms and plaza areas. Some dumping took place just south of the town, but because of the slope of the hillocks on which the dump was cast, complete data could not be gotten. The best and deepest refuse on the ruin came from two localities; the first was that found in the kiva, and the second was to be found in the south and east plaza sections where extensive dumping took place, just outside the main dwellings. It was also customary to build rooms over refuse in many parts of the ruin.

The bulk of glazed decorated pottery in the West House and the territory surrounding it was late, that is to say, the types represented ranged largely in classes "D" and "E." Glaze "F" was represented, but not in such large amounts. Very few earlier types occurred, and these were mostly glaze C.

The South House, together with the plaza dump to the north of it, revealed a definite upper middle and late preponderance of glaze types. Shard counts from the East and North Houses showed the same situation to be true. It would, therefore, seem that every section of the town was occupied at about the same period. However, it is possible that the South House, the southern tips of the West and East Houses, were the last to be occupied, for it was in these three localities where the most European influence was to be noted.

Perhaps, the best stratification on the entire ruin was that contained in the kiva. Just how long the kiva had been abandoned when dumping began cannot be definitely stated. However, it must have been abandoned when a good part of the town was still occupied. One piece of Spanish porcelain was removed almost at floor level. The shards from the kiva were studied according to stratigraphic levels. Glaze F was, by far, the most abundantly represented, with glaze E following next. Some glaze D was encountered, while few glaze C shards appeared. It should be mentioned that many variants of known Rio Grande glazed decorated rim forms were encountered here and elsewhere on the site, and that Kidder's Pecos numerical system and Mera's Rio Grande alphabetical system of classifying glazes worked about equally well, for variants occurred regardless of which was used.

In the kiva and those portions of the ruin which seem to have been occupied last in the town, were found shards of plain polished red or black ware not unlike types being reproduced at the present in such modern pueblos as Santa Clara, San Ildefonso and San Juan. Soup plates of plain red, Tewa polychrome, and some decorated in degenerate glazes E and F were also found in the kiva and these sections. Scant amounts of Tsia polychrome, Tsankawi black on cream, Jemez black on grey, and Abiquiu and Bandelier black on grey appeared.

Mention should be made of the extremely interesting shard material that came from the two pit structures. Specimens from this group were kindly checked by Dr. H.P. Mera of the Laboratory of Anthropology. Many interesting hybrid black on grey types were encountered as well as pieces of Pitoche rub-ribbed, Los Lunas smudged, Santa Fe black on grey, Mesa Verde black on grey, Tularosa black on grey, Heshotuathla, Saint John's polychrome, and Los Padillas polychrome. One black on grey shard, possibly Pueblo I, was removed from one of these structures, and the culinary shards accompanying the above examples were also a mixture, showing the same influences.

Just outside the east wall of the Spanish structure was a refuse heap, containing more Spanish porcelain than any other one thing. The entire area surrounding this structure as well as the interior, was covered with the same ware. Five pieces were also removed from the kiva, and fragments of porcelains were found in rooms in the South and East wings of the town. This ware was identified by E. de F. Curtis of the Pennsylvania Museum and School of Art, who said that most of it belonged to a group of early Spanish tin enamels made in Spain in the early 1600's. The remainder, he said, was probably made in the New World.

In addition to pottery other articles were executed in clay. A good number of clay pipes and cloud blowers were found, some excellently made, and in good condition. Fragmentary clay pipes occurred frequently in the excavation of both rooms and refuse. Some of these pipes were undoubtedly ceremonial. They were executed in light grey, buff, dark grey, dark brown, and black. Some were plain, others were decorated with incised or punched designs, and some had designs placed on their broad sides in relief. The majority were of a simple tubular type. One large specimen had been formed by moulding the clay around a corn cob, but many seemed to have been shaped around a cylindrical object like a stick or large reed.

A number of small, crudely formed undecorated objects were found consisting of birds and small animals. A small clay horse's head was removed from the refuse of the Spanish structure. A number of fragmentary candle holders were found in the refuse of the Spanish structure, and in rooms of the West and South Houses. They were undecorated and were buff, light red, and grey in color.

Numerous small, badly made undecorated clay vessels were found and would appear to be the work of children. Literally hundreds of potsherds worked into various forms were excavated in every part of the ruin. The most common forms were round, oval and rectangular. Some were perforated, and others had been shaped to be used as scrapers and small scoops. The glazed decorated variety far exceeded those of culinary and intrusive wares. . . .

In spite of the obvious European influence at Bandelier's Puaray, the culture was still essentially that of a Stone Age people at the time of its abandonment. The stone work on the whole was poor, but adequate. Stone types consisted of manos, of both the single and two-handed varieties, metates (all non-grooved), axes, hammers, mauls, hoes, fleshers, club-heads (?), pottery and floor polishers, griddles, pot lids, projectiles, including arrow and spear points, drills, awls, scrapers, abraders, fetishes, lightning stones, discs, arrow shaft straighteners, kiva ringing stones, one large stone ring, mortars, pestle and stone dishes (one which originally had three legs) etc. In addition to actual artifacts and ceremonial stones listed above, the Puaray Indians also collected concretions and minerals. Most of the tools were manufactured from the abundant local supply of small river rocks, many of which showed very little workmanship. Metates were, for the most part, roughly rectangular, flat on the grinding surfaces, and with a tendency to be concave in the middle, depending on how much usage they had had. They were similar in appearance to those being used today in some of the Rio Grande pueblos. Projectile points were scanty and poorly made for the most part. Little, or no evolutionary sequence could be noted in the bulk of the stone work from the ruin, and generally speaking, it fell in one main class, namely late Regressive Pueblo.

Bone objects also made up a valuable class of implements on the ruin. Likewise animal bones found were considered equally important since they revealed much concerning the fauna in the vicinity of the village. Specimens from different parts of the ruin were labeled and sent to [the] Smithsonian Institution, Washington, D.C., for identification. The following types may be tabulated as having come from Bandelier's Puaray: domestic dog, bison or cow, antelope, deer, jack rabbit, turkey, Rocky Mountain sheep, little brown crane, domestic sheep, beaver, Ferruginous rough-legged hawk, cottontail, squirrel, gopher, fish, turtle, bear and lynx. Domesticated sheep bones came from the kiva, from two rooms in the South Wing of the town and from the refuse adjoining the Spanish structure. Many of the animals listed here are obviously not local, hence the inhabitants of Puaray had to go either to the Jemez Mountains, the Sandias, or the Mount Taylor district. The securing of bison must have necessitated trips to the New Mexico Plains area. These animals were very important to the community, first as [a] necessary part of its diet, and second, skins, hides and bones were converted into various household objects and clothing. Worked bones coming from the excavation included flutes, whistles, beads, flakers, raspers, weaving tools, piercing tools, scrapers, handles and some unidentifiable material, which [was] either partially worked, or too fragmentary for identification. Both bird and mammal bones were used, but on the whole, bone tools were surprisingly scanty considering the size of the ruin. Mention should be made of several bones excavated which bore abrasions, probably made by metal tools.

Ornaments found during the excavation of this site were very few. They were simple and consisted largely of turquoise and shell. One clay bead was found. Dr. A.O. Woodward, Pomona College, Claremont, California, identified the shell material, and reported the following shells used: conus, olivella, abalone, and the beak and hinge of a heavy, pearly oyster-like shell. Turquoise was fashioned into rectangular or oval pendants and cylindrical beads. A large conus tinkler was found in one of the rooms, and from the kiva came two abalone pendants, the only two found. Olivellas were found with two of the burials, and appear to have been necklaces, and likewise, turquoise ornaments found with burials were invariably in the neck region. A half pint cache of turquoise was removed from one of the walls of a room.

Little in the way of perishable material was recovered from the ruin, but what was found was sent to Mr. Volney Jones of the Ethnobotanical Laboratory, Museum of Anthropology oUniversity of Michigan, who has kindly identified the specimens sent. Nearly all of the specimens of weaving came from graves, and vegetal remains came generally from rooms. One piece of burned basketry came from the kiva, and represented a portion of the bottom. It had been formed with small bundles of fibre by the coil technique.

Some of the dead would appear to have been wrapped completely in finely woven fabric with several folds in some cases, and others seemed to have been placed on coarse mats, but generally only the outline of the weaving remained. The majority of graves, however, contained no vestiges of textiles. No attempt will be made here to give a full account of Mr. Jones' report, but a list of specimens identified by him is given; *Vegetal:* abundance of charred corn kernels, cobs and ears, Hopi cotton, cotton fibre, yucca, bear grass, cottonweed, chenopodium (goosefoot), bur-reed, two varieties of beans, apocynum, and a peach seed from the Spanish structure. Animal remains showed that the people of Puaray utilized bird and animal sinew and skin to make a finely woven fabric. Several pieces of leather appearing to have been tanned were also found. Portions of feather robe, and bird-down fabric were also listed. What appeared to be buffalo and deer hair were also used in cloth making. . . .

NOTES

1. Many historians and some archaeologists now feel that Bandelier was wrong.

2. Puaray means "the village of the worm, or insect."

3. I quote Dr. E.L. Hewett, who mentions finding them in his excavations in the Pajarito Plateau.

4. Marjorie Tichy, "Observations on the Mission Uncovered at Puaray," *El Palacio*, vol. 41, pp. 63-67.

5. E.R. Forrest, *Missions and Pueblos of the Old Southwest*.

6. Remarkable frescoes were found in two rectangular, subterranean kivas at Kuaua, about one and one-half miles north of this site.

7. Note ground plan, and particularly square ante-chamber on the north side. This might possibly have been a tower. The length of the building, including this ante-chamber, is about seventy feet.

8. R.G. Fisher, Archaeological Survey, Vol. I, No. I, 1931.

9. G. Vivian, in his *Re-Study of the Province of Tiguex*, U.N.M., 1932, pp. 59, 60, 61, 62, 63, believes Site 13 to be the Puaray of 1681. His reasoning is logical, although he does not mention finding any definite "mission like" remains. However, he found post-Spanish pottery, etc.

PLAZA CIRCUITS OF
TEWA INDIAN DANCERS[1]

BY GERTRUDE P. KURATH

VOLUME 65, NUMBER 1
FEBRUARY, 1958

Outdoor ceremonial dances of the Rio Grande Pueblo Indians take place in spaces between house blocks, commonly called plazas. In the course of a day the groups of singers and dancers follow a prescribed circuit, theoretically counter-clockwise, and in accordance with the four cardinal directions. The pattern differs for each pueblo, even among the four Tewa pueblos of San Juan, Santa Clara, San Ildefonso, and Tesuque. These are within a few miles of each other, and intercommunicate.

The plazas[2] and the counter-clockwise circuits[3] have been frequently mentioned in the copious literature on the Pueblo Indians, but the circuit diversity has, to my knowledge, not been investigated. Personal observations will be analyzed and illustrated in this paper, to show the variations and to advance some reasons for the local patterns of the four Tewa pueblos just mentioned.

SAN JUAN PUEBLO

San Juan, about thirty miles north of Santa Fe, has been occupied since 1300.[4] Its several plazas generally form a parallel street pattern, but there is one at right angles to the others, and there are many peripheral homes. The public dances use two large parallel plazas, one north of the other, and the small one at right angles to them, just to the east. Access from one plaza to another is by way of narrow spaces between building blocks. The order and direction of the circuit is fixed and consistent for all public dances. A typical procedure is shown on Fig. 1[5]—the Deer Dance of February 10, 1957. [See Illustrations.]

The performers assembled in the dance house (4), which served the combined moieties. This was not the kiva, which lies to the north. The game chief led forty men and boys into the south plaza and halted near one of two small spruce trees holed in for the occasion. The dancers lined up between these trees, with the game chief to the north, one drummer (x) to the south, and the singer-dancers in the middle. For an introduction they faced south, for their first song all faced west, then for the remaining songs they faced E W E W, while the game chief shifted his position. After the fifth song he led them to the north plaza for an identical repeat. Then he led them to the east plaza, lining up south-north. Then he guided them back into the dance house for a fourth performance. The spectators watched from everywhere—from within the homes, along the walls, under a tree, close to the dancers, preferably in positions parallel to the dance line.

The circuit recurred four times during the day. A fifth appearance was intercepted because the deer fled to the hills, escaping the pueblo girls. During the second to the fourth circuits two clowns called Apaches wandered around the dance line as hunt mimes, and joined the circuit from plaza to plaza.

From the illustration it is apparent that the circuit is clockwise. This puzzled even a well-informed San Juan native, and has for the present no explanation. The theoretical four appearances, however, took place, the fourth one in private.

SANTA CLARA PUEBLO

Santa Clara is only a few miles from San Juan, to the southwest, just below Española. Founded in the fourteenth century, it has accumulated many winding side streets, and presents a confusing ground plan. One large plaza adjoins the kiva; others, less well-defined, surround this. Four plazas of varying sizes are used during the dances, as shown on Fig. 2. [See Illustrations.]

On all observed occasions the singers' chorus led the dance group from the moiety dance house to an east plaza, then to a small southerly space, then to the north, then to the large westerly plaza, always in that order, 1 to 4. During the first circuit the procession included all four locations; during the second and third each group had its own version of two plazas; during the last each group used the first three plazas and finally the space in front of its dance house. The pattern for dancers of the three dancing factions was as follows—

	Sun Basket Dance	Buffalo Dance	Buffalo Dance
	February 24, 1957	March 3, 1957	April 21 (Easter)
	Progressive Winter moiety	Progressive Summer	Conservative Winter
I.	1 2 3 4	1 2 3 4	1 2 3 4
II.	2 4	1 3	1 4
III.	1 3	2 4	2 3
IV.	1 2 3 W	1 2 3 SP	1 2 3 SC

The conservative summer moiety used to press II, 2 3, III. 1 4.

As to the position of the singers and the first position of the dancers in each location, this used an alternative orientation, that is, in plazas 1 and 3 the singers faced east, the dancers west; in plazas 2 and 4 they faced south and north respectively, as shown on the figure. Needless to say, the dancers constantly changed their orientation and relationship to the chorus during each performance, which received identical rendering in each plaza. Spectators occupied three sides of the plaza, the fourth being reserved for the singers. In plazas 3 and 4 the southerly ends were preferred because they gave the best views. Some men stood on house tops for a balcony effect.

Though a reliable Santa Clara elder stressed the counter-clockwise theory, the performers adhered to this only within each plaza. The progression from plaza to plaza followed a zigzag course, by means of a path which was sometimes clockwise. The only explanation offered was that this was the customary procedure.

SAN ILDEFONSO PUEBLO

San Ildefonso lies near the highway to Los Alamos, not far south of Santa Clara, but on the other side of the Rio Grande. It is divided into two huge plazas, occupied since about 1300. The smaller south plaza has been expanding towards the highway in the course of the twentieth century. Three adequate passageways connect the plazas. The inhabitants of each plaza perform entirely within their own precincts, sometimes on the same day, sometimes on different days; thus on the Saint's Day, namely January 23, and on Easter Sunday they perform simultaneously. Within each plaza the performers follow a consistent circuit by the cardinal points. For the final appearance the north plaza dancers conclude in front of their dance house, but the south plaza dancers choose the northern house block, at least as observed. Fig. 3 [see Illustrations] shows the circuits of two typical dances on Easter Sunday, 1957, performed concurrently. Each circuit surrounds a cairn. The directions W S E N correspond to 1 2 3 4 in the order or progression.

	Buffalo Dance North plaza	*Squash Blossom Dance* South plaza
I.	1 3	1 3
II.	2 4	2 4
III.	1 3 5	1 3
IV.	2 4 5	1 2 3 4

These two dances represent two types of orientation. The dance line is always parallel to the four sides of a square, but sometimes the dancers face the center, sometimes they have their shoulders to the center. The Buffalo dance predominantly uses the second type, also other dances, as the Women's Bow and Arrow Dance.[7] The singers respectively face the dance line or are themselves the dancers. The self-accompanied Squash Blossom Dance follows the second type at first, then the face-center type in its second part, as also the Men's Rain Dance and others. That is, the focus is east and west in 1 and 3, north and south in 2 and 4.[8]

The spectators in San Ildefonso string themselves along the walls, and also form large arcs on the south sides of both plazas. In fact, many of them sit in a semi-circle of cars, for comfort and protection from the whirling dust. Due to the spaciousness of the plazas, they never crowd close to the dancers, as do the spectators in other pueblos.

The circuit in both plazas adheres not only to a rhythmic placement according to the heavenly directions; it follows rigidly the theory of counter-clockwise progression. Even during the exits and re-entrances of the kiva and the migration from location to location, the path remains against the sun.

TESUQUE PUEBLO

Tesuque, only twelve miles north of Santa Fe, a short distance from U.S. Highway 85, has remained conservative in its layout and circuits. The homes, many of which date from around 1300, still are grouped mostly around one spacious plaza. In the single observed dance, men from both moieties, plus three *kossa* and *kwírena,* joined in the Spring Dance. This was during Lent, on March 23, 1957.

The circuits were confined to this one plaza, on the plan of San Ildefonso, but starting at the north, thus N W S E. The afternoon plan differed from the morning circuit. On the first emergence from the kiva south of the plaza the men lined up near the northern house block. They proceeded all around an imaginary square, N W S E (1 2 3 4). In the first position the men started facing west, in position 2 they faced south, and so on, as shown in Fig. 4. [See Illustrations.] Each performance in each location involved many face-abouts, as the men tromped to their own singing.

An accompanist with a scraping-stick stayed near the center of the square, in the middle of the dance line. Of the clowns, the *kossa* filed in with the dancers; *the kwírena* emerged during I. 3, from a dance house in the south wall, for their summer moiety. All three "ad libbed" their positions.

The afternoon appearance from the winter dance house did not follow the square circuit through, as had San Ildefonso's dancers. The men proceeded to the south wall, made a counter-clockwise circuit, and lined up facing south in position 5. After five song repeats with face-abouts they received gifts and then reiterated the quintuple repeat. Then they filed into the plaza dance house (6) to finish their song series.

The complete plan hence was—

I.   1 2 3 4
II.   1   3
III.   5
IV.   6

The indoor completion was attributed to the bitter cold weather. This also held the plaza crowd to a minimum, sometimes to the author's solitary figure.[9] The few spectators sat or stood anywhere, in the morning. In the afternoon they kept clear of the south wall. Most of the residents peered out from their windows on all sides.

These diversities pose two prime questions. Is it possible to establish a fundamental Tewa circuit type? What are the reasons for the considerable differences?

Before approaching these questions it is necessary to distinguish the essentials. There are many variations due to accidents of weather,[10] bringing curtailment or extension; to choreographic causes, and to esoteric reasons. For the present purposes these must be disregarded, though they form interesting topics. In particular, the dancers' utilization of the space at each station and the many elaborate patterns distinguishing the ceremonies, are important subjects. But they do not materially affect the present problem of movement from station to station.

This movement is of two types, which group together the more northerly and the more southerly pueblos:

1. Circuit from plaza to plaza, at San Juan three plazas and house in exact recurrent, at Santa Clara four plazas with a set and fairly complex pattern of complete and alternate settings.

2. Circuit within one and the same large plaza, with a pattern of complete and alternate stations.

Type 1 does not adhere to the theory of counter-clockwise direction, San Juan running just the opposite, and Santa Clara adhering in part. Type 2 always proceeds counter-clockwise. Type 2 also emphasizes the cardinal directions more clearly than Type 1. Both types stress the number four in the number of appearances during a day; and two or four within each appearance. Both types are essentially migratory.

These common properties assume more importance in comparison with the Keresan pueblos immediately south of Santa Fe. These use one large plaza and occasionally certain other places, such as giving a terminal performance in front of the dance house. In this respect they resemble the two southerly Tewa pueblos, especially Tesuque. But the Keresan dancers do not circuit around a square, with a performance at each cardinal point. Within observation, they repeat at the same place, perhaps in reversal, or at times at the other end of the plaza. For the four or eight appearances the performers may emerge from different kivas, but each moiety lines up at the same location for each appearance. They thus differ particularly from San Juan.

On the basis of Tewa theory, inter-Tewa likenesses and Tewa-Keresan differences, one might suggest a Tewa circuit prototype. This would be a station-to-station repetition in counter-clockwise circuit, with four dance appearances during the day, two in the morning, two in the afternoon.[11] The basic pattern could be something like—

I.   1 2 3 4
II.   2   4
III.   1   3
IV.   1 2 3   5 (moiety dance house space)

This is more clearcut in San Ildefonso and most complex in Santa Clara. In San Juan, as noted, all repeats are alike.

REASONS FOR DIVERSITY

There are doubtless many factors involved in this diversity. Three main causes seem apparent:

1. Geographical location. The two southerly pueblos more closely approach the Keresan one-plaza type. The two northerly ones may have been influenced by the street processionals of their immediately adjacent Spanish neighbors in Chamita and Española. This explanation is entirely hypothetical.

2. Architectural ground plan. The number, shapes and sizes of the spaces between the house blocks have an obvious effect on the circuit plan. The multiple plaza type implies several adjacent plazas, large enough for the groups but not necessarily huge. These conditions are fulfilled in San Juan and Santa Clara. One plaza in each provides a rather tight squeeze, but the rest are adequate, including the spaces in front of the Santa Clara dance houses. In San Juan in particular the shapes are ideal for the line formation favored in that pueblo, what with the parallel street arrangement.

The single plaza type requires a large central plaza of sufficient size to accommodate a circuit square. For this the Tesuque plaza is just right. The San Ildefonso plazas could accommodate three such squares, particularly the northern side. In the other two pueblos the plazas are too small or too long or both. The eastern space in Santa Clara would be large enough, but it is not a true central plaza, being open on the east side. Also, its ground slants downward perceptibly towards the east, while the ground of all other plazas in all the pueblos is fairly level.

This physical distinction unquestionably has played a role in the development of the two circuit types and some of the variations.

3. Inter-moiety relationships. The moiety pattern has a profound effect on the circuits, as generally on the choreographic manifestations. The moiety situation is not visible to the casual spectator. It produces subtle as well as obvious effects. Some of the relationships and effects have been assembled from native and written sources and fitted to the circuit patterns as follows.

In San Juan the winter and summer moieties operate in harmony. The decisions are in the hands of a unified governing body, with one Governor and one War Chief, although the pattern calls for two caciques. The moieties unite in the dances. They use the same dance house and circulate through the plazas together, without any outward distinguishing marks. At the Harvest Dance they take turns in one long event.

Santa Clara is split into four parties, each moiety being divided into conservatives and progressives. The government is highly organized and even drew up a constitution on December 10, 1935.[12] The Council operates efficiently, under one Governor (in 1957 the very able Juan Chavarria), and a set of officers; it admits women to meetings. The four factions are taken care of by the annual rotation of officers and by the election of eight representatives. The War Chief has religious duties.

The two parties of the winter moiety dominate ceremonial activities from November to April; the summer parties take the helm April to November. But both moieties can dance at any time of year. This follows an all-Tewa custom.[13] However, Santa Clara parties arrange separate public dances and give them on separate dates. Each party has its own dance house. All parties follow a set circuit, but each party has its special variant of the second and third appearances and terminates in front of its house. However, only three circuit variants are now operative, because the conservative winter faction has lost too many of its singers and dancers to sponsor a dance.[14]

San Ildefonso has another kind of internal split. Members of both moieties live around both plazas, but a larger population inhabits the northern section. The Governor, therefore, has more frequently been elected from that section. This and other causes provoked open quarrels and secession of the southern half. On February 10, 1943, an agreement on Governor election in alternate years gave the two sides equal rights and somewhat assuaged the bitterness.[15] Each side now has two representatives in the Council. But the north and south plazas operate their ceremonies separately. The dates are set independently and commonly fall on different days, but on special festivals the two plazas compete. The old kiva in the south plaza is now seldom used, and each plaza has its own kiva in the second story of a house block. This also serves as dance house, hence for entrances and exits of the dance group.

In Tesuque the two moieties cooperate yet preserve their identity. Officers are selected by headmen from both moieties.[16] Although accurate information is difficult to obtain, it seems that at present there is a separate kiva for each moiety and also a combined dance house, all three of which can be used in one day. Each moiety can schedule a separate dance, starting from its own kiva. But the central plaza is the main site for the frequent combined activities. In these joint ceremonies, one half can be conducted from one kiva and the other half from the other kiva. As in the one-plaza centralization, the dual harmony of the Tesuque dances is closer to the Keresan principle than are the dances of the other Tewa pueblos.

DOMESTIC SETTING AS SANCTUARY

For the duration of a dance ceremony, the adobe-colored space between houseblocks is transformed into a sanctuary, full of life and color. No special distant place is set aside for the deities that come down from the mountains. On certain occasions the deity representatives, who are family members, circulate among the houses and are regaled with gifts and feasts by the inmates. The inmates provide the dance audience.

Though some recent schisms tend to disrupt the pattern, the ties between family and plaza ceremony are doubtless ancient, at least as ancient as the clustering around a single plaza[17] or two plazas[18] in thirteenth century Rio Grande pueblos. Age-old circuit customs have increased their diversity during changing domestic situations.

N O T E S

1. To the Wenner-Gren Foundation for Anthropological Research, thanks for funds to study Pueblo dances and music during the spring semester of 1957. To Dr. Edward P. Dozier, thanks for suggestions.

2. The plaza is evident to popular and scholarly observers. See, for instance, Bertha P. Dutton, *New Mexico Indians and their Arizona Neighbors,* Santa Fe, 1955, pp. 11-14.

3. The repeated fourfold dance circuit carries through esoteric as well as public ceremonies. See Elsie C. Parsons, *Pueblo Indian Religion,* University of Chicago Press, 1989, I:385 ff., and Leslie A. White, *The Pueblo of Santo Domingo,* American Anthropological Association Memoir 43, 1935, pp. 142 ff.

4. The dates of occupation are quoted from Stanley A. Stubbs, *Birds' Eye View of the Pueblos,* University of Oklahoma Press, 1950, pp. 39, 43, 47, and 55 for the four pueblos.

5. The ground plan drawings, executed by Ellen Kurath, are a composite of the writer's field sketches and of the house plans in Stubbs. For clarity the house walls are drawn in outline, only the kivas and dance houses being partitioned. The spectators are not shown, their positions being arbitrary.

6. Dutton, p. 14.

7. The women emerged for six appearances, recapitulating I and II, allegedly because it was a fine day and they were in a dancing mood.

8. A circuit recalling the Santa Clara zigzag is reported for the Pinto Dance by William Whitman, *The Pueblo Indians of San Ildefonso,* Columbia University Press, 1947, p. 136.

9. Also, this was a very sacred dance, and not publicized.

10. Traditionally, the weather has never influenced a dance to the point of postponement or cancellation. But of late this may happen, according to Charles E. Lange, "Tablita, or Corn, Dance of the Rio Grande Pueblo Indians," *Texas Journal of Science,* 1057, 9; 59-74, p. 73.

11. The morning appearances now begin at 11:00 or 12:00 A.M. and they continue until a late lunch. Then the afternoon circuits begin.

12. S.D. Aberle, *The Pueblo Indians of New Mexico, Their Land, Economy and Civil Organization,* American Anthropological Association Memoir 70, 1948, p. 37.

13. Dutton, p. 6.

14. Dr. W.W. Hill, who kindly allowed my perusal of his significant manuscript on Santa Clara, describes the moiety structure, but does not relate it to the circuit patterns.

15. Whitman narrates the internal conflict and also briefly describes some dances, but he does not connect these with the circuit problem. For comments on the San Ildefonso situation, see Aberle, p. 36, n. 62.

16. Aberle, pp. 47 and 49.

17. Alfred V. Kidder, *The Story of the Pueblo of Pecos,* Papers of the School of American Research, No. 44, 1951, pp. 3, 5, 9.

18. John L. Sinclair, *The Story of the Pueblo of Kuaua,* Papers of the School of American Research, No. 45, 1951, p. 4.

WHERE DID THE PUEBLO PEOPLE COME FROM?

BY FLORENCE HAWLEY ELLIS

VOLUME 74, NUMBER 3

AUTUMN, 1967

During the period of excavations on Wetherill Mesa (1958-1965), it became apparent that a number of related studies, not in the standard program of dirt archaeology, would be of great value in interpreting the data collected from the excavations. One of these studies was the attempt to determine whether traditions still existent among the living Pueblo peoples could provide some light on which of them would claim ancestors who had lived in Mesa Verde country, an area far larger than the Mesa Verde itself. As I had been working with several of the Pueblo tribes in gathering information on early settlements pertinent to their land claims, I was asked to take over the study of native traditions, concerning ancestral migrations. But, thoroughly aware that archaeological and linguistic relationships must substantiate, disprove, or aid in interpretation of tradition, I stipulated that such material be part and parcel of the study. Moreover, if we were to discover material leading to hypotheses of who came out of Mesa Verde, at the same time we necessarily must discover something of who did not, for separation of the tribes *a priori* obviously was impossible.

A lengthy project involving considerable collection and checking of legendary material thus evolved, and a number of trips were made to the Mesa Verde country with informants, though only after they had demonstrated their understanding of verbal tribal history. There had been some apprehension that everyone might want to claim the finest ruins as ancestral homes, but this turned out to be anything but a problem. These people were as honestly concerned as any anthropologist in making factual evaluations of data. Pueblo peoples are not history-minded in the sense of assigning even relative dates to the various events of their past. Their account begins with the story of emergence from the underworld, if not with the first creation. But this religious mythology is followed by tradition, as such: the migrations which led to their present locations, the cause of migration, types of leaders, and events concerning the formation of new religious societies in patterns given them by the supernatural beings temporarily present in person to give aid and deline-

ate "proper" behavior and social structure from which they never must deviate in
any future time. If one knows Pueblo culture well enough to be able—with the aid
of informants—to skim off some of the frosting of symbolism, there remains a
framework of events to be checked against sequences in related pottery types, much
better known for specific Pueblo groups now than before.

A further aid not previously used in tracing migration is information on the
now-distant shrines, presumably once reached on foot with relative ease, and
either known or traditionally stated to have been used by ancestors even while they
were living in present pueblo sites.

Before presenting here in briefest form the gist of our conclusions from this
study, we should reiterate that we do not believe that traditions—or the data from
archaeology, linguistics, or ethnology—can be used alone, safely, in attempting
a reconstruction of Southwestern prehistory. But let us stress equally that all data
utilized should have come from field studies on the specific peoples and sites with
which one is concerned, not from assumptions presumed to pertain to "all peoples" or even merely to "all Pueblos." The field studies may date from the past or
the present and must be evaluated, but substitution of generalities, whether backed
by machine age analysis or philosophical hunches, for precise data is even more
risky than reliance on any single anthropological discipline.

CULTURAL COMPONENTS AND AREAS OCCUPIED BY ANCESTORS OF LIVING PUEBLOS

Hopi: The Hopi, who now reside on or at the base of their three mesas in northeastern Arizona, are the only living Pueblo peoples of Arizona today and their
ancestry is so mixed that we might speak of the Hopi country as a Pueblo melting
pot. Their basic nucleus seems to have been a combination of people speaking
Hopi and/or closely related Shoshonean tongues who moved to the mesas at about
A.D. 1300 or slightly before, from three areas. One group was that from Kayenta,
who had been living in the general vicinity of Marsh Pass and whose culture is
referred to as of the Tsegi focus or phase. The second was the closely similar people, so far as yet known or published, who had been occupying some of the territory quite close around the Hopi mesas. The third consisted of people who had
moved into northeastern Arizona from small sites in southern Utah, northwestern
Arizona (north of the Grand Canyon), and the Moapa Valley of southern Nevada,
all of whom produced similar painted pottery. Their arrival in the Kayenta area
would have dated before A.D. 1100 or 1150, and the reason for abandoning their
former territory generally is thought to have been growing fear of the Paiute ancestors recently arrived from the west.

This basic nucleus of three components was joined by a contemporary migration of people of Mesa Verde culture, from the eastern side of the Chinle drainage

and from southeastern Utah, especially from the Beef Basin and Navajo Mountain districts. These people were identified in old Hopi tradition as Keresan-speaking, and for some years archaeologists have thought that the Keres were the major occupants of the Mesa Verde and carriers of Mesa Verde culture.

The third major addition to the Hopi consisted of people immediately from the Little Colorado-White Mountains region of eastern Arizona, though at least a portion of these migrants had come from yet unidentified districts farther south. They were relatives of some who were becoming or about to become a part of the Zuni amalgamation. Their language probably was Tanoan or a proto-Tanoan tongue carried by people whose late Mogollon or Western Pueblo culture had been considerably influenced through Mexican contacts.

The fourth addition consisted of some of the Sinagua from the Flagstaff area, whose language more probably was Yuman or Piman than any other known for the Southwest, though the problem is unresolved.

The fifth comprised several groups from the Rio Grande, including the famous Asa clan (a migrant unit apparently made up of Keresan as well as Tanoan-speaking people, in part from a pueblo on the Chama but picking up additions as they moved). Of Rio Grande Tanoans who reached Hopi later, during the Pueblo Rebellion and Re-conquest, the Tiwas and Towas returned to the Rio Grande in the mid-18th century, but the Tanos remained to become part of the Hopi tribe. This is the only foreign amalgamating unit to retain its own language.

Zuni: The original inhabitants of the Zuni area were of Anasazi culture very similar to or duplicating that of what now is known as the Acoma area. In fact, we would classify these early people as a part of the Keresan-speaking ancestral Acomas. Between the 13th and the 15th centuries those who did not retreat toward Acoma were submerged by immigrants who came in from eastern Arizona. The language of the newcomers was Zuni, tentatively classified at present as one of the divergent California Penutian tongues, or Tanoan. Some of the culture traits of the western peripheral Acomas continued to exist in the amalgam resulting from that forceful addition of people from the triangle west of the Zuni river, a point checked by archaeology as well as tradition.

Keres: These people basically were descendants of people carrying the San José variant of Desert culture, as suggested by Dittert, and quite possibly related to the Pinto phase of California Desert culture, which extended, somewhat sparsely, across the northern Southwest. The Keres seem to have developed through successive phases within a large area extending from the Rio Puerco and probably the Rio Grande westward to Holbrook or the Jeddito, and from Alamocito Creek and the Rio Salado, south of Acoma, northward to include the Acoma-Cebolleta-Zuni Valley country (the latter only before 1300 A.D.), the Red Mesa-Chaco-Aztec region, the southern Chuska, and the Mancos-Mesa Verde area in part. During Pueblo I and especially in Pueblo II, some of these people from the Acoma-Zuni district had infiltrated the Reserve-Upper Gila-White Mountain area to the south to such an extent that the original Mogollon inhabitants lost their cultural identity in the ensuing phases, primarily Anasazi in profile.

Tanoans: Our hypothesis is that the early Mogollon people and the early people of southern Arizona (later represented by the relatively simple Desert Hohokam) both sprang from a common background of Cochise culture and spoke related languages, the one Tanoan and the other Piman. That portion of Pimans who received an early increment of Mexican migrants developed into the Basin Hohokam, Pima ancestors. Some of the Mogollon peoples moved northward. Their two routes, one via the Rio Puerco of the east and one by the Upper Gila or White Mountains and the Chuska Valley, led some Tanoan bands into the Upper San Juan, where by the time of Basket Maker II they were making small amounts of brown-paste pottery. By Basket Maker III most of the pottery was gray or white, the change resulting from experiments with locally prevalent clays and changed firing techniques. Some of the more eastern Tanoans settled in the Gobernador-Rosa-Largo-Gallina country where their language differentiated into Towa. Between A.D. 1100 and 1200 they moved into the Jemez drainage. The people of the Piedra country probably spoke Tewa, though it could have been Tiwa; in the 12th century some or all of them moved eastward to join a scattering of original Rio Grande peoples in the Taos area. The latter probably were the northern and rather countrified outpost group of the Rio Grande Tiwas, a remnant of the northward-moving Tanoans or descendants from local variants of the Cochise people such as are represented by the Atrisco sites (related to Cochise) outside Albuquerque. The Tewas developed their distinctive branch of Tanoan somewhere on the eastern San Juan, either in Mesa Verde country or farther upriver.

Tewa occupation of the Upper Rio Grande came in two or possibly even three waves. The western group which settled on the Chama and northern Pajarito arrived in the 13th century, and pushed some old local residents, Keres, into Frijoles Canyon and to the south, where their relatives had been living for some time. The eastern group of Tewas seems to have traveled via the upper San Juan to where they could cross the Conejos and reach the upper stream of the Rio Grande. They—or a part of them—spent some time in the edge of the Plains country, probably killing and drying meat to serve for food during further travel. Then they came down the east side of the Rio Grande to settle in the Nambe district in the 14th century. It is possible that there was a third migration consisting of Tewas en route to the Galisteo Basin, where they came to be known as the Southern Tewa or Tano, though Tewa legends state that the Galisteo people broke off from the Pajarito group and also that they broke off from the Nambe-Pojoaque group. It seems probable that Tanoans from both districts saw economic opportunity in the Galisteo and the resulting unit may have developed their small variation in Tewa dialect *in situ*. The eastern Tewas, like the western, had displaced resident Keres around the Santa Fe country, and they displaced at least some of those (such as the Santa Anas) who had been living in the Galisteo Basin. The Tewas may have amalgamated with other Keres there. The displaced Keres took up their stand in the Middle Rio Grande Valley, where relatives had been living.

The southern Tiwas of Tiguex, the Albuquerque-Bernalillo district, apparently were local Tiwas with additions from Taos, from the Piro-Jornada area to the south, and from the Piro-speaking peoples who occupied the southern group of the Saline pueblos east of the Manzano Mountains. There also was a migration in from southern Acoma territory, possibly of Tanoan-speaking increments who had left the Reserve-San Augustín region, or possibly of Keres. In this case we know more of the pottery than of the language, and people, but there is evidence of considerable Keresan influence, through additions or contacts, in the social organization of Isleta.

THE PUEBLOS' OWN STORY OF THEIR MIGRATION

Although some of the more or less acculturated modern Pueblos like to explain that the mythological statement of their emergence from a lake or cave leading from the underworld, or their later crossing of a great river, refers to migration via the Bering Straits, most of the older accounts clearly speak of the Pueblos stating that their people "emerged" in the northwest, often specifically identified as southwestern Colorado. The events of the several creations and destructions of the world and its inhabitants before this emergence are derivations from the borrowed Mexican myth of origin, most clearly seen in the version given by Laguna Pueblo. To the Pueblos, their place of early development was "White House," where they tarried for sometime, hunting, farming, building villages, and learning the secrets of curing and, finally, those of weather control. But ultimately there was crop failure and such a food shortage that masses were starving. According to Laguna, a drought had been caused by Mother Earth because the people paid too much attention to gambling rather than to religious ceremonies and had remained at White House instead of moving on southward to the place she had decreed for them— Laguna. The White House area became so dry that there were no birds, no corn, no bees, no animals. The people could not make the required religious prayer offerings because the necessary feathers, corn husks, and wild honey were not to be had. Mother Earth, relenting, sent a messenger to show where such items were to be obtained, in the Laguna area, and the people gathered what few possessions they could carry and came southward by way of a route east of Mt. Taylor and past the present site of Paguate on its southwest slope.

Acoma's version refers to jealousy between the people and the katcinas, the "people" apparently being those who followed the old "medicine cult" and the latter those who had taken up the newly introduced katcina cult. (Such jealousy had been constant in the historic period.) After a battle between the katcinas and the people, the former announced that they never again would visit the pueblos in person but would provide aid in the form of rain and fertility, their specialties, if the proper ceremonies were performed. The hungry people angrily argued that someone was at fault for not handling the ceremonies properly, a predictable Pueblo reaction to any change in religious pattern. The account mentions an attempt to build a tower to reach the sky. This was where the katcinas lived. It also was where the more important supernaturals who are identifiable as Pueblo versions of the god of water (Tlaloc in Mexico) and the god of wind (Quetzalcoatl in Mexico) resided. The tower never could be completed because the groups quarreled and began to speak different languages so they no longer could cooperate. They separated, some moving to the Rio Grande and others to Acoma, Laguna, and Hopi. Was this the never-completed tower in Sun Temple, Mesa Verde's latest religious center, possibly planned in a desperate attempt to propitiate the supernaturals who were withholding moisture for crops? Similarity between this myth and that of the Tower of Babel are recognizable, but the Pueblo tale is a part of the native myth as a whole, and there seems little reason for a Christian insertion.

The unit which reached Acoma from the north came via Chaco, and in the upper reaches late Mesa Verde-type sites of short occupation are found. They went around the west side of Mt. Taylor and reached the rock of Acoma, where they found an inhabited village, which they joined. This story fits our archaeological knowledge, even to the presence of Mesa Verde potsherds in the Acoma dump, though not in proportion to those locally produced. There is Hopi tradition of some of the Keres from their area having moved to Acoma, and our guess is that Pottery Mound, on the Puerco, became the home of these migrants, who added Hopi pottery and Hopi style in kiva murals to the traits of the Acoma nucleus they were joining.

Zia and Santa Ana are specific and consistent in their account of the migration. Both seem to have left the San Juan country by way of the Gobernador. Zia passed Stinking Lake (Lake Jedionda) and came southward, meeting the Jemez in transit and moving along beside them, so that each could see the smoke of the other's fires. Jemez confirms this legend and claims to recognize a symbol pecked into a rock near Dulce (Jicarilla agency), which is not far from Jedionda. The Zias tell of stopping for a while, periodically, and we would suggest that this may have been in Pajarito Plateau country, as indicated by the pottery they still were making when they arrived at the site which was to become that of Zia itself. In the meantime, they settled for a period in the Kittichina pueblos which they built on a mesa some miles to the north of their present location. The next move was to where they built Zia on the volcanic mesa, and to another a short distance up the Jemez river. As their population grew, they constructed other pueblos in their immediate area; the Spaniards found five, all identifiable ruins today. For a time during the period of the Pueblo Rebellion, the Zias moved to the top of Red Mesa, near the present Jemez Pueblo, but at the time of the re-conquest they were persuaded to return to their partially ruined pueblo on the volcanic hill still occupied today.

The people of Santa Ana wandered farther afield before making a final settlement. After leaving the northwest and reaching the Santa Fe area or the Pajarito Plateau where they remained for a time (probably very near Zia ancestors, as their languages are very similar), they moved into the Galisteo Basin. After some years there, the people went on into the valley of the Rio Grande, where they noticed good ground for agriculture just north of the present Bernalillo. But they did not settle there at this time. They divided, one portion moving back into the southern end of the Galisteo, at Paako (or had these people merely remained there?). The others went up to live beside the Zias in one of the Kittichina pueblos, and when the Zias moved south, these Santa Anas did the same. They built a pueblo at the confluence of the Salado and the Jemez rivers. (This is not that Salado south of Acoma.) When differences arose between them and the Zias, the former moved down the Puerco to reside for a while in Acoma territory. Later they came east to the Rio Grande, picked up the Paako people (some time after the desertion that pueblo seems to have been re-occupied by Tanos), and moved, with them, to establish Tamaya, the large Santa Ana pueblo, and a number of small sites. These, in part, were farm villages at their presently used village of Ranchitos north of Bernalillo, in Corrales, and elsewhere along the west side of the Rio Grande, across the Tiguex. This tradition is verified by potsherds.

We are less sure of the origin of the Middle Rio Grande Keresans, San Felipe, Santo Domingo, and Cochiti, than of any of the others, for legendary material is almost unknown for Domingo and San Felipe, the ultra-conservatives, and Cochiti could not trace its ancestry farther than an early home in Rito de los Frijoles, even in Bandelier's day, though emergence in the northwest was mentioned. That all three of these Pueblo peoples lived in this southern portion of the Pajarito Plateau is most probable. There is an old account which states that they were driven south and thus to their present homes by incoming Tewas who took over the northern portion of the Plateau, as well as the Chama and the Santa Fe area, but a more common tradition is that they left for their present homes because of drought and crop failure. In the early 1900's these Middle Rio Grande Keres still made visits to a cave representing Shipap, the opening of emergence, slightly north of Ojo Caliente. This had been Tewa country since the 13th or 14th century, so the original Keresan use of this cave probably antedates that influx.

The Tewas are less specific in their reasons for leaving the northwest but note food shortage and excessive cold (too short non-frost season) for farming, which led to migration in two units, one of which came from the northwest into the Rio Grande via the Chama. The other went up the San Juan, crossed the Conejos, did their necessary hunting, and came down the Rio Grande past Taos and on to the Nambe foothills. People from the Mesa Verde, and probably from elsewhere on the upper San Juan, had hunted in the Rockies before, as indicated by types of animal bones in refuse, and the dried meat from hunting en route was a practical staple to carry when corn was lacking and a choice of location for new homes still to be made. The Chama and Pajarito Tewas, who are as specific as the Cochitis on the subject of Keres lived as their neighbors in the Frijoles and vicinity, left the plateau, they say, because of drought. Dating by potsherds places this move to the bottomland of the Rio Grande in the late 15th century. The Tewas of the eastern foothills moved down from their ridgecrest pueblos when they felt relatively safe from attacks; they had been farming in the valleys before and now built their homes there or joined others already living near the Rio Grande and its tributaries.

With the knowledge that all of the ancestors of all of the living Pueblos did not come from the northwest, as areas presently occupied and many other areas, as well, were inhabited before the Four Corners area was abandoned, one well might wonder how it happens that the White House episodes and the migration accounts came to be integrated into the traditions of all the tribes with the possible exception of Isleta. Our explanation is that these stories became a part of the legends of whatever people the migrants joined, as well as being retained by the migrants themselves, for such an experience of physical and psychological suffering, magnified by fear that a religious error had been committed, would have produced a soul-shaking saga. Such problems, with recriminations, splitting, and migration, though on a smaller scale, are known to have occurred when drought struck modern pueblos. The similarity between Hopi, Zuni, and Keresan accounts, though with appropriate migration route variations, suggests that certain units which joined each of these tribes must have been closely associated in their past. The appreciable contrast in the Tewa tale indicates movement of this group in another direction. But still there is enough basic similarity between the Tewa story and others to suggest that all of these peoples once had lived as neighbors (as the Pueblo stories all stipulate), though in some cases separated by some dozens of miles. Not so the Tiwa. And not so the Jemez, who tell of having been in the Four Corners country too briefly and too long ago to have built pueblos there, though they had a shrine on "Banana Mountain" (wild bananas being a common native appellation for the sweet yucca fruit), apparently Ute Mountain, earlier known as Yucca Mountain. From there the Jemez moved southwest to settle on "Yellow Mesa," the Gallina country around Cuba, and then in the Jemez Mountains. This account is quite in accord with relationships worked out for derivation of Jemez Pueblo IV pottery and structures from those of the Gallina.

The direction of movement (or lack of direction) from place of origin as stated in the religious myth, substantiates present archaeological knowledge. The southern Tiwa did not come from anywhere in particular, according to tradition. Their lake is not located (the borrowed concept being rather vague), and there is no statement of direction of travel to their present homes. If these people had their basis in the old Middle Rio Grande culture, their moves were minor. They do insist that some of their people came down from Taos and others from the south, the latter being the Piros who had lived for a time in the Saline country across the mountains from the Rio Grande after coming up from the Jornada area.

Pueblo people, like others, are very much against moving their sacred shrines, though, when necessary, substitute locations are designated by the old names. Until the first years of the 20th century, the religious leaders of Acoma made semi-annual treks, with offerings packed on the backs of burros, to an old shrine in the Chaco and then on to the tall monument formerly known as "Chimney Rock" and now as Jackson's Butte at the Mancos Canyon footpath entrance to the Mesa Verde. From there they made a day's trip to the northwest to their symbolic Shipap opening to the underworld, presumably a small body of water such as a spring or pond (with which this area abounds), possibly with a cave in association. The Jemez religious leaders formerly made trips to their "Banana Mountain" shrine. The Tewa and Taos (partly Tewa in background) had a Shipap shrine in the area of the Great Sand Dunes National Monument in Colorado, probably itself a substitute for something farther west. All lakes and springs are connected underground, according to Pueblo belief, and katcina rain spirits may be summoned from any of these and the spirits of the dead may descend through any of them to reach the afterworld below.

Occasionally some contemplative archaeologist asks the question: "Unless the Mesa Verde was seriously menaced by enemies, why didn't the people who left return later to their old homes? Drought and temperature changes pass after a few years."

It seems to me that the very problem of moving, without transportation, and of reconstructing houses would be enough to dissuade peoples from all but mandatory migrations. But, to see whether there was more to be said on this matter, I posed the question to the Cacique of Cochiti and received the same serious answer Tewas had given Hewett years ago when trying to explain the cause behind an especially trying period of hard times.

San Ildefonso, ill-advised and perhaps pushed by witches, had created a new plaza to the north of that used before. Epidemics, strike, and a population decline which threatened to extinguish the tribe followed. Theirs was the penalty of breaking an age-old tabu. The north plaza was abandoned fortunately, in time. Births increased and the tribe prospers today.

"Pueblo people never move to the north," the Cacique told me, "Any other direction is O.K. for moves. But not to the north. The people came here from the north. If they move back toward the north it brings terrible bad luck. Pueblos *never* would do that!"

HISTORY

Through the articles in *El Palacio*, which has entertained and educated the citizens of New Mexico and the country for over seventy years, one can trace the evolution of the study of history, anthropology, folk art, and fine arts in the Southwest. The four articles selected for inclusion here all show the eclectic nature of the journal, its readability, and the success of its mission to bring scholarly material to a general audience. All four articles touch on the Spanish colonial period of New Mexico history. New Mexico focused on its Hispanic colonial past earlier and with greater fervor than was done elsewhere in the Southwest. This may have been because the colonial monuments and artifacts that survived appealed to the romanticism of late nineteenth-century America.

As early as 1882, the New Mexico Historical Society petitioned Congress to preserve the Palace of the Governors as a monument for the history of the territory, and by 1885 the Palace had museum exhibits in its east wing. Colonial monuments and colonial history also were a major factor in the developing tourist industry in New Mexico, an industry that became in important part of northern New Mexico's economy as soon as the railroad connected it to the East Coast in 1880. The New Mexico Historical Society and the Museum of New Mexico put a great deal of effort into collecting artifacts, books, and manuscripts relating to the colonial period. In the process they created one of the finest artifact and library collections in the United States.

One of the early pioneers in the field was the author of the first article, Ralph Emerson Twitchell, a lawyer by training but a historian by avocation. Twitchell produced a prodigious number of articles and volumes about the history of New Mexico. The article printed here is typical of his work and represents the early period in the study of Spanish colonial history. In his somewhat flowery and uncritical style, Twitchell explains to his audience who Don Gaspar de Villagrá was and describes Villagrá's history of the conquest in New Mexico.

The second article, by Arthur J.O. Anderson, also looks at the colonial past, not from the New Mexico perspective but rather from that of the initial Spanish conquest of Mexico. Anderson, a highly trained linguist, is best known for his translation and publication of Fray Bernardino Sahagún's *Florentine Codex*. The background research for this monumental study of Aztec culture was the source for the article included here. His fascinating essay reminds all of us that European scholarship on the North American continent did not begin at Harvard or on the East Coast but, very early, in the valley of Mexico, undertaken by the missionaries who came as part of the Spanish conquest.

In the third article, T.M. Pearce explores one of his major interests, New Mexico place names. He examines the lives and careers of the two Dukes of Alburquerque who served as viceroys of New Spain. Pearce mixes the larger concerns of the viceroyalty with events in New Mexico to give us a detailed background of the founding and naming of what is now New Mexico's largest city.

The final selection is an exciting and thought-provoking article by archeologist Charles DiPeso. Beginning in 1958, DiPeso directed a major research project at the Casas Grandes ruins in Chihuahua, Mexico. This research made him very much aware of the need for a multi-disciplinary approach to understanding the history and prehistory of northern Mexico and the American Southwest. This approach also demonstrates how artificial the distinctions between history and prehistory are. His article, first delivered as a paper to the Western Historical Association and written towards the end of his work at Casas Grandes, eloquently explains his approach.

— MICHAEL WEBER

CAPTAIN DON GASPAR DE VILLAGRÁ
AUTHOR OF THE FIRST HISTORY OF THE CONQUEST OF NEW MEXICO BY THE ADELANTADO DON JUAN DE OÑATE[1]

BY COLONEL RALPH E. TWITCHELL

VOLUME 15, NUMBER 8
OCTOBER 15, 1924

New Mexico enjoys the unique distinction of being the only state in the American Union having a soldier-poet as chronicler of the events transpiring during the first decade of European contact and settlement. It is also the only commonwealth whose first chief executive bore the title of Captain-General and Adelantado. The subject of this paper was a better chronicler than poet, and, as a junior officer under Oñate excelled in his chosen profession. His name lives in history as one of the most prominent of the conquerors and earliest explorers and settlers of New Mexico. His book, the first edition of which is exceedingly rare, not more than four copies being in the great libraries of the United States, and only three in Mexico, was published first in Alcalá de Henares in the year 1610, just twelve years after his first acquaintance with the "Kingdom and Provinces of New Mexico" as a captain under Oñate. The book is a small octavo containing 24 folios of preliminary certificates and endorsement, letters, etc., followed by 287 folios of hexameter verse — an epic which has preserved to posterity in attractive form an accurate relation of the events comprising the Oñate conquest.

In 1900, the Mexican government through the agency of the Museo Nacional de Mexico published a reprint in two volumes, supplemented by an Appendix containing the Memorial of Fray Alonzo de Benavides, copies of documents in the *Archivo Nacional* made by Padre Fischer, some fragments of a work by P.M. Fr. Juan Gonzales de Mendoza and the *Mercurio Volante* by Don Carlos de Siguenza y Góngora.

The book received the royal approval, the phraseology of this formal sanction being more than usual in interest, portraying as it does the safeguards of the period protecting authors and the Crown as well in publications of this character. In granting the license the King declares:

> Whereas, on your part, Captain Gaspar de Villagrá, it has been stated that you have written a book, in blank verse, entitled New Mexico, which has been duly exhibited and which has cost you considerable labor, care and

attention; and having served as a soldier in the discovery, pacification and settlement of the said New Mexico, the story of which we have been discussing and which has been thus by you reduced to a real history and as thus prepared and written you have petitioned and prayed that we grant you license for its publication during a period of twelve years so that no other person may be able to print the same, or as it may suit our royal pleasure. . . .

Thus considered we grant you license and authority for the period of ten full years next succeeding the date of this our decree, and henceforth you or the person you shall authorize, and no one else, may print and sell the said book, reference to the use of which is herein made. And we do now grant permission and authority to any printer of these kingdoms named by you for the purpose during that time of publishing the same from its original, in which on each page, signed at the foot will appear the rubric of Francisco Martinez, our clerk; and one of which will be deposited with our Council, so that, prior to its sale, you shall bring it before them, together with the said original in order that it may be ascertained if the said publication is made accordingly and shall produce testimony in public form by the proof-reader by us appointed that the said publication has been examined and corrected from the original. . . .

And we decree and ordain that during said period no person whatever, without your permission shall sell or print the same, under penalty that he who may do so shall lose whatever books, forms and apparatus which he may have had, and shall also be liable to a fine of fifty thousand maravedi for each time which it may be done to the contrary; and of the said penalty one third part shall go to our royal council, the other third part to the judge imposing the penalty and the remaining one third to him who shall be the informer or shall denounce him.

And we ordain that the members of our Council, president, alcaldes or judges of our Audiencia, alcaldes, constables, house, court and in chancery, and whatsoever remaining justices in all the cities, villages and places of our kingdoms and domains, and each one in his jurisdiction, as well those now as also those of the future, that they shall keep and comply with this our decree and will, which we now make, and you shall not oppose it nor avoid it nor allow it to be avoided in any manner whatsoever, under penalty of our royal will and of ten thousand maravedi for our royal council.

Given at Madrid, on the seventh day of the month of March, one thousand six hundred and ten years.

THE KING

By decree of the King, Our Master.
JORGE DE TOVAR.

In a letter to the King, which is also published in the book, the poet lauds his
royal master to the skies after the style and fashion of a true courtier for his mag-
nanimous efforts in bringing about the discoveries in New Mexico and the dispens-
ing in that far off region the doctrines of the true faith among its many barbarous
peoples and bespeaks for his Majesty many felicitous years in the exaltation of "our
Holy Catholic Faith and the eradication of the grievous errors and despicable idolatry which the devil, our mortal enemy, sows and scatters in this and far-off regions where souls invoke and clamour for the catholic aid and refuge of your Majesty." This gallant Spaniard was in truth a most distinguished soldier, a descendant of the illustrious family of Perez, of Villagrá, a village in the Province of
Campos, in Spain, from which also came the celebrated Captain and warrior, Don
Francisco de Villagrá, who was a "terror and fright to the indomitable and war-
like Auracanians."[2]

It is not known exactly when or where Villagrá was born, but is believed that
his birth occurred between the years 1551 and 1555. The portrait in his book was
made when he was 66 years of age and was, of course, painted prior to the publication of his book in 1610. He was educated at the celebrated University at
Salamanca from which he was graduated with the degree of Bachelor of Letters.
It is not known just when he came to New Spain where he is prominent in seeking enlistments in the City of Mexico under the banner of Oñate, eager for the conquest and pacification of the "kingdom and provinces of New Mexico." The maes-
tre de campo, Don Vicente Zaldivar tells us that in the year 1604 Villagrá was about
53 years of age, more or less, and, in a description of his person, declares him to
have been "of small build, heavy-set, robust, with well-set limbs, heavy grayish
beard, bald head, with two deep wrinkles, one larger than the other, extending
from eye-brow to eye-brow, over his nose and rising to the forehead."[3]

The services rendered the Spanish Crown by Villagrá can not be over estimated. As a loyal subject he spared no expense and made every possible sacrifice
in keeping with his financial means. There were occasions when, in company with
the exploratory forces of his commander-in-chief, he marched more than six thousand miles over mountains, plains and deserts. In some of these in fierce combat
with the Indians, the most notable having been in the assault upon the Peñol de
Acoma where fighting side by side with eleven of his comrades whose names are
immortalized in his poem, he performed prodigies of valor, at times at the very
threshold of destruction in ferocious hand-to-hand combat with the Indians. He
was indefatigable; hunger, heat or cold, long journeys, dangers uncounted, floods
or storms he feared not and always showed himself the gallant leader and captain
which he was. Upon one occasion, having fallen into a trap set by the "barbarous
enemy," into which both he and his horse had fallen, dauntless and intrepid he
arose and thus dismounted, with his boots reversed (*con los zapatos al reves*),

made his escape, the Indians thus being unable to follow his trail to the camp of his command.

Thus valiant and meritorious, to all of which his companions in arms gave testimony, he received the grade of Captain of Cavalry, was appointed Procurador-General of the army of occupation and Juez Asesor in all ecclesiastical matters, a member of the Council of War and Factor of the royal exchecquer in the newly conquered kingdom. He was rewarded also by a grant from the Crown making him and his descendants Hijosdalgos with all the privileges, prerequisites and position of those of that class. In addition, he was appointed mayor of Guanacevi and given the title of Captain of the Tepehuanes in the province at that time designated as Nueva Vizcaya, now the state of Durango, the duties of which he most efficiently discharged, being well acquitted and approved in the residencia which followed his incumbency. After thirty years of service under the vice-royalty of new Spain, which he performed during the last third of the 16th century, having sought a certificate of merit for a benefice from the royal audiencia of Nueva Galicia for an appointment as governor of some province, or as corregidor of Zacatecas, he sailed for the mother country in the first years of the 17th century, where he resided eleven years, during which, in 1610, his poem was published. After its publication he returned to New Spain carrying a commission as Alcalde Mayor in Guatemala, given him by the King, and departed this life suddenly while on the voyage. We are unable to give the exact date of the passing of this gallant Spaniard, but in a royal cedula the date is given as 1625, although in the last will and testament of his son-in-law, he is mentioned as being alive in 1638. This must be an error, however, or the testator was not advised of the death of his father-in-law at the time the will was executed.

Captain Perez de Villagrá left a widow, a son, José de Villagrá and a daughter, Doña Maria de Vilches Saldivar y Castilla, who married the Captain, Don Cristobal Becerra y Moctesuma, great-grandson of the Emperor Moctesuma. Captain Becerra left many curious statements and information in his will relative to his ancestors.

In the estimation of noted Spanish historians, Villagrá's poem is one of the greatest historical value, favorably compared by them with the letters of Hernando Cortéz, the Relación of Bernal Diaz del Castillo and the work known as the Conquistador Anonimo de D. Andres de Tapia and the Fray Francisco de Aguilar "cronistas-conquistadores," who grasped the pen equally with the sword. Captain Gaspar Perez de Villagrá promised a second part of his Historia, but it was not published if it was ever written.

Bancroft was the first historian writing in English to call attention to the value of Villagrá's work, having made an examination of the same as early as 1877, stating also that the Spanish historian Cesareo Fernandes Duro in his Don Diego de

Peñalosa-148-160 gave, in 1883, a most excellent summary of Villagrá's work.[4]

In an exact reproduction of the measure one of historian Bancroft's many assistants gave a literal translation of the 1st canto of the poem, which is very much worth while and inasmuch as Bancroft's work is out of print is reproduced here for the benefit of those who have interest in the subject:

HISTORY OF NEW MEXICO
BY
CAPTAIN GASPAR DE VILLAGRÁ
First Canto

Which makes known the argument of the history, and the situation of New Mexico, and knowledge had of it from ancient monuments of the Indians and of the departure and origin of the Mexicans.

> Of arms I sing and of the man heroic;
> The being, valor, prudence and high effort
> Of him whose endless, never-tiring patience.
> Over an ocean of annoyance stretching,
> Despite the fangs of foul, envenomed envy
> Brave deeds of prowess ever is achieving;
> Of those brave men of Spain, conquistadores
> Who, in the western India nobly striving,
> And searching out all the world yet hidden,
> Still onward pressed their glorious achievements,
> By their strong arms and deeds of daring valor,
> In strife of arms and hardships as enduring
> As, with rude pen, worthy of being honored.
> And these I supplicate, most Christian Philip,
> Since of New Mexico thou are the Phoenix
> Of late sprung forth and in thy grandeur risen
> From out the mass of living flame and action
> Of faith most ardent; and whose glowing embers
> Thy own most holy father and our master
> We saw inwrapt, devoured by sacred fervor—
> To move some little time from off thy shoulders
> The great and heavy weight, that these oppresses,
> Of that terrestrial globe which in all justice
> Is by thine own strong arm alone supported;
> And giving, gracious king, attentive hearing,
> Thou here wilt see the weight of weary labors,
> And grievous calumnies with which is planted

The Holy Gospel and the Faith of Jesus
By that Achilles, who, by royal order
Devotes himself to such heroic service.
And if I may be rare excess of fortune
Have thee, most noble Philip, for a hearer
Who doubts that with a universal impulse
The whole wide world will hold its breath to listen
To that which holds so great a king's attention?
Then, being thus by these so highly favored,
Since it is nothing less to write the story
Of deeds that worthy are of the pen's record,
Than to achieve deeds that no less are worthy
Of being put by the same pen is writing,
Nothing remains but that those men heroic,
For whose sake I this task have undertaken,
Should still encourage by their acts of valor
The flight ambitious of a pen so humble,
For in this case I think we shall see equalled
Deeds by the words in which they are recorded.
Listen to me, great king, for I was witness
Of all that here, my lord, I have to tell thee.

Of those who have given their time to historical research in the story of Spanish
America and the earliest efforts toward the colonization of southwestern United
States of today during the Spanish period, Adolf [sic] F. Bandelier was the first
from New Mexico to make a critical examination and translations from Villagrá's
work. Engaged in the City of Mexico in searching the archives for information as
to Spanish land grants in this section, under the patronage of the late Thomas B.
Catron, Bandelier was the first to make known here the existence of the great quantity of material relating to the history of New Mexico which was afterwards "discovered" by Dr. Herbert Eugene Bolton of the University of California. It was Bandelier who learned of the existence of the copy of Villagrá's Historia de Nueva
Mexico, in the libraries of our sister republic, installed at the Museo Nacional de
Mexico, and having been accorded the privilege he made a verbatim copy, folio
by folio, with all the curious "tail-pieces" and illuminated initial lettering which
Bandelier reproduced in water coloring. This copy was delivered to Senator Catron
and probably is now to be found in the library which was left to his children . . . .

NOTES

1. Paper read before the New Mexico Historical Society, October 21, 1924.

2. Lopez de Haro, *Nobilario Genalogico*, lib. X de la segunda parte, fol. 414.

3. *Historia de La Nueva Mexico,* Gaspar de Villagrá, Reprint, Mexico, 1900, Introduction.

4. H.H. Bancroft, *Arizona and New Mexico,* page 115, note 5.

THE EARLIEST AMERICANISTS

BY ARTHUR J.O. ANDERSON

VOLUME 52, NUMBER 5

MAY, 1945

To found a college in which the Red man could teach something of his civilization to the conquering White, while he, in turn, indoctrinated the Red, would be a truly Utopian form of acculturation. Something nearly like this happened in the early years of Spanish rule in Mexico. In that project the most brilliant workers were Franciscan missionaries who came with the Conquistadores, joined later, when the initial spark had cooled, by Jesuits, who planted their Order in Mexico in 1572. They taught in colleges, they studied Indian life and language, they learned much from the Indians.

There are many who could be numbered among the earliest Americanists. The present paper, after first considering the more generalized efforts of the schools, will mention the significance of Olmos, Molina, and Sahagún (Franciscans); Rincón and Carochi (Jesuits); and Gastelu, a secular priest.[1]

SAN FRANCISCO DE MÉXICO

An incident in the subjugation of the Aztecs of Tenochititlán was the founding by Fray Pedro de Gante, in 1523, of the School of San Francisco de México. In its first fifty years, under Gante, it gave a thousand students, including Indians, an elementary education and religious training. Latin and music came later, and still later—for adults—vocational training.[2]

SANTA CRUZ DE TLATELOLCO

The importance of the Academy of Santa Cruz de Tlatelolco[3] lies in three circumstances. One is that it developed into a college in which both the Spanish missionaries and the Indians exchanged their expert knowledge. It did so—the second point—largely because it was broadly conceived, not only by Zumárraga, Bishop of Mexico, Mendoza, the viceroy, and more remotely by Charles V, who on the whole was pretty broad-minded, but by a circle of guiding geniuses, remarkably well and diversely trained—Basacio, Focher, Cisneros, Coana, Olmos, Sahagún. In some respects its curriculum was not unusual; it had religion, ethics, reading and writing of Spanish, Latin grammar, rhetoric, logic, philosophy, and music. Study of Mexican medical lore, however, showed the live interest of its faculty in using the products of Indian civilization; in men like Sahagún it had professors broad enough to recognize the value of saving what was good in Mexican civilization.

From the first, the policies of the Academy of Santa Cruz de Tlatelolco struggled against those reactionaries who argued the inherent superiority of Spaniard over Indian. Eventually such opposition helped ruin the venture. But the college proved that the Indian could easily grasp and use any offering of Old World university education. Contemporaries, including Sahagún, found the Indian students in these pioneer times unfit for the priesthood: they tested some promising young Indians out. From this standpoint, the experiment could have been dubbed a failure. Yet if the fascinating discussion in lib. X, cap. XXVII, of Sahagún's *Historia* recorded common clerical experience in the sixteenth century, the intellectual strength of the Indian was fully realized, the achievements of Aztec civilization were fully appreciated, and the weight of ancient traditions and mores—unfitting recent converts for the priesthood— were accurately assessed. The third significant contribution of this school was that its students helped preserve knowledge of the ancient life. They were among the amanuenses, collaborators, and printers who made philological works of the sixteenth century possible. They were among the native teachers who taught Nahuatl. To the more alert and fair-minded of the learned Spaniards they taught Aztec history, religion, and sociology. Policies represented by the College of Santa Cruz de Tlatelolco fostered such Indian chroniclers as Chimalpahin, Ixtilxóchitl, and Tezozomoc, and inspired the exhaustive analysis represented in Sahagún's *Historia*.

SAN JUAN DE LETRÁN AND THE UNIVERSITY OF MEXICO

Mendoza, the viceroy, who was active in founding the school discussed above, also founded two others.[4] The Academy of San Juan de Letrán cared for mestizo children, many of whom were illegitimate and abandoned by their parents, and was intended to prepare teachers of similar children of future generations. The University of Mexico was another of his endowments (1551);[5] in the same year, Charles V further endowed it; later (1599) the Pope gave his confirmation and the title of Pontifical. Instruction in Nahuatl was early in its list of courses.

JESUIT COLLEGES

Still later, the Jesuits started their activities.[6] Having established the Company of Jesus in 1572, they founded their most celebrated college, the Academy of San Pedro y San Pablo, in the next year. In time, it became the Colegio Máximo. Other schools followed: San Miguel and San Bernardino were ultimately fused into one—San Ildefonso. San Gregorio educated Indians exclusively. The seminary at

Tepotzotlán specialized in Indian languages, particularly Nahuatl and Otomí; but all of them stressed Latin and philology, with thoughts of the widespread evangelization for which the Jesuit Order was noted. The colleges of San Pedro y San Pablo and at Tepotzotlán, as well as others in Valladolid and Puebla, were all founded in the first ten years of Jesuit activity.[7]

In naming and discussing six philologists who studied and taught Nahuatl and Nahua civilization, this paper cannot claim to be exhaustive. However, the three Franciscans—Olmos, Molina, and Sahagún; the Jesuits—Rincón and Carochi; and the secular priest, Gastelu, can lay claim to much of the credit for complete study and systematization of the language.[8] All of them were eminent men—founders of convents, churches, hospitals, schools; professors in the colleges. They laid the basis of all present knowledge of Nahuatl. All of them became experts in the civilization of the Indians, and in writing the confessionaries and other religious aids which accompany some of their *Artes* showed that they knew well the pre-Conquest traits which survived.

ANDRÉS DE OLMOS (CA. 1491-1571)

"A Franciscan Spaniard of holy memory," an "indefatigable preacher,"[9] Olmos was born at Oña (province of Burgos), and educated and ordained at Valladolid. Zumárraga chose him to accompany him to Mexico (1528) and to assist him in his episcopal duties. His assistance was prodigious. He traveled afoot continuously over several provinces; he founded seven convents. Mountains, forests, hostile Indians were no obstacle; neither were the various Indian languages which he encountered. He mastered Tepehua, Totonac, Huaxtec, and especially Nahuatl; he wrote grammars and dictionaries of the last three tongues. He taught Latin at the College of Santa Cruz de Tlatelolco.

His known writings in Nahuatl are the grammar of *Arte,* a vocabulary, *The Last Judgment, Conversations Which Mexican Lords Had with Their Sons, The Book of Seven Sermons, Treatise on the Seven Mortal Sins and their Progeny, Treatise on the Sacraments, Treatise on Sacriliges* [sic].'Similar works in Huaxtec are said to survive; possibly also some in other tongues. But the bulk of these are thought to be lost. Both Clavijero and Siméon[10] mention a treatise on Mexican antiquities, also lost.

Of these works the only one certainly surviving—probably his most important —is the Mexican grammar (1547), a remarkable achievement considering that when he wrote it, Olmos had been in Mexico less than ten years. Complete, clear, exact, orderly, it is the basis of almost all subsequent studies of Nahuatl grammar. It has faults: the Latin model which he followed (Lebrixa's)—like that of any European language, for that matter—is ill-adapted to Nahuatl; though in adapting Nahuatl to a Latin mold he makes the language understandable. Though he faltered

occasionally as in failure to recognize the commonly used ligatures in certain combinations, or to present correctly the system of numeration, his work is still a mar-
vel of clarity.

For the mind trained in Latin, thinking of languages in terms of Latin was
doubtless inevitable. The method has serious limitations. Nahuatl lacks true infini-
tives, gerunds, and participles, for instance. For these and other problems, the
grammars provided cumbersome circumlocutions: one is never sure how much
foreign influence has crept in.[11] But all six priests here considered followed the
same track—Rincón the least slavishly, and, notably, he was at least part Indian.

Olmos' grammar is the least ecclesiastical in its language and examples. Others
stress the sermon and the confessional; Olmos, one feels, thought of Indians and
Spaniards. But generally, in rules and examples, all later grammars owe much to
Olmos.

ALONSO DE MOLINA (1511[?]-1585)

An ususual circumstance brightens the early life of Molina.[12] When Friars
Pedro de Gante, Juan de Tecto, and Juan de Ayora, among the Franciscans to arrive
in Mexico in 1523, first attempted to convert the Aztecs, their complete ignorance
of Nahuatl was a tantalizing obstacle. Finding a widowed Spanish woman, who
came with the Conquistadores and had two sons who had grown up with Indian
children, solved the problem. One of them, Alonso, became the Friars' companion
and interpreter, and he preached their sermons. When of age, he became a Franciscan friar himself. Molina is the earliest link between the Indian mind and that
of the Spaniard, at least on an intellectual level.

The written works of Molina were products of prodigious labor. The *Castilian-
Mexican Vocabulary* first appeared in 1555; the *Mexican-Castilian Vocabulary*,
a longer work than even the enlarged and revised *Castilian-Mexican Vocabulary*
with which it was published, appeared in 1571. An *Arte Mexicana* is also dated
1571. These were the first significant works on the Nahuatl language to be printed.
Molina's statements about the vocabulary[13] indicate that the work was laborious
and hard; he stresses that he had to acquire mastery by slow degrees. The work is
careful, and he was well aware that his vocabulary lacked much because he did not
know all there was to know. The project of publishing a dictionary was one which
the authorities aided him in doing. It was ordered by his superiors (*"mis
prelados"*); it was printed by the viceroy's orders and at his expense —a most
unusual assistance.

BERNARDINO DE SAHAGÚN (CA. 1499-1590)[14]

Bernardino Ribeira became Fray Bernardino de Sahagún on entering the Order
of Franciscans some years before he left for Mexico (1529) with Fray Antonio de

Ciudad Rodrigo and nineteen other friars. On shipboard, using Aztec personages returning from their commanded exhibition in Spain, he began the study of Nahuatl which he continued to the end of his days. He soon mastered the language as well as any non-Indian might—surpassing all other Spaniards except, perhaps, Father Molina. Controversies over his *Historia universal de las cosas de Nueva España* and his enlightened attitude toward the Indians whom he taught led him through an eventful career at the end of which sorrow must have been deep. Mainly, however, he occupied positions of considerable *eminence—guardian* of the monastery at Tlalmanalco (1530-1545), Superior of the Convent of Tlatelolco (1546), Dean of the College of Santa Cruz de Tlatelolco (1560), Professor of Latin and Nahuatl at the same college (1536-1540, 1570-1590). He ended more than ninety years of most remarkable achievement—even if it remained unknown for 250 years—probably lost in the feeling that his work had been futile, because of circumstances connected with his ambitions for the College of Santa Cruz and, perhaps more, because of the convictions reflected in his *Historia*.

The only work of his pen known to have been published during his lifetime is a book of Christian Psalmody;[15] his list of writings is, however, long. The following[16] is probably incomplete: in religion, besides the one mentioned, *Commentary on the Epistles and Gospels for Sunday* (Nahuatl); *Sermons; Evangeliarum, Epistolariu, et Lectionarium*; *Life of San Bernardino of the Seine* (translated into Nahuatl); *Daily Exercises in the Nahuatlan Language*, *Manual for the Christian*; *Christian Doctrine* (Nahuatl); *Treatise on the Theological Virtues* (Nahuatl); *Book on the Coming of the First Fathers and the Discourses They Had with the Priests of the Idols*; *Catechism of the Christian Doctrine*; *Post-Baptismal Talks to Children*; *Spiritual Light*; *Spiritual Guidance*; *Precepts for Married People*; *Doctrine for Physicians*; in philology, an *Arte* of Nahuatl; a *Trilingual Dictionary* (Spanish, Latin, Nahuatl); a *Calepino* (Latin dictionary); and finally the remarkable *Historia universal de las cosas de Nueva España*—perhaps rather an encyclopaedic ethnological work than a history. A bibliography is hard to pin down, and much has been lost.

Although Sahagún's points of view as a priest must not be forgotten, nevertheless his work at the College of Santa Cruz de Tlatelolco and his writing in the *Historia* ran strongly counter to the prevailing orthodox, conservative, and highly restrictive policies of commanding Spaniards of his time. At the College, he was of the group which highly respected the abilities of the Indian students. His recognition of the achievements of the Aztec civilization is shown by championing study of Mexican medical lore, by use of picture-writing to inculcate religious principles,[17] or, in discussing problems in educating Indian children, by tributes to the pre-Spanish social and educational systems.[18] He found the Indian mind able to absorb and use all the higher learning of the Old World; and he was one of the experimenters who presented much of it to the more capable Indian students.

Thanks to Sahagún, Molina, Olmos, and others like them, there were trilingual Indians (Spanish, Latin and Nahuatl) with whom Sahagún could collaborate in the writing of the *Historia.* The attempt, in which Sahagún had a hand, to make priests of the best-prepared Indian students was a failure: the weight of tradition and many other factors was too great. But Sahagún proved that there was no limit to what the Indians could be taught, and much of official Spain held his success against him.[19]

These same aspirations and convictions stand out in a number of pages of the *Historia.* Probably the obstacles he met in completing the work as he had planned, and of putting it to use, stemmed from personal animosities of other priests, perhaps frustrated by their difficulties with the Indian mind, and also from official desire to emphasize only the Spanish version of the Conquest.[20] It is notable, too, that Sahagún was free in his praise for many aspects of the Aztec civilization which the Spaniards were fast destroying—government,[21] the fine qualities of the language,[22] the art, science, and so forth, of which he speaks in lib. X, cap. XXVII.

Magnificent though Sahagún's success was in writing the *Historia,* it is doubtful that the enormous labor—the ten versions[23]— produced what he had hoped for. He speaks[24] of a work in three columns (not just the two of the Florentine Codex)— Spanish, Nahuatl, and a third clarifying Nahuatl words. He appears to have planned a treatise on grammar and a vocabulary to close the work.[25] He counted on producing a work which would give his colleagues and successors an exact knowledge not only of the language (which all writers of Nahuatl grammars and vocabularies set out to do), so that the Christian Faith could be effectively and authoritatively spread among the Indians, but also of the customs, practices, and daily life of the Indians.[26] Priests must know not only how to avoid preaching without error, or even unintentional heresy or sacrilege; they must know custom and tradition contrary to Christian doctrine and morals, in order to combat them. As is well known, his plans were upset by jealous colleagues and suspicious superiors. Enemies came into office long enough to foil him. The more broadminded policies of Charles V gave way to the more restrictive rule of Philip II. His works were taken away from him. His grammatical treatise and vocabulary may exist, but are unknown. It is doubtful whether even the Great Florentine Codex, complete though it is, represents what Sahagún planned.

Some of the most competent and thorough study of Nahuatl comes from the pens of Jesuit priests. The Order was established in Mexico after the first flush of enthusiasm over conquest (in 1572). It was a highly disciplined institution. Religious policies were firmly established in the New World; and the Jesuits flourished following a steadier pattern than that of the Franciscan experimenters.

ANTONIO DE RINCÓN (D. 1601)[27]

One of Rincón's greatest distinctions is his Indian ancestry. He was the descendant of the chiefs of Texcoco, where he was born; he had Nahuatl from birth. One year after the Jesuits established themselves, he became one of the Company (1573), and spent his life teaching grammar (Nahuatl) and other subjects to students at the College of San Gerónimo, teaching the Indians and tending their spiritual needs, combating idolatry, changing their customs, preaching in church, hospital, and prison, and to forced labor groups. Later, about 1594, he was associated with the Seminary of San Gregorio. His later years, during a decade or more of which he compiled his *Gramática y vocabulario mexicanos* (1595), were made miserable by a paralyzed side.

Rincón's Indian ancestry and, presumably, a childhood spent in a distinguished Texcocan family give his *Gramática* a rather special place. It cannot rank with the treatises of Olmos or Carochi, for all Peñafiel's enthusiasm for it;[28] it is too slight a work. But it is unusual for being first to emphasize the inadequacy what the Nahua knew as the beauties of their tongue: Sahagún fully realized that Nahuatl was inevitably to suffer from contact with Spanish and the disappearance of the civilization, including its leading men, which would perpetuate its finest qualities. Rincón was brought up among Texcocans speaking that finer kind of language, and was of the group which no doubt spoke the finest. That in his love and mastery of the tongue he was more deeply inspired than even the best Spanish masters shows in several characteristics of his little book. One was his attempt, probably the first serious one, to indicate the proper pronunciation of Nahuatl words by means of accents. His method and terminology can be seen to have affected Gastelu and Carochi, for instance. Another characteristic is his examples of poetic and refined expression, some of which are well-known today because he recorded them.[29]

He still presented the language in the rigid Latin cast. But, considering the education of the priest of those days, it was unavoidable; and the need of presenting it so as to be understood by others similarly educated would have made any other method difficult if not futile. The vocabulary is concerned only with the terms used in the *Gramática*.

HORACIO CAROCHI (1580-1662)

The most eminent of the Jesuit Nahuatl scholars was without doubt Padre Horacio Carochi (or Carocci).[30] Born in Florence, Italy, he became a Jesuit at the age of twenty-two. In his sixty years as priest, he became one of the most learned of Jesuits in the New World, eminent in history, geometry, philosophy, theology, and music; in Latin, Greek, and Hebrew; and preeminent in Nahuatl, as well as Otomó and Mazahua. In these Indian languages he wrote various works; but he is remembered for the Nahuatl grammar of which a later Jesuit, Paredes, made a compendium. In his work as priest Carochi was known for his zeal and humility;

no great traveler, he remained content in the comparative obscurity of the College of Tepotzotlán.

Carochi's *Arte de la lengua mexicana*, first published in 1645, was soon recognized as a leading work. Eventually it became unobtainable, along with other works on Nahuatl, and in response to the repeated demands of students, Paredes undertook a reedition which he somewhat shortened and rearranged,[31] publishing it with the title of *Compendio del Arte de la lengua mexicana del P. Horacio Carochi* (1759). Like all such works, it was written in order to train priests in the correct understanding and use of Nahuatl in preaching and confessing the Indians. For such study it is perhaps the best work which Colonial Mexico knew. Seventeenth and eighteenth century scholars so recognized it; and, indeed, in giving detailed explanations of Nahuatl constructions and usage, it is probably preeminent.[32]

The *Compendio* is in three divisions: first, the general rules and syntax; second, the combinations; third, adverbs and other devices for refinements and "*para la transicion.*"[33] The authors felt that mastery of the first part alone would give the student a sufficient command of the language; the next two parts would give him added grace, fluency, and understanding. In many ways, the work is invaluable for its methods of presentation and for its exactness and correctness, in which it surpasses even Olmos' *Gramática*. In appreciation of the grace and poetry of Nahuatl which one finds in Rincón, however, it is lacking. Carochi's interest in Nahuatl was in the efficient, business-like proficiency in the current ecclesiastical Nahuatl necessary for saving Indian souls. His knowledge of Nahuatl was nevertheless profound, and a good many of the examples of Nahuatl expressions show a considerable knowledge of Aztec civilization.

Like Rincón and Gastelu, Carochi developed a system of accents or marks to denote differences of pronunciation which the European alphabet alone could not reproduce. The scheme is essentially the same as, and was probably based upon, Rincón's. But whereas neither Rincón nor Gastelu use the marks in their texts, except to explain their use, Carochi does so rigorously.

ANTONIO VÁSQUEZ DE GASTELU

Antonio Vásquez de Gastelu, Bachiller, was professor of the Nahuatl language at the Royal Colleges of San Pedro and San Juan, in the seventeenth century, at Puebla de los Angeles.[34] Clavijero[35] speaks of him as a secular priest. As author, he wrote a *Catecismo breve* and *Lecciones espirituales para las tandas de ejercicios de San Ignacio*, both in Nahuatl.[36]

The *Arte de lengua mexicana* was first published in 1689, and according to the Bachiller Juan de León Coronado,[37] filled a widely-felt need in dispelling the darkness into which the study of Nahuatl had fallen. That the book went through probably three editions (1689, 1716, and 1729) speaks well for its usefulness. It is, however, a slight work when compared with either Olmos or Carochi. The wealth of example, used so well by those linguists, is lacking; presentation is concise to the point of barrenness. Carochi's skill in using the system of accents which he perfected to try to indicate correct pronunciation is also lacking. What gives it its greatest interest is its appendix, with a Nahuatl catechism and confessionary, which must have been of major importance for the remotely-stationed priests. Gastelu's *Arte* is not the only one of the *Artes* or Gramáticas which contain such aids. But this specimen indicates the kind of anthropological training which the colleges and seminaries of the time provided. And so there is a "Confessionario breve, en la lengua mexicana, y castellana," with its examination of the penitent's observance of the Ten Commandments, and its inquiry into the mortal sins, part of which is translated into Spanish; a "Catechismo breve de lo que precissamente deue saber el Christiano, en lengua mexicana," in Nahuatl; and a few pages of "Correcciones que se les podran dar a los penitentes mexicanos de algunes pecados en el confessionario," with a "Correccion para despues que el penitente se aya confessado." It was necessary to search the Indian's soul for sin and heresy, and the priests had to know what to look for.

To men like these priests, but particularly to the few here discussed, subsequent study of Nahuatl is due. On a background of the first schools and colleges, Olmos moves as the pioneer. His work affected those who followed, even though it remained unpublished until 1875, when Rémi Siméon, the celebrated French linguist, discovered and edited it. Though there are other dictionaries, that of Fray Alonso de Molina is still the indispensable classic for those who study ancient Nahuatl. Gifted to begin with, and favored by his epoch, by his superiors, and by up-bringing, he compiled a vocabulary of Nahuatl as spoken before the Conquest. His, too, was the first published major work dealing with Nahuatl. Sahagún, though his grammatical treatise and vocabulary are lost, succeeded despite great obstacles in writing his systematic, encyclopaedic ethnological work, the *Historia,* in Spanish and in a pure Nahuatl free of the barbarisms, adulterations, and errors common to much of the literature in that tongue.

The imaginations of the Jesuit Fathers were less free than those of their Franciscan predecessors; they settled into tracks by then well established. In the time they flourished (1572-1767 in the Spanish Colonies) a sort of ecclesiastical Nahuatl had developed, and though, to judge by comments and admonitions of the experts here mentioned, the average missionary's use of the language was shockingly inexact, and there is extreme variation in orthography and expression, the norms of a "standard accepted" Nahuatl for church use were well established in centers of learning. So although the later grammarians were more preoccupied with theology, while the earlier Franciscans and Jesuits dealt more with everyday people, the culminating *Compendio* (Carochi-Paredes) is fuller, more complete, more precise than any, and despite the cramping effect of the Latin tradition, easy to understand and not impossible to apply. The Jesuit Nahuatlists appreciated the beauties and flexibility of the language, but their business was first to apply it to confessional and pulpit, and second to systematize it.

The Caucasoid mind works differently from that of the Indian;[38] so much so that all grammars, vocabularies, and translations are to a certain extent in vain. Partly, Caucasians have not wished to understand—as witness Sahagún's enemies. Where there has been the wish to understand, there has also been the wish to impose changes. Even Sahagún was fundamentally thus motivated. Partly, the work of Colonial Mexican linguists was molded according to this urge; hence the circumlocutions and, one sometimes suspects, the distortions in even so objective a work as Molina's *Vocabulario*. The catastrophe of the Conquest stopped Nahuatl in its bid to become the reigning language in Mexico,[39] but what we have and what we may yet recover of Nahuatl we owe to these men, the earliest Americanists.

NOTES

1. Calavijero, 1787, Vol. II, p. 414, lists Ximenes, Olmos, Sahagún, Molina, and Tapia Centeno as writers of grammars and dictionaries, and Rangel, Rincón, Carochi, Mercado, Davila Padilla, Betancurt, Páez, Toval Montezuma, Paredes, Castelu, Pérez, Cabrera, Aldama y Guevara, Focher, and Cortes Canal as writers of grammars only. The list is not chronological. Peña, 1943, p. 127, mentions in addition Pareja, Larios, and San Buenaventura (17th and 18th centuries).

2. Peña, 1943, p. 4.

3. *Ibid.*, p. 5; Emmart, 1940, pp. 17 ff.; Sahagún, 1880, p. xii (Jourdanet's introduction: Sahagún, 1831, lib. X, cap. XXVII.

4. Peña, 1943, pp. 5, 7-8.

5. According to *ibid.*, p. 7, n. 1, its operation was continuous until after Mexican Independence (1551-1833); subsequent service extended from 1834 to 1865. As the National University it has been open since 1910.

6. *Ibid.*, p. 6.

7. Dunne, 1944, p. 6.

8. It is a matter of additional interest that the Library of the School of American Research possesses, besides the Sahagún editions by Bustamante and Jourdanet-Siméon, a Molina (1571), a Gastelu (1726), and a Carochi-Paredes (1759). The writer is grateful to Miss Murphey, Librarian, and to Dr. Hewett, Director, for permission to use those works. Moreover, the School of American Research possesses photographic copies of the Great Florentine Codex.

9. Clavijero, 1787, Vol. I, p. xv. See also Siméon, 1875, pp. iv ff., or Emmart, 1940, pp. 21-22.

10. Clavijero, 1787, *loc. cit.* Siméon, 1875, p. x, citing Torquemada (*Monarquia indiana*, lib. I, cap. XI, pp. 31-32), says that he used an old Indian as informant on the past civilization of Texcoco.

11. See Rincón, 1885, lib. II, cap. 2; lib. IV, cap. 5, for examples. Also Siméon, 1875, pp. 85-88, 90-91; 3ª Parte, caps. 7-8, and *passim;* Carochi, 1759, 1ª Parte, cap. 8, par. 3. In all of these, there are many suggestive examples.

12. Peña, 1943, pp. 10-11.

13. Molina, 1880: from the Archbishop's license, the Epistola Nuncupatoria, and Prologo al lector, Part I; and Prologo al lector, Part II; pp. unnumbered.

14. Clavijero, 1787, Vol. I, p. xv; Emmart, 1940, pp. 23 ff.; Hewett, 1944, *passim;* Peña, 1943, pp. 30-31; Sahagún, 1880, pp. xi ff.

15. Peña, 1943, p. 31.

16. *Loc. cit.*

17. Sahagún, 1880, p. lxiii.

18. Sahagún, 1831, lib. X, cap. XXVII.

19. *Ibid.,* p. iv and *loc. cit.*.; Sahagún, 1880, pp. vii-viii; Emmart, 1940, pp. 23-24.

20. Hewett, 1944, pp. 7, 9.

21. Sahagún, 1831, p. iv.

22. Sahagún, 1880, p. xi.

23. Peña, 1943, pp. 32-33; see also Hewett, 1944, pp. 6 ff.

24. Sahagún, 1831, p. vii.

25. Sahagún, 1880, p. lxii.

26. *Ibid.,* pp. lxi-lxii.

27. Rincón, 1885, pp. iii ff.; Alegre, 1841-2, Vol. I, pp. 73, 179, 197-198, 275. Peñafiel, in his introduction to Rincón, 1885, also cites Oviedo (*Dicc. univ. de hist. y geog.*, T. 6, Mex., 1885, p. 617).

28. Rincón, 1885, p. iii.

29. *Ibid.,* lib. IV, cap. I, contains some good examples distinguished for being non-ecclesiastical— probably pre-Hispanic. Carochi and Olmos, however, also recognized the distinction between aristocratic and common expression.

30. Alegre, 1841-2, Vol. I, pp. 426-427.

31. Carochi, 1759, "Razon de la obra al lector" (pp. unnumbered).

32. *Ibid.,* "Parecer de D. Domingo Joseph de la Mota" (pp. unnumbered).

33. *Ibid.,* "Razon de la obra al lector" (pp. unnumbered).

34. Gastelu, 1726, Secretary's Statement (pp. unnumbered).

35. Clavijero, 1787, Vol. II, pp. 412, 414.

36. Information kindly supplied by Librarian, Harvard University, citing *Enciclopedia universal ilustrada Europeo-Americana*, Vol. 67.

37. Gastelu, 1726, "Densura de Juan de Leon Coronado" (pp. unnumbered).

38. Hewett, 1944, pp. 1-2.

39. Hewett, 1943, p. 63.

BIBLIOGRAPHY

Alegre, el P. Francisco Javier
1841-2 *Historia de la Compañia de Jesús en Nueva España aue estaba escribiendo el P. Francisco Javier Alegre al tiempo de su espulsion*. Publicala...Carlos Maria Bustamante...3 vols. Mexico: Imprenta de J.M. Lara.

Clavijero, Abbé D. Francesco Saverio
1787 *The History of Mexico Collected from Spanish and Mexican Historians, from Manuscripts, and Ancient Paintings of the Indians*. Illustrated by Charts, and Other Copper Plates...Tr. by Charles Cullen. 2 vols. London: G.G.J. and J. Robinson.

Emmart, Emily Walcott
1940 *The Badianus Manuscript (Codex Barberini, Latin 241), Vatican Library. An Aztec Herbal of 1552*. Baltimore: The John Hopkins Press.

Carochi, Horacio
1759 *Compendio del arte de la lengua mexicana del P. Horacio Carochi de la Compañia de Jesus...dispuesto...por el P. Ignacio Paredes, de la misma compañia*...Mexico: En la imprenta de la Biblioteca Mexicana.

Dunne, Peter Masten, S.J.
1944 *Pioneer Jesuits in Northern Mexico*. Berkeley and Los Angeles: University of California Press.

Gastelu, Antonio Vásquez
1726 *Arte de lengua mexicana*. Puebla: Imprenta de Francisco Xávier de Morales y Salazar.

Hewett, Edgar L.
1943 *Ancient Life in Mexico and Central America*. New York: Tudor Publishing Co.

Hewett, Edgar L.
1944 *Fray Bernardino de Sahagún and the Great Florentine Codex*. Santa Fe, New Mexico: School of American Research.

Molina, P. Fr. Alonso de
1880 *Vocabulario de la lengua mexicana, compuesto por el P. Fr. Alsonso de Molina*. Publicada de nuevo por Julio Platzmann. Edición facsimilaria. Leipzig: B.G. Teubner.

Peña, Carlos González
1943 *History of Mexican Literature*. Revised edition, tr. by Gusta Barfield Nance and Florence Johnson Dunstan. Dallas: University Press.

Rincón, Padre Antonio del
1885 *Grammática y volubalario mexicanon, por el Padre Antonio del Rincón, 1595*. Reimpresión de 1885. [Ed. by Antonio Peñafeil.] Mexico: Oficina Tip. de la Secretaría de Fomento.

Sahagún, le R.P. Fray Bernardino de
1880 *Histore générale des choses de la Nouvelle-Espagne*. Tr. et annote par J. Jourdanet...et par Rémi Siméon. Paris: G. Masson, éditeur.

Sahagún, M.R.P. Fr. Bernardino de
1831 *Historia universal de las cosas de Nueva España. Antiquities of Mexico*...by Lord Kingsborough. 9 vols., Vol. VII. London: Robert Havell, 77 Oxford Street; and Colnaghi, Son and Co., Pall Mall East.

Siméon, Rémi
1875 *Grammaire de la langue nahuatl ou mexicaine, composée, en 1547, par le Franciscain André de Olmos*, publiée avec notes, éclaircissements, etc., par Rémi Siméon. Paris: Imprimerie Nationale.

TWO DUKES OF ALBURQUERQUE

BY T.M. PEARCE

VOLUME 61, NUMBER 6

JUNE, 1954

The only title to appear twice in the registry of the viceroys of Mexico is that of the Duke of Alburquerque. The first of these names, Don Francisco Fernández de la Cueva, the twenty-second viceroy, who ruled from 1653 to 1660, was probably that of the seventh Duke of Alburquerque, for Don Francisco de la Cueva Enríquez, who held the vice-regency from 1702 to 1710, is certified by the *Enciclopedia universal ilustrada* as the eighth.[1] No full biography of either of these illustrious men seems to be available; but the evidence favors Don Francisco the earlier as the grandfather of Don Francisco the later. Both were successors to Don Beltrán de la Cueva, the first Duke of Alburquerque, who established the dukedom in 1464.[2] These two men are of interest to New Mexicans, for each has been credited with founding the *villa* of Albuquerque and each was active in defending the frontiers of New Spain against outside foes. A sketch of their activities will shed light on some of the internal and external problems of both New Mexico and New Spain in those troubled days.

The first Duke of Alburquerque to become viceroy of Mexico made his entry into Mexico City just four months before Cromwell became Protector in England.[3] During most of the administration of Francisco Fernández de la Cueva, the Viceroy was faced with the growing naval power of England, spurred on by the Puritan zeal of Oliver Cromwell. An English monk, named Thomas Gage (who had lived in Guatemala and Mexico) turned apostate, and carried to Cromwell information on the military and naval installations of Spain in the New World. In 1654 Cromwell equipped two great fleets, one to carry on war against Spain in the Mediterranean and the other to attack the Spanish colonies in the West Indies. The first squadron, under Admiral William Blake, intercepted a flotilla of Spanish vessels bound for America and put all the ships to the flames. The second English squadron, under William Penn, the father of the Penn who was to found Pennsylvania, made an unsuccessful foray against the island of Hispaniola (modern Dominican Republic and Haiti) and then went on in May of 1655 to occupy Jamaica. The governor of that island petitioned the Duke of Alburquerque for troops, and in the following year the Viceroy sent a small force which joined a command sent from Cartagena (Colombia) and the islanders still holding out against the English. At first the Mexican forces held the advantage, but they suffered considerable losses which they were unable to replace. The English were reinforced from the Bermudas and finally destroyed their opponents. The greater part of the islanders fled with what they could transport to New Spain and the other islands.[4]

Several of the historians describe Francisco de la Cueva as a patron of arts and letters: *"protector de los sabios y de las artes"* is the phrase used by one of the writers;[5] *"muy decidido por el adelanto de las ciencias, las letras y las artes"* are the words of another.[6] His palace was described as a model of elegance and good taste in the city. On the dark side of the picture were the robbers and bandits who flooded the highways, so that no one dared to travel unaccompanied. Against these malefactors the Viceroy took stern measures; and after apprehending and executing many of them, the remainder gave up their way of life, and travel and commerce again flourished on the roads of Mexico. Don Francisco was notably pious, assisting at the festivals of the churches and making liberal contributions toward the completion of the Cathedral. It was, therefore, a matter of great concern to him when a notable ecclesiastical scandal occurred in Puebla in the middle of his first *trienio.*[7] The monks of three religious orders, Augustinian, Dominican, and Mercy (Merced), were jealous of their place in the Corpus Christi procession. They petitioned that the Cross of the parish of Saint Joseph in Puebla should not precede them in the order of march. When the Vicar General ruled against them, they left the procession, standing in doorways and streets, to the great desecration of the Faith. For this obstinacy, the Vicar General placed the names of their Superiors on the list of excommunication. The names were later removed, however, upon intervention of the Viceroy.

Don Francisco also had to intermediate in a battle for precedence between the Tribunal of the Inquisition and the Secular Council of the City of Mexico. On the day when the Bailiff of the Inquisition was to carry the Edicts of Faith for posting, the Mayor of the Municipal Council claimed the best position, with the Bailiff on his right, the other councilmen accompanying the Mayor. The officials of the Inquisition were to take second place to the civil magistrates. Six days before the *Auto de Fe* (edict for punishment of heresy and other religious violations), of February 28, 1655, the Municipal Council sent the Viceroy a royal decree, which declared that the Secular Council was always to be preferred above the Ecclesiastical when both were attending an *auto de fe* and, furthermore, the Councilmen were to be exempted from attending the Cathedral when the Inquisition published its decrees. This was to avoid what happened five years before, when the Council had to walk behind the Inquisition. The Duke Francisco decided in favor of the Municipal Council, as his Royal Master had decreed in 1650, but the evidence of strife between Church and State is clearly written out in this *acontecimientos.*

The same struggle was being enacted in New Mexico, between the governors of the province and the *custodios* of the missions. In 1659, Governor Bernardo López de Mendizábal engaged in an irreconcilable dispute with Fray Juan Ramirez, Custodio of Missions, over who was to command the soldiers escorting both dignitaries in the caravan from Mexico to Santa Fe. After reaching the capital of New Mexico, the argument was heightened over the disciplines of the Indians, their ceremonial dances and services in field and craft. Mendizábal was investigated by both secular and religious authorities, finally appearing for trial before the Holy Office in Mexico City in 1663. His trial lasted into 1664 and was ended, so far as Mendizábal was concerned, by his death. Judgment in the case was suspended until 1671, when the trial was declared closed and the memory of Mendizábal absolved of blame.[8] The Duke of Alburquerque, however, was not a party to the difficulties of Governor Mendizábal, although he did receive the report from the friars concerning the Governor's derelictions. He left office before Mendizábal was brought down the trail to stand trial, along with his wife, Doña Teresa, for both private and official matters in their way of life in Santa Fe.[9]

After seven years as viceroy, Don Francisco Fernández de la Cueva was replaced by Don Juan de Layva de la Cerda, Conde de Baños, but before the Count de Baños took possession on September 16, 1660, the Duke of Alburquerque nearly met his end in the very cathedral to which he had devoted so much of his religious faith. As was mentioned earlier, Don Francisco was accustomed to attend the festivals of many of the churches in the City of Mexico. He aided in the completion of La Merced, one of the more important churches of the city, and in the afternoons he usually made a daily visit to the great Cathedral which, after nearly a century of work, was nearing completion.[10] After inspecting the progress of workmen, the Viceroy would retire to the chapel of La Virgen de la Doledad and say his prayers. On the afternoon of March 12, 1660, as he knelt at a prie-dieu *(reclinatorio)*, a young soldier leapt from the shadows, drew his sword and struck the Duke a blow, crying, "I vowed to Christ that I would kill you!" The Viceroy rose and holding the prie-dieu before him, grabbed for his own sword, while he exclaimed, "What mean you?" The assailant answered, "To kill you without hearing Mass." Before the man could repeat his attack, the men accompanying the Viceroy overpowered him. After he was carried off, the Duke finished his devotions and then returned to the palace.

The attack created a sensation in the city, for not only was the threat to the Duke very great, but the attack was made within the sanctuary of the Cathedral. A trial was held the same evening and at that time it was declared that the man was a Spaniard named Manuel de Ledesma y Robles and that he was a soldier intended for the expedition to Jamaica. He was nineteen years old, and he testified that he had not really intended to kill the Viceroy (as he could easily have done) but meant only to show his nobility *(hidalguía)*; Ledesma did not show penitence, or weakness, nor was he able to give the judges a clear explanation of his motives for the deed. Later commentators point out that Ledesma was a minor, that his mind was obviously confused if not deranged, that he had no time to prepare a defense, and was provided with inadequate legal representation. One of the advocates of the Audiencia spoke on his behalf. Judgment was pronounced the next morning: Ledesma was condemned to be drawn from prison behind two horses; put in a cage and carried through the streets of the city; then hanged on a gallows in the Plaza Mayor; after this his head was to be cut off and placed on a pike where all could see, and the right hand was to be severed and displayed with the sword which struck the Viceroy. The sentence was carried out to the letter, with the added detail that the mutilated trunk of the victim lay all day at the foot of the gallows. Ledesma not only failed to make confession to a priest, despite the exhortations of a multitude of the clergy and monks who accompanied him, but he refused to call upon the name of Jesus at the moment of his execution.[11]

So ended the second *trienio* of the twenty-second viceroy of New Spain, Don Francisco Fernández de la Cueva, Duke of Alburquerque. The sentiment was universal, according to one commentator, that the colony had lost "a father and a zealous governor of the kingdom, who knew how to combine piety and magnificence and was a protector of writers and a promoter of studies in the University."[12] After leaving Mexico, Don Francisco returned to Spain, en route to Sicily, whose new viceroy he was to become by appointment of Philip IV. Three Mexican historians credit this Duke of Alburquerque with the founding of the Villa of Alburquerque, New Mexico, in 1658,[13] but archives from New Mexico preserved in the National Museum of New Mexico show that this honor should be reserved for the later duke of the same name, whose rule as viceroy was to begin just forty-two years after the first viceroy named Alburquerque had departed.

It is somewhat confusing to the reader of Mexican history to find the thirty-fourth viceroy referred to as the second Duke of Alburquerque. This phrase, "the second duke," seems to indicate that Don Francisco Fernández de la Cueva Enríquez was the second descendant of the family name to hold the title, Duke of Alburquerque, whereas he was the eighth member to hold the title. True, he was the second of the Dukes of Alburquerque to become viceroy, and this made him the second duke by this name to live and hold office in Mexico. But the reader of New Mexican and Mexican archives with notes in this period needs to translate "the second duke" as the "eighth duke" and "second viceroy named Alburquerque" if he wishes to keep proper perspective on the Alburquerqueños and their dukedoms.

The eighth Duke of Alburquerque arrived at Vera Cruz on October 6, 1702; he had been a passenger on a French fleet which safely ran the gauntlet of the British squadrons harassing naval transport between Spain and her colonies. The Spanish crown had just suffered a devastating loss at Vigo, a port on the northeast coast of Spain, where English and Dutch ships barricaded the harbor, then landed men and destroyed all the vessels and cargo of the great merchant flotilla which had just arrived from Mexico and the West Indies. The War of the Spanish Succession had just begun, in which England, Holland, Portugal, Austria, and most of the German States were united against France and Spain. When the sick and childless Hapsburg Charles II died, he chose the grandson of Louis XIV as his heir, Philip V; but rival claims were put forward by Prince Charles of Austria, son of The Holy Roman Emperor Leopold I, whose line went back to the daughter of Ferdinand and Isabella. Treaties between England and France had arranged to support Prince Charles, but Louis XIV decided to support the will of Charles II, at the cost of renewing a struggle which had torn Europe apart in the previous decade. Into this maelstrom of rival claimants, both in Spain and in New Spain, stepped the thirty-fourth Viceroy, Don Francisco Fernández de la Cueva Enríquez. Having reached the port of Vera Cruz, he entered Mexico City on November 27, 1702, and took possession of the government.

The alliance with France and French prestige at the court of Philip V were reflected in Mexico by a change the Viceroy made on January 6, 1703. On this day the uniform of the palace guard became that of the French army. The appearance of the soldiers in French military attire was a signal for the wearing of French styles of dress by the civilian population. The leader in this manner was, of course, the Viceroy. Duke Francisco Enríquez was courtly and affable in his manner, but he was also a man of action, working to strengthen the fortifications of the coastal ports and to appoint leaders whom he could trust in the garrisons. There were partisans of the Austrian pretender active in Mexico as well as in Spain. Alburquerque strengthened the navy, encouraged the campaign against pirates in the Gulf of Mexico, and tried to recover thousands of Spanish firearms which had been distributed to the magistrates and had found their way into the possession of rebellious natives in a tumult ten years earlier. Because of the war, the Duke ordered confiscation of property in Mexico belonging to English, Dutch, and Portuguese.

In order to provide money for the prosecution of the war, Philip V decreed that the Church contribute a tenth of all its revenues to the public treasury, and he decreed that in New Spain this fund must be raised by September, 1703. The Archbishop opposed the decree as an illegal extension of the civil power, but the most influential bishops recognized the consequences of opposing it, and the Archbishop ordered instead an abundant donation to avoid conflict with the King. A contribution of fifteen percent of the salaries of all civil officials and of fifty-five pesos from all landowners was collected for the Crown, plus additional revenues from crown properties and large voluntary donations. In return for this tremendous effort, Philip V decorated Don Francisco Enríquez with the Order of the Golden Fleece.[14]

In New Mexico, at this time, the province was slowly recovering from the devastation of the Pueblo Revolt in 1680 and the warfare subsequent to the reconquest by de Vargas in 1692. Don Diego de Vargas was first appointed governor of New Mexico in 1691. His successor, Pedro Rodríguez Cubero, supported by the Council in Santa Fe, brought charges against de Vargas of embezzlement and undue severity in the punishment of Indians. When these charges were laid before the Duke of Alburquerque in Mexico, the Custodian of Missions in New Mexico championed the side of de Vargas and the Viceroy restored the ex-governor to his former post. Thus, the Viceroy, in the first year of his administration, took a firm hand in settling the jealous rivalries in New Mexico officialdom. De Vargas resumed office at Santa Fe on November 10, 1703. In the following spring he led a campaign into the Sandía mountains against Apaches, and falling ill, was brought to Bernalillo, where he died on April 4, 1704. The great Conquistador was buried at Santa Fe "in the principal church." A lieutenant, Juan Páez Hurtado, was designated by de Vargas in his will as successor until Francisco Cuervo y Valdez assumed office as governor in March, 1705.

In Cuervo y Valdez, the Duke of Alburquerque selected a military man to fill the unexpired second term of de Vargas. Valdez was a knight of the exclusive Order of San Diego and moved in aristocratic circles in the capital. One wonders if he was a close friend of Francisco Enríquez, for at the beginning of the second year of his stay in New Mexico, he founded a villa in Don Francisco's honor. This was the Villa of Alburquerque, placed with thirty-five families on the banks of the Río del Norte and named San Francisco de Alburquerque. The name "Francisco" happened to be Cuervo y Valdez's given name, as well as the Duke's. In reporting this establishment, Governor Valdez asked the Viceroy for a chalice, religious ornaments, and other things needed for the church at Alburquerque. When the letters of Valdez were read on July 28 to the General Assembly in Mexico, the Assembly voted to send the equipment to the Church, but Valdez was reproved for naming a villa after the Viceroy without consulting him. Secretly, the Viceroy must have been pleased, but there was a complication in that a royal decree was before the Council at that time authorizing the establishment of a villa in honor of the King, Philip V. The Council found a way out of this dilemma by changing the title of the new villa to San Felipe de Alburquerque, thus honoring both the King and the Viceroy.[15] The church of San Felipe in Old Albuquerque bears the name of the Viceroy, except for the lost *r*, which disappeared somewhere before the opening of the Santa Fe Trail: the narratives of Zebulon Pike, 1807; George W. Kendall, 1841; J.F. Meline, 1866; and W.W.H. Davis, 1869; all record *Albuquerque,* and not *Alburquerque.*[16]

Before returning to Mexico, Cuervo y Valdez concluded a treaty of peace at Santa Fe with Comanches and Utes, and he called in the military garrisons from a number of the Indian pueblos, where they had produced more friction than security. As Valdez passed through the adobe village he had founded and named for the Viceroy, he must have felt that it was a humble memorial to the brilliant grandee who waited to welcome him after his exile in the primitive areas of New Mexico. In the capital of Mexico, despite the threat of the English navy to the coast and of savage Indians to the frontiers, social life had been at a pinnacle ever since the arrival of the Duke and his wife. The luxury of the wealthy residents was uncontrolled by the needs of society. One of the most extravagant members of capital society was Don Francisco Medina de Picazo, Treasurer of the Mint. In order to win favor from the Viceroy-Duke, Señor converted an entire building into a theatre and presented a comedy, after which he offered a sumptuous banquet, presenting the Viceroy and members of his family with gifts of a thousand pesos each, and a hundred pesos to every guest. All the servants received twenty-five pesos—in the line of "tips," one might say today. This lavish entertainment was followed by a fiesta at his country house, where there were three days of bullfights and the food and amusement for the guests came to twenty thousand pesos. One of the dramatic spectacles provided was a golden pine tree, said to have cost three thousand pesos to prepare. By way of return for this and like courtesies provided them, the Viceroy and his wife entertained at the Palace with great pomp, inviting the celebrated personages of both Church and State to enjoy comedies, music, and splendid banquets.

One of the scandals during the regime of the thirty-second Viceroy concerned the daughter of Don Jaime Cruzat, ex-governor of the Philippines and a man of tremendous wealth. The young woman, whose dowry was reputed to be more than six hundred thousand pesos, was called *La China* by the public. She was sought as a bride by the Count of Santiago, by a judge named Uribe, by Don Domingo Sánchez de Tagle, and by Don Lucas de Careago. The Archbishop of Mexico favored Tagle, but the other authorities opposed this match. The tutors of *La China* had ideas, too, about her marriage and carried her off to a house in the district of San Cosme. While she was being hidden, a lawyer presented an indictment against Tagle on behalf of another woman to whom he was pledged. The Archbishop thereupon excommunicated the lawyer, and accompanied by a band of armed men removed Señorita Cruzat from the place of concealment to the convent of San Lorenzo. There the Archbishop married her to Tagle. The Viceroy sent his own troops, accompanied by the brothers of *La China*, in an effort to stop the ceremony, but the monks of San Lorenzo closed the doors of the convent and prevented an entrance. In retaliation, the Viceroy seized the bridegroom at night, fined him twenty-thousand pesos, and banished him to Vera Cruz. The father of the groom was also fined in the same amount and banished to Acapulco. A brother of Tagle

had to pay only ten thousand pesos for his part in the affair. The Duchess of Alburquerque, *la vireina*, was a friend of Tagle, and she was so put out with her husband
that she separated from him. A great lawsuit resulted, in which the Viceroy, *la
vireina*, the Supreme Court, the Archbishop, and the married couple with their
representatives were all involved, and perhaps the consequences would have been
grave if the father of the groom had not died in the midst of the proceedings. The
demise of Don Jaime Cruzat shocked all parties to the action and produced a
general appeasement.

While these mock-serio social disorders were troubling the life of Mexico,
famine was current among the peons, and the negro slaves ran starving and almost
naked on the highways. In spite of the religious fanaticism of that period, the
desperate poor attacked the churches, despoiling the images of jewels and desecrat-
ing the altars of sacred vessels. In punishment, there followed horrible public exe-
cutions, in which the criminals were not only killed but their bodies were mutilated, the hands of those who robbed the churches being severed and then nailed
in the streets to terrorize the passersby.

Whereas in parts of Mexico during this period, neither Church or State seemed
to be meeting their responsibilities, in Arizona and California the heroic Jesuit
priest Father Eusebio Kino was carrying out his pioneer labors, establishing a
chain of missions, which were to bring new concepts of Christian society and new
forms of agriculture and resources in cattle, sheep, and horses. San Xavier del Bac,
founded by Kino just outside present day Tucson, is still regarded as one of the
finest examples of mission architecture in the United States. The California missions in this period were suffering from lack of food and other means of subsistence; thought was even given to abandoning the territory entirely. The courageous
Jesuit missioners, Salvatierra, Ugarte, and Basaldua made trips to northern Mexico for supplies. After many broken promises, a ship was dispatched with funds
to purchase provisions from the Yaquis; and with resolute will the padres persuaded both their monks and the soldiers to remain in California.

Smallpox, hitherto unknown among the Indians, appeared in California at this
time. In 1711, it claimed Father Kino as one of its victims. There were serious upris-
ings among the Pimas in Sonora during the term of the second Alburquerque as
viceroy, and the civil authorities put the revolts down with terrible severity. Later
historians have blamed the Viceroy for tolerating inhumane and cruel acts by his
officials. Perhaps such measures, so out of keeping with concepts of civilization
and Christianity, must be judged against the background of the times and the
exigencies the Viceroy faced, confronted by both primitive and civilized forces
aiming at the destruction of Mexico.[17]

King Philip V had such confidence in the Viceroy Don Francisco Fernández
de la Cueva Enríquez that he kept him in office more than eight years, nearly three

trienios, an unusually long term of service. "He had governed New Spain with the greatest moderation and prudence," writes one historian," and had preserved it from turbulence and disunity."[18]

The two Dukes of Alburquerque who came to the New World have certain traits in common, as might be expected from the background they inherited of chivalry and good taste. They were aristocrats in both manner and action, exercising good judgment during their administrations and holding the respect of their subjects. If they were not reformers, introducing strong measures for rehabilitation in the economic problems of Mexico, they were not tyrants, destroying what remained of civil liberties in an age dominated by repressive institutions like the Court of the Inquisition. Both saw the struggle between Church and State, which was a critical one in Mexico City, reproduced on a smaller scale in the provincial colony of Santa Fe, and although both were pious men, each tried to limit the Church to spiritual rather than temporal affairs. Although both men have been associated with the founding of Albuquerque, New Mexico, the second viceroy bearing that name (with the addition of a second *r)* was actually the unintentional patron.[19] A complete study of the viceroys of New Spain, in their relations to the American frontier and its problems would be of great interest and value. In such a study, the attitudes and activities of the two Dukes of Alburquerque discussed in this article would make an important chapter.

NOTES

1. *Enciclopedia universal ilustrada Europei Americana,* Tomo IV. Bilbao, Madrid, Barcelona: Espasa-Calpe, S.A., 1905-1930. Since the name *Enríquez* is added to *de la Cueva,* it is probably that Don Francisco's daughter married an Enríquez and that Don Juan is the grandson and the successor to the title. Marriage into another family is certainly indicated by the addition of the name Enríquez to de la Cueva. In the absence of a *de* or an *y* it is difficult to determine whether this occurred either through the father's or the mother's side. A longer sketch of the Portuguese-Spanish village from which the family took its name and of the chief historical figures associated with "Alburquerque" may be found in *Diccionario geographico-estadistico-histórica de España y sus posesiones de ultramar,* by Pascual Madoz, Tomo I. Madrid, 1845. The ducal name is *Alburquerque* not *Albuquerque.* The latter is found as another Portuguese family surname (both as *Albuquerque* and *Alboquerque; cf. Enciclopedia universal ilustrada),* but the distinguished members of this family have no direct association with the two viceroys of Mexico and, therefore, no historical connection with founding of the American town which now bears their name rather than that of its true patron. Dr. L.B. Mitchell traces the etymology of *Alburquerque* back through Portuguese and Spanish to Arabic *al barquq,* "the apricot;" cf. *Western Folklore,* VIII (July, 1949), 255-256.

2. Referring to Don Francisco Fernández, Dr. Silvio Zavala writes, March 8, 1950: "Entiendo que no se ha hecho un estudio biográfico serio del Duque de Alburquerque y que la bibliografia sobre el mismo es escasa." Pascual Madoz, *op. cit.,* wrote in 1845 that (in translation): "This dukedome has continued in the sons and descendants of D. Beltrán de la Cueva." The name "de la Cueva" seems to have disappeared before the twentieth century, for in the *Enciclopedia universal ilustrada (loc. cit.)* we read (in translation): "This title in the nineteenth century passed to the house of Alcañice. The actual duke of Albu-

querque, whose title carries with it nobility in Spain, is don José Osorio y Silva Zayas Téllez-Girón."

3. The Viceroy entered Mexico on August 15, 1653. Oliver Cromwell was installed as Protector under the new English constitution on December 16, 1653.

4. Andrés Cavo, *Los tres siglos de Méjico*, publicado con notas y suplemento por Carlos Maria de Bustamente, páginas 98-100. Méjico: J.R. Navarro, 1852; D. Vicente Riva Palacio, y otros, *México á través de los siglos*, tomo II, páginas 618-619. México, Barcelona: Ballesca y Espasa, 1887-1889.

5. *Los tres siglos de Mejico*, página 98.

6. Jesús Romero Flores, *Iconografía Colonial*, páginas 78-79. México: Secretaría de Educación Pública, Instituto Nacional de Antropoligía e História, Museo Nacional, 1940.

7. *Trienio:* term of three years. This affair among the religious is described in *Iconografía Colonial, loc. cit.*, and apparently occurred either in 1654 or 1655.

8. A concise treatment of the New Mexican struggle between Church and State will be found in Cleve Hallenbeck, *Land of the Conquistadores* (1950), pp. 114-137. Hallenbeck draws upon France V. Scholes, *Church and State in New Mexico* (University of New Mexico Press, 1937) and other publications by the same author in the *New Mexico Historical Review*, which he lists.

9. Doña Teresa Mendizábal was accused of both heresy and the practice of sorcery. Servants of the *Casa Real* in Santa Fe testified that she washed her hair on Fridays and dressed gaily on Saturdays, like the Jews; that she never said grace before meals or prayers before going to bed; that she kept her writing desk locked and put pieces of onion in her shoes. She also had a book which was thought to deal with sorcery and was written in a foreign tongue. Doña Teresa answered at her trial that she kept her desk locked as a safeguard against these very household servants, that she put onions on her toes to ease her corns, and that her sorcery book was a volume of Tasso's poetry. See Scholes, Hallenbeck references in previous note.

10. According to *Terry's Guide to Mexico* (1909, 1944), p. 274, the Metropolitan Church or Cathedral of Mexico City was begun in 1573 and was completed and dedicated in 1667.

11. *México, a través de los siglos*, pp. 619-620; *Los tres siglos de Méjico*, p. 101; *Iconografía Colonial*, p. 79; Bancroft, *History of Mexico*, vol. III, p. 149.

12. Andrés Cavo, *op. cit.*, p. 102.

13. Andrés Cavo, *op. cit.*, p. 100: Cavo cites Villaseñor, *Teat. americano*, p. 2, lib. 6, cap. 17, H.H. Bancroft, *History of Arizona and New Mexico* (1889), p. 168, Note 61, cites Zamacois, *Hist. Mej.*, v.376.

14. *México á través de los siglos*, p. 758.

15. *New Mexico Archives*: Historia, II, Part, 2, p. 359 (photostat of records in Museo Nacional, Mexico City), University of New Mexico Library.

16. The Marqués de Altamire, in his report to the Auditor General of War, September 16, 1750, gives the distance of *la Villa de Alburquerque* from Texas. Cf. *New Mexico Archives, Provincias Internas*, 37, pt. 1, p. 58. Hallenbeck, *op. cit.*, p. 199, says that *Alburquerque* was spelled with two r's "up to 1780 or later."

17. *México á través de los siglos*, pp. 758-761. A very brief sketch of the thirty-second viceroy's regime is to be found in Manuel Rivera Cambas, *Los gobernantes de México*, I, 301-308.

18. *Los tres siglos de Méjico*, p. 122.

19. *Terry's Guide to Mexico* (1909, 1944) describes the grill of the Chapel of Pardon in the Cathedral of Mexico City, as the gift of the Duke of Alburquerque in May, 1730. It came from the Portuguese settle-

ment of Macao "in southern China," was of tombac (an alloy of copper and zinc), and was forty-five feet long and twenty-five feet high, designed to form an allegory of the crucified Saviour and the two Thieves. The date for the arrival of this screen may tell something about the longevity of the eighth Duke and his continued interest in the progress of the Metropolitan Church of Mexico.

3-DIMENSIONAL RECORDS IN THE SPANISH AND MEXICAN PERIODS[1]

BY CHARLES C. DI PESO

VOLUME 78, NUMBER 4

JANUARY, 1973

A century before the birth of Christ, Cicero proclaimed, "History is the witness that testifies to the passing of time; it illuminates reality, vitalizes memory, provides guidance in daily life, and brings us tidings of antiquity" (*De Oratore, Vol. II, p. 36*).

The quest for historical truth does not vary no matter where one chooses to work, be it in the Holy Roman Empire or the northern frontier of New Spain. Unfortunately and far too often this philosophical challenge laid down by Cicero defeats us, and this is indeed a sad commentary in view of the tremendously important works which have been produced by such giants of borderland history as Bandelier, Bancroft, Bolton, Bloom, Hammond and Twitchell, to mention only a few. These classical scholars, who spent their lives gleaning, translating, and annotating information concerning activities of those incredible Iberians who dared penetrate the *Gran Chichimeca* with sword and cross, unwittingly and as a product of their times favored this imperial effort to implant an alien Mediterranean herding lifeway in this northern frontier. Their endeavors all reflect a single history—that of the donor invader.

Who among us has chosen to write the complicated but interrelated histories of those native soil members—soil parasites and soil exploiters — who have occupied and still do occupy the northern fringes of New Spain? What sage, other than that fantastic scholar Bernardino de Sahagún, has offered up so much of himself to record the pre-Iberian cultures of the vanquished recipients? What scholar, glowing with a Bolton's love of Father Eusebio Kino and a military flare, will come forth to champion the Pecan Chief Bigotes, or those Sonoran chiefs who in the 1570s led the two successful native campaigns which temporarily turned the enemy from their lands? Who will truthfully bring into proper light the dignity of native histories such as a Zuni version of Coronado's attack upon Hawikuh? Without a doubt, the historians' task in the borderlands has just begun.

Francis Parkman, in his 1865 introduction to the *Pioneers of France in the New*

World, remarked, "Faithfulness to the truth of history involves far more than research, however patient and scrupulous, into special facts. Such facts may be detailed with the most minute exactness, and yet the narrative taken as a whole, may be unmeaning or untrue. The narrator must seek to imbue himself with the life and spirit of the time. He must study events in their bearings near and remote; in the character, habits, and manners of those who took part in them. He must himself be, as it were, a sharer or a spectator of the action he describes (*Proceedings of the Massachusetts Historical Society*, Vol, VIII, p. 353)."

Indubitably, the role of all participants in any historical event must be accurately balanced if one is to record truthfully the social interplay of two or more peoples in contact, and it can only be done when its time is dead and the emotionalism of its moment has abated. Assuredly, the researcher knows that the conjunctive approach will fail simply because of the magnitude of a historical continuum's gestalt. But how does a scholar glean the chronicles of a nonliterate people? In answer, one's mind turns immediately to those forceful tools such as material culture inventories produced by archeologists, folk histories recorded by the ethnologist, language affiliations noted by the linguist, and indigenous myths.

However, pre-Iberian archeology produces data which are factually gross by virtue of its group emphasis, which can only infer variations in cultural designs which are made up of multitudes of ways and means by which the human animal can and does adapt to various environments and to those who intrude into his territory. But the archeologist, unlike the historian, cannot hope to touch the shoulder of one of his study specimens, know his name, or personally learn to like or dislike him as an individual. Some archeologists within the last decade, perhaps as a result of this lack of true history in Dr. Parkman's sense, have come to consider cultural history as a mere byproduct of their discipline and, consequently, have begun to search out the basic adaptive mechanisms of social institutions (Longacre *et al.*, 1970, p. 9).

In turn, the ethnologist, using one or two informants, lives in constant fear that his collected field data are biased, for he knows that no one man embodies his entire culture, as there are too many social restrictions between sexes and age groups and too much specialization in sophisticated cultures.

The linguist working in the northern frontier is fully aware of the effective need of historical documentation in creating time depth for native language maps, but he too is constantly beleaguered with the question of reliability of such information, as many so-called barbarians often were capable of manipulating several languages—a fact not always accurately recorded by the Iberian reporter.

Then too, the oral Chichimecan histories are will-o-the-wisp records, whose accuracy depends not only on various mnemonic devices, but also upon the modes of generational transmission from one age group to the next, which often cause shading and changes in the original which are the result of shifting values in time and in allegory.

Obviously then, these various disciplines, which all seek a common goal—that is, to gain a truthful approach to an honest understanding of a historical event—must stand together as a cooperating team if we hope to achieve any real meaning to history. The results of all these approaches must be brought to bear on a single narrative in order to bring into a common focus a multi-dimensional understanding of Spanish borderland history.

To a degree, the so-called 19th century romantics such as Cushing, Bandelier, Fewkes, Hodge, and Mindeleff, used various of these disciplines to create a meaningful view of the activities of both the native recipient and the Iberian donor in the southwestern arena of frontier conquest. The Awatovi, Hawikuh, Pecos, and Gran Quivira archeological projects have brought together various data which put some Pueblo history into a realistic light, and Holder (1971) has set a meaningful amalgam of these disciplines in his *Hoe and the Horse on the Plains*. Other studies in the Pimeria Alta have, to a degree, fleshed the Upper Pima and Sobaipuri skeletons.

At the moment, I am endeavoring to bring some of these forces to play in recreating the history of the Casas Grandes people of northwestern Chihuahua. This interdisciplinary approach requires one to employ archival searches into both the conquering Iberian literature and the vanquished Mesoamerican codices, as well as archeological reconnaissance and excavations in order to physically locate in time and space specific sites such as the Sobaipuri village of Quibiri, the Jesuit mission of San Cayetano, the pueblos of Hawikuh, Awatovi, and Gran Quivira. The written accounts of Benavidez, Castaneda, Oñate, Kino, Nentvig, Pfeffercorn, Bernal, Fuente, and the entire host of Spanish chroniclers must be used in order to give life to the archeological investigations of various borderland loci. The excavation of such simple clues as cow and horse bones or peach seeds in what were once thought to be pre-Iberian archeological horizons indicate the archeologist's blind spot.

For far too many years archeological data produced in the borderlands have been terminated at the magic date of A.D. 1450, thus creating a demilitarized time zone which separated archeology from history and, in so doing, created an academic gap in the native historical continuums of Pimeria Alta and Nuevo Mexico. Fortunately, this chasm is slowly being filled by historical archeologists such as Fontana, Polzer, and Schroeder. Similarly, the tribal histories of the Upper Pima and the Sobaipuri of the Pimeria Alta have been put to the pen with the aid of archeological excavations and historical evidence wrought by Bolton, Thomas, Burrus, and many others. Rio Grande studies, which combine archeology, ethnology, and historical sources, are being pieced together for Pecos, Gran Quivira, and other locations by scholars imbued with this multiple approach, led by men like Hackett, Kidder, Schroeder, Father Chavez, and a host of others. In each case, these inspired individuals must laboriously climb upward on the time ladder, rung by rung, and involve these various disciplines in order to interweave the true fabric of historical reconstruction.

Speaking from personal experience, I have found that without the combined knowledge of the Casas Grandes archeological data, the Mexican codices, the journals of Guzman, De Vaca, and De Niza, the Coronado and Ibarra chroniclers, it would be impossible to recreate a meaningful history of the area. Without these combined data, there could be no real comprehension of the impact of conquest made by the pre-Iberian, Mesoamerican mercantile or *puchteca* systems on this borderland frontier. Like the Iberians, these sophisticated exploiters used their military and their priests to enforce control of the indigenes by implanting the religions of Tezcatlipoca and Quetzalcoatl. These conquerors, in their own time and in their own way, sought to control the northern Chichimecan indigenes with the power of their own cultural yokes.

The mechanisms of frontier conquest have been at play in the Southwest from at least A.D. 900. The Iberian intrusions of the first half of the 16th century and the seeding of Christianity were the third, or perhaps the fourth, exploitative conquest of this borderland, and on each of these separate occasions, sophisticated exploiters came to glean such mineral resources as copper, gold, silver, and turquoise and invoked considerable cultural exchange by so doing. These conquest patterns have been studied by men such as Spicer, in his *Cycles of Conquest* (1962) and Foster, in his *Culture and Conquest* (1960).

It would seem that these various donor intrusions all had a common environmental perimeter and, perhaps, each set of conquerors faced a related static indigenous or recipient population. In each instance, contact resulted in a related series of meaningful historical events, each of which must be thoroughly understood in its proper light if the true history of the Spanish borderlands is to be factually recorded.

It is ordained that the historian of tomorrow who is interested in Spanish native borderland history of the 16th century must first be cognizant of the Huitzilopochtli intrusion of the 14th century, the Quetzalcoatl conquest of the 11th century, and the Tezcatlipoca influences of the 10th century. To accomplish this, the scholar must carefully dimension his subject, i.e., measure out the length, the breadth, and the thickness of his project. To the social scientist, *length* may be thought of as the equivalent of time; the locale, or place, as the *breadth* of a subject; and *thickness* as the involved cultural mechanism.

These three dimensions, then, can be defined in any number of ways, dependent upon one's discipline or the specific mode of ordering explicit facts into a dogmatic, implied classification system. The differences between these numerous systems, their lines of reasoning, and their semantics tend to make strangers of scholars who may be interested in the same subject. Sir Karl Popper, in his book *The Logic of Scientific Discovery* (1959), best demonstrates the weaknesses and strengths of some of our systems which are based in implicit, rather than explicit, data.

To illustrate the logic of these dimensions, I shall draw upon my most recent work, which involves the reconstruction of the Casas Grandes nonlineal historical continuum, which dates back some 10,000 or more years in the northwestern corner of the present state of Chihuahua, Mexico. These people were variously involved, through time, in the human survival roles of soil members, soil parasites, and soil exploiters and, at various times in their sequence, were put upon by various donor invaders, including the Quetzalcoatl puchteca and the Christian Iberians.

The first dimension in this social science exercise, that of length, or time, was determined by a number of methods invented by the natural sciences which, by definition, deal not with human society, but rather with observable, natural phenomena such as are classified by physics, chemistry, and biology. In order to obtain a correlation with the Christian calendar, we used, as already mentioned, written history where feasible, and extended any pertinent dates back into pre-Iberian horizons with the aid of dendrochronology—a primary dating method evolved by the happy accident of mating the discipline of astronomy with that of botany in the mind of the late Dr. A.E. Douglass of the University of Arizona. His curiosity regarding the relationship of sun spot activity and its effect on the earth's vegetation led him to discover the basic principles of tree-ring dating.

Thanks to his colleagues, a Casas Grandes dendro-calendar, the first of its kind to be developed in the Republic of Mexico, was devised from explicit physical data, i.e., hundreds of charred building timbers taken from the ruined city of Casas Grandes. These growth patterns were programmed in a computer along with similar data taken from a number of already proven ring growth calendars, and the end result was a set of correlated calendrical figures which formed the Casas Grandes system (Scott, 1966).

This dating method was supported by still another dating technique, originally developed by the physicists, Drs. J.P. Arnold and W.F. Libby, of the University of Chicago (1949), in their original study of the half-life of the radioactive 14th isotope of carbon. In the course of the pursuit, they created another explicit dating tool, not as specific as dendrochronology, but nonetheless a most useful time correlator. These two methods were used along with such tertiary aids as obsidian dehydration, thermoluminescence, and palynology to pinpoint certain historical events which occurred in the Casas Grandes area in terms of the Gregorian time tabulation. The result shocked our preconceived speculations concerning the lifespan of Casas Grandes, for the physicists and chemists, and not the social scientist, told us explicitly that the Paquime culture appeared full-blown in the Casas Grandes Valley about A.D. 1060, the year when the work crews were ordered to the mountains to cut building timbers.

The thrill in this newly acquired knowledge involved the fact that this was also the time during which the Late Bonitians of Pueblo Bonito, located in the Chaco Canyon, were gleaning their wooden master beams—a fact inconceivable in the framework of prior archeological constructs, which had placed the two cultures 300 years apart. What is more, the Carbon-14 evidence indicated that the city was destroyed ca. A.D. 1310 plus or minus 30, a date which we had presupposed to be its beginning. This correlation was derived from samples of carbon found in the ceremonial pit ovens, which were found filled with agave hearts.

To indicate the involvement of seemingly unrelated clues associated with this time dimension, permit me to carry the factoring a step further. The codices informed us that mescal, made from the heart of these plants, was drunk only on ceremonial occasions; ornithologists informed us that our macaw breeding cages contained remains of young juveniles, 11-12 months of age; and the visiting astronomers noted that a cross-shaped mound, also excavated on the city's premises, was oriented in such a way as to determine the time of the equinoxes and solstices. Now, by assembling these hints, i.e., Carbon-14, the knowledge of the Mesoamerican ceremonial calendar appertaining to the vernal equinox, the native rules regarding intoxicating beverages, and the breeding schedule of the *Ara macao*, it becomes possible to imply that the city of Casas Grandes was destroyed by enemy people at a time when the townfolk were preparing for their annual spring ceremonials, i.e., sometime during the third week of March. This, of course, is a gross statement, but it demonstrates the possible manipulation of a number of explicit and seemingly meaningless pieces of data exposed by natural and physical scientists, which we, as social scientists, can legitimately use in reconstructing a historical time framework.

The city was destroyed ca. A.D. 1340, but the culture continued to exist in the western highland border of the Sierra Madres, a fact attested to by further archeological investigations which brought to light four Carbon-14 dates associated with Casas Grandes culture which measured between the mid-16th and 17th centuries in the area historically defined as the homeland of the Jova and the Jocome. These implications were very thrilling, for if these correlations were correct, then it could be suggested that remnants of the Casas Grandes culture existed well into historic times and that some of its bearers may have been seen by such men as de Vaca, who apparently described them as "people of the permanent houses;" by de Niza, as the "Kingdom of Marata;" and by Ibarra's chronicler, Obregón, as the "People of Caguaripa." The sum of these exciting data is being gathered for presentation in the forthcoming Amerind publication in a desire to bridge the disciplines of archeology and history of this time block. This historical continuum, then, will carry the Casas Grandes culture component well into the historic borderland horizon, and suggests that the remnants of this elaborate semihydraulic culture is variously identified before A.D. 1050 as Mogollonlike, after A.D. 1050 as Casas Grandian, after A.D. 1600 as Jova/Jocome, and after A.D. 1700 as Apache!

The second dimension, that of breadth, or the spatial component, was variously studied in terms of the physical distribution of the Casas Grandes cultural elements in space. To this end, the tools of the civil engineer had to be used in determining the size of the city and the design of the public water and sewer systems, as well as that of the irrigation systems which were installed by the Paquime architects. The sovereignty area, in this case, was determined by means of mapping, aerial photography, and surface locations of satellite towns, pyral communication towers, roads, and frontier defenses which contained similar concentrations of Casas Grandes material culture.

Further, ceramic trade goods, which were used as indicators of economic contacts, inferred that the market distribution of Casas Grandes pottery was widespread, as it involved Mexico City in the south, and Mesa Verde, Colorado, in the north. However, it took the malacologists working with the marine shell found in the city's warehouses, the ornithologists who identified the bird remains, the geologists and the physicists working with minerals and their trace elements found in the workshops, to aid us in our understanding of the extracting industries and the exploitation level of the Casas Grandes economy. Shell from the Gulf of California, *Ara macao* from Vera Cruz, Mexico, obsidian from Durango, Mexico, ricolite from New Mexico, meerschaum from Arizona, and alibates flint from Texas, were all found in the ruins, and their presence implied not only the existence of a sophisticated local artisan class, but also supported the concept of a Mesoamerican form of mercantile system which involved Casas Grandes as one of a number of established Northern Frontier trading centers.

As noted in the discussion of the time dimension, this economic system continued to exist into historic times, and may have been referred to in de Vaca's description of the economic activities of "the people who lived and traded in the land of the permanent houses," which may refer to the Casas Grandes progeny; and, in turn, to Obregón's (in Hammond and Rey, 1928, p. 281) reference to the Mexican Culguas, or Alcolhua,[2] also mentioned by the members of the Chamuscado and Espejo expedition when they were in the Rio Grande Valley, below El Paso, where they noted the presence of copper and "red coral" objects which had been traded from the Culguas who lived "13 days inland" (Obregón in Hammond and Rey, 1928, pp. 280-281).

The first two dimensions, time and space, i.e., length and breadth, can be made meaningful with the aid of the natural and physical sciences, and it is upon the exposure of these facts that the third dimension, thickness, or social mechanism, can and must be generated. This is the very area to which, I believe, Cicero referred as "illuminated reality" and Parkman as "bearings near and remote." The underlying problem in amassing these ideas from physical data is that they are, for the most part, intangible inferences based upon explicit artifact associations and, as such, can be variously interpreted within the same logical framework and, hence, are unprovable.

The physical anthropologist can give us those data which appertain to the height and shape of the Casas Grandians and permit us to evaluate their death ratios as determined by age and sex. They can attest to growth arrest lines and other pathological incidents, but together these data cannot tell us how these people thought! The architectonics of the people can be ascertained by detailed excavations, comparative descriptions of buildings and other public works, but who divines what went on in the houses, the ceremonial structures, and the public areaways? Social organization is elicited, however, by comparing architectonics—the innate and ordered knowledge of structural skills—and associated material culture. Archeology certainly has elaborated and can continue to elaborate upon the minute details of individual artifact design, but who has the wherewithal to place the indigenous value on these objects?

It can be done by compiling laborious classification systems and relating association factors. To demonstrate, hundreds of Scarlet Macaws were found, carefully buried in the plazas of Casas Grandes. These birds were foreign to the area and were trafficked in from Vera Cruz or some location further south of his northern habitat perimeter. They became a very valuable religious commodity in the eyes of the indigenes, as Father Marcos de Niza noted; but in the local macaw, the green *Ara militaris*, for some reason did not. In turn, the "god stone" (Sahagún in Dibble and Anderson, 1963, p. 224) turquoise became highly valued in Mesoamerica during the lifetime of Casas Grandes. This semiprecious stone is fairly common in the Southwest, but is very rarely found south of the Tropic of Cancer. This economic factor of natural scarcity appears to have involved a powerful exploitative exchange in the borderland area, which can be likened to the sociopolitical mechanisms which involved the Hudson's Bay Trading Company, as both for a time, succeeded because of the delicately balanced value systems of two cultures in contact.

The determination of this most important third dimension is the most difficult but by far the most exciting of assignments—difficult because it requires the repeated analysis of masses of permanent minutiae, which must be ordered time and time again into meaningful programs. To do this properly, of course, we have need of the mathematician, the statistician, and the programmer—all of whom can talk to that divine calculator, the computer. These men supply the mathematical logic of their disciplines, but it is the social scientist who can best program and evaluate multiple vector studies designed to interpret social action.

The logic of randomness, regression, Chi square, and the tenets of the economist, the sociologist, and the psychologist must all be brought to bear upon any historical reconstruction if the challenge of this, the third dimension, is to be properly met. And meet it we must, if we hope to bring life to the past which will illuminate universal realities in man's interactions with himself and nature—the understanding of which is desperately needed to aid in tomorrow's survival.

NOTES

1. Western History Association Conference, October 14-16, 1971.

2. See Hammond and Rey (1928, p. 2, Fig. 6) and Santamaría (1942, vol. 1, p. 435) who felt that this reference was to the Alcolhua tribal name of those Toltecs who fled the destruction of Tula and who, according to Peterson (1959, p. 76), returned to the region of Coatlichan in the mid-13th century.

BIBLIOGRAPHY

Arnold, J.R. and W.F. Libby
1949 *Age Determination by Radiocarbon Content: Check with Samples of Known Age.* Science, Vol. 110

Foster, George McClelland
1960 *Culture and Conquest: America's Spanish Heritage.* Viking Fund publications in anthropology, No. 27. Wenner-Gren Foundation for Anthropological Research, New York.

Hallenbeck, Cleve
1940 *Alvar Nuñez Cabeza De Vaca: The Journey of the First European to Cross the Continent of North America, 1534-1536.* Arthur H. Clark, Glendale, California.

1949 *The Journey of Fray Marcos de Niza.* Southern Methodist University, University Press in Dallas.

Hammond, George Peter, and Agapito Rey
1928 *Obregón's History of 14th Century Explorations in Western America.* Wetzel Publishing Co., Los Angeles.

Holder, Preston
1971 *The Hoe and the Horse on the Plains: A Study of Culture Development Among the North American Indians.* University of Nebraska Press, Lincoln.

Longacre, William A.
1970 *Reconstructing Prehistoric Pueblo Societies.* School of American Research Advanced Seminar Series. University of New Mexico Press, Albuquerque.

Nuñez, Cabeza De Vaca, Alvar
1922 *The Journey of Alvar Nuñez Cabeza de Vaca and His Companions from Florida to the Pacific, 1528-1536.* Translated from his own narrative by Fanny Bandelier, together with the Report of Father Marcos of Niza and a letter from the Viceroy Mendoza. Allerton Books, New York.

Parkman, Francis
1865 Pioneers of France in the New World. *Proceedings of the Massachusetts Historical Society,* Vol. 8.

Peterson, Frederick A.
1949 *Ancient Mexico, An Introduction to the Pre-Hispanic Cultures*. G.P. Putnam's Sons, New York.

Popper, Karl
1959 *The Logic of Scientific Discovery*. Harper and Row, New York.

Sahagún, Bernardino De
1963 Historia General de Las Cosas de Nueva España, Book 11—The Earthly Things. In *Florentine Codex*, edited and translated by Charles E. Dibble and Arthur J.O. Anderson, Monographs of the School of American Research. The School of American Research and the University of Utah, Santa Fe, New Mexico.

Santamaría, Francisco Javier
1942 *Diccionario General de Americanismos*. Editorial P. Robredo, Mexico, D.F.

Scott, Stuart D.
1966 *Dendrochronology in Mexico*. Papers of the Laboratory of Tree-Ring Research, No. 2, University of Arizona Press, Tucson.

Spicer, Edward H.
1962 *Cycles of Conquest*. University of Arizona Press, Tucson.

Rito de los Frijoles, Bandelier National
Monument. At the bottom of the ladder stands
Charles F. Lummis with a scarf on his head.
Courtesy Museum of New Mexico, Neg. No.
42070.

*Paul A.F. Walter at work in the Palace of the
Governors in the early days. Courtesy
Museum of New Mexico, Neg. No. 13129.*

*Marjorie Ferguson Tichy stands in the Puaray
Ruins, 1934. Courtesy Museum of New
Mexico, Neg. No. 127722.*

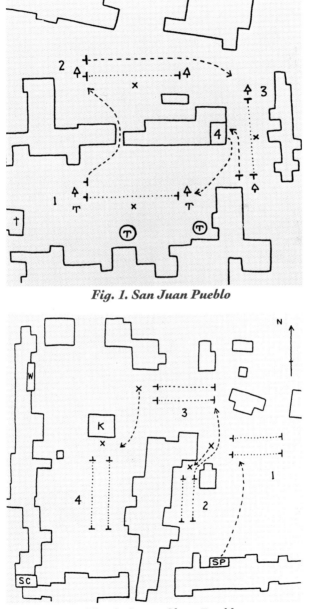

Fig. 1. San Juan Pueblo

Fig. 2. Santa Clara Pueblo

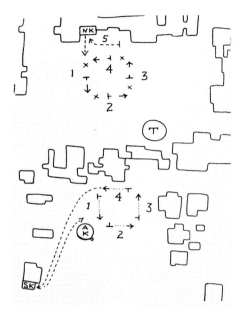

Fig. 3. San Ildefonso Pueblo

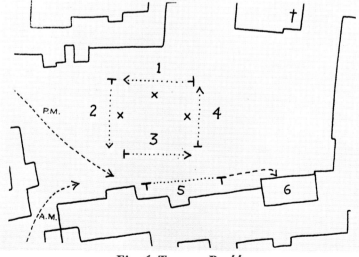

Fig. 4. Tesuque Pueblo

*Casas Grandes, Chihuahua, Mexico. Courtesy
Museum of New Mexico, Neg. No. 41058.*

LEGEND FOR FIGURES

solid line . . . . outline of house block

broken line . . . . circuit path

dotted line . . . . dance line

arrow . . . . circuit direction

X . . . . instrumentalists

1, 2 etc. . . . . stations

T . . . . tree

K . . . . kiva

AK . . . . abandoned kiva

NK . . . . north kiva

SK . . . . south kiva

W . . . . winter moiety dance house

SC . . . . conservative summer moiety dance house

SP . . . . progressive summer moiety dance house

All figures are oriented with north at the top.

94

*Ernest Blumenschein, Taos,
New Mexico, 1932. Photo by
Will Connell. Courtesy
Museum of New Mexico, Neg.
No. 59758.*

*Peter Hurd, 1968. Photo by Bob
Nugent. Courtesy Museum of New
Mexico, Neg. No. 43555.*

Raymond Jonson with one of his paintings.
Photo by T. Harmon Parkhurst. Courtesy
Museum of New Mexico, Neg. No. 73938.

Randall Davey at work, Santa Fe, New
Mexico. Courtesy Museum of New
Mexico, Neg. No. 20335.

*Gustave Baumann, Santa Fe, New Mexico,
1932. Photo by Will Connell. Courtesy
Museum of New Mexico, Neg. No. 59739.*

*Little Market, Guatemala City, 1913. Photo
by Jesse L. Nusbaum. Courtesy Museum of
New Mexico, Neg. No. 60068.*

Mid-nineteenth-century majolica platter. Photo by Jim DeKorne. Courtesy Museum of New Mexico, Neg. No. 49830.

Pantepec, Puebla, Mexico, women wearing the elaborate, traditional quechquemitl. *Photo by Donald Cordry first appeared in* El Palacio 81, no. 4, p. 6.

EL PALACIO

— HISTORY — ARCHAEOLOGY — ETHNOLOGY —

VOL. I.   SANTA FE, NEW MEXICO, NOVEMBER, 1913   NO. 1.

Making Earth Yield Her Secrets

GOOD WORK WELL DONE

ACHIEVEMENTS OF SCHOOL OF AMERICAN ARCHAEOLOGY.

Built on Broad Foundations It is Making Notable Contributions to Science. Museum of New Mexico in Historic Palace Prove Great Attraction.

The School of American Archaeology at Santa Fe is an institution primarily for research. It selects but directs and supervises archaeological expeditions not only in the Southwest, but as far south as Guatemala and as far north as Alaska. Its director is expected to spend much of his time on the "firing line," whether it be in the torrid zone or in the frozen north, organizing the scientific expeditions that bring to light the secrets of prehistoric cultures and gather treasures for museums and laboratories where scientists and students may study, dissect and compare them.

The School of American Archaeology has such a Museum and such a laboratory at Santa Fe, New Mexico, and offers its facilities not only to the comparatively few who make of the study of archaeology a life work, but to that wider audience of men and women who desire by actual contact with library, museum and laboratory and field work to gain a broader knowledge of prehistoric man. For such, the summer school each August offers especial facilities, being held in a section of the Southwest rich in prehistoric ruins and remains.

The School of American Archaeology was established and is maintained by the Archaeological Institute of America as one of its four archaeological schools, the classical schools being at Athens and at Rome, and the Oriental school at Jerusalem. A fifth school is to be established in China. Not one of these schools has what might be termed a large resident student body, as all are primarily schools of research. The school at Athens, in the report for its thirty-first year, enumerates six students and four associate members, four regular students and fifteen associates, the school at Jerusalem, seven enrolled students, none of whom remained eight months, four of them staying less than two months.

Publications.

Among the tangible results of the initial work of the School of American Archaeology, in addition to truly

(Continued on Page 2.)

ALL THE WORLD LOOKS THIS WAY

Distinguished Visitors from Abroad as Well as from United States Register at Museum.

"Juan Riano, Minister of Spain to the United States of America," he wrote explicitly, yet modestly, on the register of the Museum of New Mexico on October 7, although his titles are many and he is soon to be elevated to an ambassadorship. Don Riano was much interested in the work of the School of American Archaeology and the exhibits of the Museum. He proved himself well informed on the early history of the Southwest and his rapid fire questions indicated that his interest was more than "pro forma."

"A. L. Harmsworth, London, England, (Christ Church, Oxford); John Mackie, London, England (Connaught Club, Marble Arch, W)," were two other inscriptions among three hundred written on the register during October. Mr. Harmsworth has just graduated from Oxford and is a near relative of the publisher of the London Times. Mr. Mackie is an author and was formerly with the Northwest Mounted Police. He declared that ever since boyhood, he had a great desire to visit Santa Fe and the Cliff Dwellings.

"Percy E. Quinn, M. C., 7th District of Mississippi," and Mrs. Quinn of Natchez, were two other distinguished visitors.

"Werner Osthaus, Hagen, Westfalen, Germany," was a tall, handsome, blue-eyed German, who almost missed his train in his enthusiasm over the Museum. H. Kaspholz, Cassel, and H. Moyh, Hendeburg, were two other visitors from Germany and Vittorio G. Alfredo Doran registered from Carrara, Italy.

Then there were the noted Indian, "Dr. Carlos Montezuma, Chicago," the pride of his race, and "Marshall D. Ewell, Chicago," a distinguished jurist and author.

"Hap Kinealan" and "G. Kendorian," of Armenia, almost wept tears of homesickness as they turned the leaves of the many Armenian and Syrian books in the Finck library of the School of American Archaeology, and they would have camped day and night with those treasures during their three days' stay in Santa Fe, had the rules of the institution permitted.

Thus the world travelers pass through the museum doors in the Palace of the Governors and carry Santa Fe's fame to all climes.

THE EXPEDITION TO GUATEMALA

Soon after New Year's day Dr. Edgar L. Hewett, Director of the School of American Archaeology, will leave, accompanied by Mrs. Hewett, for Guatemala, to prepare next year's work at Quirigua. Newly engaged in this scientific work so successfully begun by the School, will be Ralph Linton of Swarthmore, and Earl Morris of the University of Colorado, both of whom received archaeological instruction in the Santa Fe School. A foreign scientist of great renown will probably join in the work. Because of climatic conditions, a medical director will be attached to the staff.

STARTING THE WORK AT QUARAI

The upper panel shows members of the Summer School of American Archaeology beginning excavation at the ruins of Quarai; the middle panel gives a view of the ruins of the mission church and the lower panel illustrates the formal transfer of the ruins to the School. Director Edgar L. Hewett accepting the deed from State Senator W. W. McCoy. The photographs are by Dr. Charles F. Lummis, a member of the Managing Committee of the School of American Archaeology.

ANCIENT QUARAI RUINS TAKEN OVER BY MUSEUM

With ceremonies simple and yet unique and impressive, the mission and Pueblo ruins of Quarai were formally transferred to the Regents of the Museum of New Mexico on Wednesday, August 21. State Senator William M. McCoy, who with J. P. Dunlavy and J. W. Corbett deeded the ruins and 40 acres of land to the school, made the presentation and Director Edgar L. Hewett delivered the speech of acceptance. The old Spanish custom of throwing earth, stones and grass into the air by the parties to the transfer was observed.

The Archaeological Institute of America and the School of American Archaeology were represented by Prof. Mitchell Carroll, general secretary of the Institute; Dr. Charles F. Lummis of Los Angeles; Dr. R. W. Corwin of Pueblo, Colo.; Prof. L. B.

Peton of Hartford Theological Seminary of the managing board, and Dr. E. L. Hewett, director of the school.

Quarai mission was founded among the Tiguas, at the base of the Manzano mountains, not far from the present Manzanal, Torrance County, by the Franciscans in 1629. It was abandoned in less than 50 years because of Comanche and Apache raids. The ruin is an especially fine one and is 150 years older than the oldest California mission.

Excavations were begun immediately by the School of American Archaeology and every step will be taken to preserve the splendid ruin. Out of the burial mound fine specimens of pottery and other utensils and relics have been taken, besides a number of

(Continued on Page 2.)

El Palacio as it appeared in its first issue—Vol. 1, No. 1, page 1.

County Courthouse, Lincoln, New Mexico, in the old days. Courtesy Museum of New Mexico, Neg. No. 54418.

Board meeting at Puye, 1909. Left to right: John R. McFie, Frank Springer, Edgar L. Hewett, Charles F. Lummis, R.W. Corwin, Nathan Jaffa. Courtesy Museum of New Mexico, Neg. No. 13328.

*Mary Austin and Ernest Thompson Seton
at Mrs. Austin's house, Santa Fe, 1927.
Photo by Carol Stryker. Courtesy Museum
of New Mexico, Neg. No. 14248.*

*Artist John Sloan
marches in the Santa
Fe Fiesta parade.
Courtesy Museum of
New Mexico, Neg. No.
45750.*

Patio of the Palace of the Governors, Santa Fe, during Fiesta, 1925. Left to right: Nathan Jaffa, Oskenonton, Edgar L. Hewett, José Sena. Courtesy Museum of New Mexico, Neg. No. 7271.

Charles Lummis and his son Quimu in
Quirigua, Guatemala, ca. 1911. Photo by
Jesse L. Nusbaum. Courtesy Museum of New
Mexico, Neg. No. 61336.

Artists gather in the La Fonda hotel, Santa Fe, 1933. Left to right: Carlos Vierra, Datus Myers, Sheldon Parsons, Theodore Van Soelen, Gerald Cassidy, Will Shuster. Courtesy Museum of New Mexico, Neg. No. 20787.

FINE ARTS

It has always struck me as remarkable that from the original group of anthropologists and historians who gathered in the Palace of the Governors and founded the Museum of New Mexico, there was a widening of interest that came to include the fine arts. Led by Dr. Edgar Lee Hewett, the Museum, which started in 1909, had built a fine arts building by 1917.

There were a few artists working in Taos and Santa Fe at the time. In 1909 Warren Rollins had asked former Governor Prince if he could have an exhibit of his paintings in the Palace. Prince agreed, but doubted that there would be much interest in art in Santa Fe. The Panama-California Exposition in San Diego in 1914 saw the construction of the New Mexico Building to house New Mexico arts and crafts. That building provided the impetus for the Museum of Fine Arts in Santa Fe, and indeed was the model for it.

Santa Fe rapidly gained a reputation as a community friendly to artists, and the Museum helped any of them who moved to town. The new Museum of Fine Arts sat on the plaza, which—long a center of government and commerce—became the end of the trail for artists too. *El Palacio* reported on the fine arts from the first. The interest of both the Museum and *El Palacio* in being an open forum for ideas is reflected in the following articles, with their wide range of subjects and approaches to art.

Ernest Blumenschein, a founder of the Taos art colony, was a fine writer as well as a gifted painter. His article is one of the best ever written about the powerful emotional effect of the New Mexico land and people on Eastern- and European-trained artists. The exciting new subject matter caused an explosion of color, shape, and light on their canvasses.

From the beginning the Museum had open, unjuried annual art shows, and major New Mexico artists entered them and sold their works from what was still one of the few commercial outlets for art in the town. *El Palacio* reported faithfully on these events and others in the art world. By the time Alfred Morang reviewed the 25th Annual Show in 1938, Santa Fe was well established as a major art center, with a nationwide reputation.

Newly arrived from the East in 1937, Morang was an excellent reviewer— besides his talents as a painter and musician, he had already had considerable success as a writer. Morang, who fulfilled everyone's idea of a Bohemian artist, had a radio program on art for fifteen years in Santa Fe, as well as writing a newspaper column and a book on art and running his own art school. He had a broad knowledge of international modern art and art history, and continued to write his sensitive and constructive reviews of the Museum's annual shows for a number of years.

By the post-War years art was prospering not only in Santa Fe and Taos but in art groups and schools in other parts of the state as well. One of the noted painters was Peter Hurd, who worked from his ranch in the Roswell area. His skillful realistic paintings of the landscape and glowing light of southern New Mexico and his sensitive depiction of its peoples brought him fame and respect throughout the United States. The article on Peter Hurd is written by one of New Mexico's best-known writers, John Sinclair, who also introduces the Monuments section of this book.

Another important painter, Raymond Jonson, who was a pioneer in abstract art, worked in Santa Fe from 1924 to 1949, and then in Albuquerque. Jonson had a studio at the University of New Mexico and taught for many years there, developing a remarkable body of work from Cubism to non-representational painting. He had an enormous influence on generations of students, including Ed Garman, who wrote the appreciation of him that appears here.

Randall Davey, who arrived in Santa Fe in 1918, entered with gusto into the life of the town and loved it so much that he stayed there for the rest of his life. Davey's painting, which, as David Gebhard observes, was in the French tradition, continued in the same style, full of élan and verve, though his subjects became Southwestern. His *joie de vivre* was reflected both in his work and in his life, and he cut a dashing figure those times when he burst into the Museum of Fine Arts in his tweeds and boots, enthusiastically talking about art.

The article by well-loved artist Gustave Baumann is very much like Gus himself— full of honesty, empathy, humor, and close observation. It is the text of a talk he gave at the Museum of Fine Arts under rather unusual circumstances, though he didn't know it at the time. I recall that it was winter, and as he talked a sudden melt of a snowpack on Marcy Street filled the storm sewer, which backed up into the Museum's plumbing system and flooded the Fine Arts basement where the paintings were stored. As Fine Arts director Bob Ewing and I stood listening to Gus at the back of the auditorium, near the elegant candle-lit buffet that had been set up to follow the talk, we had a growing realization that things were not as they should be.

The talk went on, Gus all unheeding, while the Museum maintenance crew and city fire department began to pump out the basement. At the buffet following the talk, people were quietly taken aside, apprised of the situation, and asked to go home, put on boots, and return to form a bucket brigade that would dump out the accumulating sludge and sewage. All the paintings were saved, the sandwiches from the buffet fortified the feverish workers, and we managed to have a wonderful evening. Somehow Gus went home after his talk and missed all of this, but he would have loved it, as well as the community spirit that it typified.

—EDNA ROBERTSON

ORIGIN OF THE TAOS ART COLONY

BY ERNEST L. BLUMENSCHEIN

VOLUME 20, NUMBER 9
MAY 1, 1926

In the years before we came several artists had seen the Taos Indian village. Some stayed a few days or weeks to sketch, then wandered on. Henry Sharp was one of these. he told me of his visits to different tribes when I met him in Paris in '96, saying that, as I was interested in Indians, I should be sure to visit the Taos Pueblo. Shortly after this conversation I returned to America, and, with great enthusiasm for the discovery of fresh material, I induced Bert Phillips to accompany me on a painting trip to the Rockies.

Notice, please, the desire for "fresh material." We were ennuied with the hackneyed subject matter of thousands of painters: windmills in a Dutch landscape; Brittany peasants with sabots; French roads lined with Normandy poplars; lady in negligee reclining on a sumptuous divan; lady gazing in mirror; lady powdering her nose; etc., etc. We felt the need of a stimulating subject. This, and the nature of youth, brought us to the west.

Although we were the greenest of tenderfeet we pitched into Western life: bought horses, a wagon camp outfit, and left Denver for unknown adventures. Taos was only a name to us, a place we should visit in our travels. We painted and camped in Colorado for three months, had our first experience with horses, cloudbursts, cooking, sleeping in the open, and the many delights of outdoor life in the Rockies. After the summer months had passed, we started south with the intention of going into Mexico. After crossing high mountain passes, during which we lost a horse, broke our light wagon in many places, ran short of money, and depended chiefly on wild doves for the "piece de resistance," we came to the high plateau country of New Mexico. Never shall I forget the first powerful impressions; my own impressions direct from a new land through my own eyes. Not another man's picture this, not another's adventure. The great naked anatomy of a majestic landscape once tortured, now calm; the fitness of adobe houses to their tawny surroundings; the vastness and overwhelming beauty of skies; terrible drama of storms; peace of night—all in beauty of color, vigorous form, everchanging light.

After a hundred miles in New Mexico we reached the sordid mud village of Taos, curious to see the pyramidal pueblo. We drove right out to the foot of Taos peak prepared to camp at the pueblo itself, but the Indians refused us permission to locate in their midst and also wanted considerable money for the privilege of sketching. So back we went to the Mexican village, three miles away.

No artists were here then. No artists were in Santa Fe. In 1898. And in that year in September, we two rovers who had met in Paris at the Academie Julien, decided that we had found what we had traveled long to reach. We abandoned the idea of going to Mexico, sold the horses and wagons, moved into an adobe house—and then and there began the Taos Art Colony, now famous all over the world.

It doesn't matter if five or six artists had visited Taos before our arrival. They had nothing to do with this colony. Only one ever returned and that was Sharp, some years after we had begun to make the place known by our work. Phillips is the foundation on which the Taos group built. He has lived in Taos ever since that day we dropped in from the north, while I returned many summers to paint the mountains and deserts and Indians and Mexicans, before I could induce my wife to risk her life and complexion on the frontier.

Many artists came and as our paintings began to attract notice, Taos became the subject for many articles in the press. Our painters were receiving prize after prize in the big exhibitions in New York, Philadelphia, Chicago, Washington, and Pittsburgh. The Taos Society of Artists was formed and later the New Mexico Painters. Each year these organizations send out circuit exhibitions which tour the principal cities, carrying the impressions of our artists' lives to many people. Last year the New Mexico Painters had two circuits, on the West Coast, the other throughout the East, while the Taos society had a circuit show through the Mississippi valley. Walter Ufer had a one-man show in New York; Victor Higgins one in Chicago and California and Hawaii. Half a dozen of the Taos paintings were shown by invitation at Venice, Italy, two years ago; half a dozen more are now touring South America.

Needless to say, our colony is famous in the art world. Our recognition is complete and thoroughly established on a sound basis. Yet we have not reached our top form, by any means. With our European education, our own natural talents, and the great benefit our overcultivation receives from the healthy vigor of the Indian's art— his pottery, blankets, jewelry, music, superb dances—there is no doubt that this art group and the equally famous one of Santa Fe will be serious and honorable factors in the development of New Mexico.

TWENTY-FIFTH ANNUAL SHOW

BY ALFRED MORANG

VOLUME 45, NUMBER 19

AUGUST 31, 1938

One of the most significant phases of American cultural development is the rapidly growing interest in art. The time has passed when the complex experiments of abstract and non-objective artists are generally regarded as the products of muddled brains. Even the most casual visitor to the exhibitions understands the need of distance to blend the intricacies of heavily applied pigment. The old obsession that a work of art must rival the camera is happily drifting away, with the wordy literature of the eighteen-hundreds.

This increased awareness of painting is doubtless closely connected with the growing appreciation of creative writing and music. When we take into consideration that the public now attends concerts where the most extreme of the moderns are played, and that the popular magazines print work depending upon the most lyric of life values, it is not surprising that artists who until a few years ago refused to exhibit because of a lack of popular appeal are now the favorites with at least a broad cross-section of the American public.

The various museums throughout the country are not limiting themselves to any one school or approach to art. Non-jury exhibitions have done a good deal in developing a broader conception of the many phases possible in painting. Even a casual glance at any magazine will illustrate the fact that modern advertising experts are fully aware that art has progressed a long way since the Barbizon days.

The museum at Santa Fe is one of the most progressive in the country, and perhaps its most promising exhibition of the year is the annual Southwestern show, where painters of every style hang their work, burying, at least for the time being, the hatchet of conflicting artistic theories.

This year the Southwestern show is unusually interesting. The walls vibrate with the two elements, life and death, both integral parts of existence.

Any detailed description of this exhibition is impossible in a short article. Certain painters must be selected as representing trends that range from highly complex non-objective compositions to paintings depending upon purely illustrative values.

Leading the semi-conservative painters, Randall Davey's pastels are splendid examples of the use of this medium; works that show this fine artist steadily developing, when more than one man of his place in the artistic sun is content to repeat himself.

Jozef Bakos' oils, at least to this reviewer, are disappointing when seen in relation to memories of many of his previous very excellent paintings.

Teresa Bakos is developing that Redon-like sense of the dream-consciousness that has marked many of her previous pictures. In her case there is no mannerism in this nebulous approach. Her paintings of stars in the exhibition are highly satisfying elements in a personal conception of the cosmic whole.

Will Shuster's landscapes are filled with a gusty pleasure in attacking problems that could easily defeat a less highly trained painter. Painted in earth colors, they achieve the quality of solid land that will remain basically unchanged through the seasons. . . .

The water colors by Olive Rush combine that sureness of touch and the imaginative qualities for which she has become nationally famous. And when we realize that she can carry those highly personal elements into the complexities of mural painting, her work becomes doubly significant.

Brooks Willis is an artist who grasps the American scene without falling into the easy trap of the picturesque. His work is firmly painted, his design never sacrificed to details that lead many painters using the same type of subject into dubious mannerisms.

E. Boyd seems more concerned with subject than with plastic values, but in her case not to the detriment of her work. There is a vast difference between illustration and her deeply moving approach to an unvarnished phase of life.

Vernon Hunter's painting, American Murals—In Old Mesilla—is a plastically conceived record of the past. He has succeeded in grasping this phase of the Southwest without lapsing into self-conscious humor, and has shown himself an artist capable of sensing beauty in the fragments of decay, a feat demanding the utmost sincerity.

Albert Schmidt's Church is a beautifully conceived pattern, and, more important, a successful attack upon the problem of pictorial form combined with a definite use of tonal color.

Fremont Ellis' richly painted landscape possesses a very decided pigment luster. He is one of those painters who find the natural scene sufficiently important to forego any conscious effort to attack abstract problems. . . .

Sheldon Parsons is showing landscapes that demonstrate the command he has achieved through the surface upon which he paints and the use of his familiar subject matter. It is interesting to see this veteran Santa Fe painter in the same exhibition with John Sloan, that other veteran of American art.

McHarg Davenport's Bull Heaven may not be the spirit of all butchered bulls ascending to the bovine fields of a higher world, but it certainly is impressive enough to be. Among American painters concerned with satire, Davenport ranks high, and this is a splendid example of his bitter sympathy.

Datus Myers exhibits a portrait of Sally Green that is stiff and awkward without the grace that stiffness lends to, say, the work of Carl Hofer. But his painting of the lady with a guitar is a good example of his feeling for rhythm and decorative treatment.

Louise Morris manages to give a very complete statement in the simplest washes of water color. Her design never tries to leap out of the confines of the paper, and her color has a kind of lyric charm.

John Cornin strikes a note reminiscent of Marc Chagall. These horses never grazed on earthly grass. At any rate these creatures of Cornin's seem to emanate a strange beauty of their own. . . .

The work of the abstract and non-objective artists is decidedly interesting. Gina Knee achieves that balance between the real and the imagined that is the keynote of all successful abstraction. Her washes of vibrant color sing with inner life. One may say Marin has influenced her, but his influence has been a good one. She stands in the front rank of women painters because she never allows charm to overcome more solid values of design and color strength.

Nancy Thompson reminds one of Dufy. She loses the form, and at times her design is insecure, but the abundant life in her water colors overcomes to a good extent these marks of immaturity.

The non-objective artists are undoubtedly headed by Raymond Jonson and Agnes Pelton. Jonson's large composition, Chromatic Contrasts, forces aside the boundaries of the material world and opens the door to a sphere of pure sensation, in this particular piece closely akin to certain atonal music. Agnes Pelton's small canvas, Tomorrow, is a kind of poised emotion bathed in light certainly not derived from the sun or the moon. It is an experience in pure painting, without the slightest dependence upon the external scene.

Robert Gribbroek is a non-objective painter who has pushed far into Transcendental fields. One of the most promising talents in the country in this phase of art, his work in the Southwestern show exhibits his imaginative and technical skill to a high degree.

Bill Lumpkins is an artist who approaches non-objective problems with a scientific mind. His work may lack the passion of that of some of the other Transcendental works, but the remarkable sense of order in his canvases places him in a unique position.

Stuart Walker's Composition projects mentally conceived forms with the solidity of seen shapes. He combines a materialistic approach with a clearly defined spiritual impulse.

Dane Rudhyar is a remarkable artist. His drawing is alive with the color of organic life that mingles with an element of purely spiritual exaltation. . . .

The painting of the cross by Georgia O'Keeffe is a good example of this famous American artist's command over symbolism used in a creative design.

The work of Cady Wells, an abstract artist, is one of the highlights of the Southwestern exhibition. Under his hands a perfect technique becomes a tool for the expression of sharply reasoned emotional reactions toward nature. . . .

Eugenie Shonnard's Indian head in sandstone catches the subdued strength of a primitive people. As in certain work of the French school, the emotional power triumphs over the inadequacy of external form.

The Twenty-Fifth Annual Southwestern Show is composed of more than two hundred entries, representing the work of 128 artists.

PETER HURD,
ARTIST ON HORSEBACK [1]

BY JOHN L. SINCLAIR

VOLUME 53, NUMBER 6

JUNE, 1946

As the crow flies in a south by east course from the Camino del Monte Sol in Santa Fe, a hundred and sixty-one miles via Pinos Wells, he'll probably perch on a fence post belonging to artist Peter Hurd who paints, rides, and sings at his "Sentinel Ranch" in the Ruidoso Valley, adjacent to the little settlement of San Patricio, Lincoln County, New Mexico.

In a cluster of trees on the bank of the river just south of the village is Pete's white ranch house with the red roof. (Everybody calls Peter Hurd "Pete" because the free and easy name ties in so well with his personality.) Southward stretch the bare hills of the lower Ruidoso, east and west meanders the valley with its orchards, fields of alfalfa and corn, north the foothills roll over and beyond the Bonito to the ten-thousand-foot peaks of the Capitan Mountains. A splendid environment for an artist and a man like Peter Hurd.

Pete went to West Point for two years. There he sold his first painting of moonlight over a guardhouse to an officer for $10 and flunked mathematics. A year later he resigned, decided to become an artist for better or worse. While attending Haverford College in Pennsylvania, Pete met the noted painter, N.C. Wyeth, who took him on an an apprentice to develop his talent. With the routine of college, working with Wyeth and attending the Pennsylvania Academy of Fine Arts, Pete was a busy man. Finally he abandoned college and gave his entire time to art.

In 1929, he married Wyeth's daughter, Henriette, a talented painter herself. They now have three children, Peter, Ann Carol, and Michael.   A commission to do a mural in the J. Ross Thomas Memorial Building at the New Mexico Military Institute at Roswell, which he once attended, brought Pete back to his home town in 1933, and he and his family have made their home on the foothill ranch near Roswell ever since.

Everything Pete does he enjoys—but painting, playing polo, and strumming a guitar while singing Spanish and Mexican songs he enjoys best. Ask the natives of San Patricio how Pete can make the Spanish language roll around his tongue!

that they remark when they see him riding with Reginald Bishop, "There goes Pete Hurd with his gringo friend."

Much has been written about the work of Peter Hurd because he is a great artist. His natural talent has brought fame his way—but all the fame humanity could give Peter Hurd would never go to his head.

Murals by Peter Hurd are in the post office building at Big Springs, Texas, and in the post office annex at Dallas, Texas. He is represented in the Wilmington Art Center and the Art Institute of Chicago. The Metropolitan Museum has purchased one of his paintings. His work has been reproduced in *The Magazine of Art* and *Life* magazine, and he has been included in Peyton Boswell's *Modern American Painting* and in the *Encyclopedia Britannica's* "Contemporary American Painting." His illustrations appear in many juvenile books published by Scribners, McKay, Doubleday-Doran, and others, and more recently in *The Return of the the Weed* by Paul Horgan and *Swift Rivers* by Cornelia Meigs. Among his awards are: first prize, landscape, Wilmington Society of Fine Arts, 1930; first prize, international watercolor exhibition, Art Institute, Chicago, 1937; honorable mention, lithograph exhibition, Print Club of Philadelphia, and honorable mention, black and white illustrations, 1937; Dana watercolor medal, Pennsylvania Academy of Fine Arts, 1945.

This season a one-man show of Hurd's work was exhibited in seven New Mexico communities on the State Museum's traveling series—Las Cruces, Santa Fe, Taos, Las Vegas, Roswell, Portales, and Clovis.

NOTES

1. Based on an article by John L. Sinclair in the *Santa Fe New Mexican*, August 4, 1940.

THE ART OF RAYMOND JONSON

BY ED GARMAN

VOLUME 63, NUMBERS 5-6
MAY-JUNE, 1956

Jonson stated his aim early in life. It was to work out his salvation. It was to live and work so that his thought might take form. He wanted his work so to become a symbol of order that it would express what he had made of his life in both body and spirit.

Working out one's salvation is the big issue which we all have to face. Jonson found his key to this main issue early. He has been devoted to life through the art of painting—not to painting for its own sake, but as a way of life, as a consummation of what intelligent and sensitive living can apprehend and express.

The growth of an intelligent, sensitive, and spiritual outlook is not based on things. It is in no way linked to materialism. Such growth is based on values, which arise from experience with life and are crystallized by insight and instinct. This we can see today, here in these galleries. We see in the beginning a group of works that show the development of a clear painterly comprehension of the world around the artist, then moving and growing through successive steps to a weighing, a visualization, and an expression just as clear of the world within the artist.

From 1912 to the present day he has followed his trail of self-revelation and emotional intensification. This is the real work of the artist. Through progressive steps, new planes of experience presented themselves. These were highly important discoveries, which unfolded into forms that were unique, without precedent in idea or predecessor in fact.

In viewing the multiplicity and variety that Jonson has presented to us, we need not be confused. The manifestations of growth in an artist are as logical as the forms of stem and leaf, flower and fruit, are to a plant.

I have found a consistency of intention in his works. I believe it to be essentially an emotional quality. There is also a consistency of style regardless of idea or process. Concepts may differ; the visual perspective may be varied; but these paintings are essentially of one character.

With their inheritance from him of his experience, thought, and sensibility, these paintings are enrichments: they are actual products. They are the distillments of a complex human spirit. They are actual and intrinsic facts, symbols of our most precious wealth: individuality and its constructive expression. His art forms are as complete and concise, as explicit, as his own personality.

It is only by understanding the individual and giving him full value that we have any hope of coming to grips with the only real wealth that life has to offer. Society does not experience or create culture. It can at best present a salubrious environment for the living personality. Only the individual can experience: only the individual can create spiritual wealth. We have in Jonson, in his art, an example of valuable experience, a creation of real wealth, for which we will be a long time in his debt.

There is something awesome, something of mystery, about the way the need for beauty and the imagination shapes and bends the character of an artist toward his own fulfillment. Jonson grew out of the basic substance of our common culture and like a sun shed light on worlds hitherto unseen.

In him a being has been achieved who has dissolved the world in his restless imagination. It was his genius to form purposes and to invent instruments for his own realization. This he has done in terms of beauty.

As an artist working in the medium of fine arts painting, Jonson undertook problems that are by their nature extremely complex. Because art is involved with life, it was necessary for Jonson to solve a number of philosophical questions before he could come to the nature of his most consistent efforts. Each artist, like every person, must solve them alone.

It was this unique personal effort, this unique birthing, that made the creative issue so often such a desperate one. There has always been an urgency about Jonson's creativity. It was urgent because as an artist he always felt himself to be on the threshold of a largeness of vision beyond anything in his current experience. He perceived it as a breakthrough to another dimension of qualitative values.

As an artist he sought, by conceptual means, to express qualities that grew out of his living experience as a man, as a sensitive intelligence, and as a painter involved with plastic problems.

The resolution of these three factors was the crux of his artistic problem. Thus we can see in the works gathered here a change and growth. We see in the early works the dependence and dominance of a subject obtained from his natural external environment. Then came motifs symbolic in nature and themes abstracted from nature. With the appearance of the first non-objective works, we see that he has caught hold of the central problem of his artistic life.

Somewhere along his path he saw the shimmer, the fluorescence, of a beauty transcending truth, a beauty manifest only in the constructive-plastic-dynamic substance of art forms. Thus he entered the aesthetic search, that stray gleam of longings to be fulfilled. It was this that kept him at his seemingly unprofitable business. It was this that enveloped him in the fresh and rugged air of the pioneer.

It was this enterprise which developed in its realization one of Jonson's dominant and vital characteristics. It is a prodigious creativity. It is a promethean force which seeks out the fresh, the various, the novel, the unique, the individual. It is a swift flame that devours the commonplace, the generality, the forced style, and the banality of varied repetition.

It is this characteristic of diversity that prevents evaluation of his art in terms of comparisons, of trends, of prevailing styles. Paintings done only a few days apart can deny relationship to each other. Appreciation must be made on an intrinsic and solitary basis. It is an art and a beauty expressing the single rapture of the unique experience and its expression. It is a beauty flowing from the interior regions of personality and experience. It is a beauty welling forth from the intimate sources of freedom and life.

The aesthetic content of a work can be seen to be not the result of the mechanics of painterly means. Its nature is organic. It is an emotional quality of fine purity, only possibly of conveyance through artistic means.

The enrichment of material which reaches so high a peak in all these paintings is still but a means to an end. We sense in the sublimation of means and method an ecstasy in the doing of them. Not sensuousness, but a keen joy in carrying the rhythms of unity and dynamic arrangement to every particle of his material.

The paintings themselves have a singing twilight quality about them, a subtlety and mood almost characteristic even in the most brilliant contrasts, the strongest arrangements of line and shape, space and mass.

No, it is not twilight. It is the fresh intensities of the dawning light powered by the new sun of a new day. It is a glowing freshness that is subtle, impressive. They have poise, a peace-giving serenity that is musically on rest.

It was Jonson's aim so to live that his life and thought might take form and express what he had made of his life. He took of life what was significant to him and with his own unique experience formed it into a shape that may cast its flame and shadow into the recesses of time.

It is a wonder to me that what has seemed strange about him should not have immediately lost its strangeness and become a familiar and assuring presence as a guiding light in the shadows of an always current materialism.

Within Jonson's uncommon striving for spiritual growth, he has reached a peak of achievement that can never again be reached. It belongs to the inaccessible realm where each individual must remain alone with an originality that is untransferable.

We are fortunate to have a record of Jonson's adventure with life. We are something more than fortunate to have this endowment of qualitative wealth.

AMERICAN PAINTING AND
RANDALL DAVEY TODAY

BY DAVID GEBHARD

VOLUME 64, NUMBER 5-6
MAY-JUNE, 1957

American painting in the twentieth century exhibits numerous broad high-ways well known to public and critics alike, but at the same time introduces many frequently visited roads and byways. It is one of the ironies of history that many times those little-known trails are marked by the most creative spirits of an age. Although we are still unquestionably too much a part of our own age correctly to appraise it, we Americans would certainly find it valuable at least to look back on the last half-century of our painting and its criticism and attempt to reexamine and judge its values, for after all each period considers the past in its own light. History is, as a great European once said, "a myth agreed upon"; perhaps by look-ing into our own immediate past we may find that a new "myth" is needed.

Certainly, one of the salient features in art criticism during the last three or four decades has been the judgment of the value of a work on the basis of its experimen-tal nature. A work was considered significant or great, not because of any intrinsic qualities in the painting, but because it presented a new and different approach. However, no one would completely disregard the value of experimental painting in the twentieth century. We are living in a period during which the most exciting and far reaching discoveries have been made in painting, sculpture, and architec-ture, since the emergence of the Renaissance in the fifteenth century.

But at this point we must inject a note of caution into this type of value judg-ment. We must be cautious, in assaying the value of a painting, that our bases of criticism do not rest solely on uniqueness or pure experimentation in painting. Oftentimes in the history of art the mature statements which have been made in a particular mode of expression have appeared long after the first or initial experi-ments. As Americans we must exercise a great deal of reserve in this regard, since we have a considerable fondness for "firsts." What we are saying here is that an object must be analyzed and judged on its own merits. It is true that this sets up a dual standard, for art history is concerned with both the experimental nature of an object and its essential qualitative value.

The twentieth century has been an age of turmoil, and to a considerable extent this turmoil has been deeply reflected in its art. The disturbed conditions of the individual and of mankind in general have been mirrored in the anguished painting of the German and American expressionists. The mechanistic view of our world has been reflected in the paintings of the constructivists, the purists, and other groups. Paintings as a vehicle of social and political criticism have flowered in both Europe and the United States. On the other hand, one always wonders whether the most valuable statements have not been made by the classicists of our age. For example, in the stylistically diverse paintings of Rénoir, Cézanne, Matisse, and Braque, we have a presentation of the serene and calm aspects of life, which we could term the classical lyricism of twentieth-century painting.

It is in this latter group that the paintings of Randall Davey would find their place, for here is a half-century of paintings that have sought to capture the sparkling optimism and joy of twentieth-century life. Man is presented to us as an individual, a thing of worth and value. In his life and painting, Davey has emphatically rejected the idea that man is a mechanical device to be manipulated by others or by his environment, or that man is an insignificant atom in the universe. There will always be some who say that this is a nineteenth-, not a twentieth-century point of view. They will go on to say that this was a view stated by the impressionists, above all by Rénoir and Monet in the last years of the nineteenth century. Perhaps in saying this, certain critics are revealing more about themselves and their philosophy than they are about the paintings. Because these men have lost hope in the dignity and worth of man, they find it disturbing and difficult to experience paintings which express faith in man.

As a painter, Davey matured in the environment of social criticism exemplified by the work of the well-known "Ash Can School." But what he learned from the teachings of Sloan, Henri, Luks, and others, was the ability to see the world around him, and to translate his impressions into painting. Davey's paintings are, above all, an impression of the world translated onto the two-dimensional canvas by color alone. Fine draftsmanship inevitably underlies many of his paintings, but the viewer is aware only of the paint as color. Davey's technique of broken color, which is best exemplified in his numerous encaustic paintings of racing scenes, portraits, and still life, also owes something to the seventeenth-century work of the Spaniard Velásquez and the Dutchman Franz Hals. By working in this coloristic, impressionistic medium, Davey has continued in his work the tradition of visual reality which these earlier painters had established.

The paintings of Randall Davey also convey to us the essential liveliness, movement, and spirit of American life. This has been accomplished partially by the colors themselves, by color placement, and also by the basic informality of the scene he depicted. There is never anything static in his paintings. Whether it is a portrait, a still life, or a scene of the race track, the painting always has its own inner life and force. Thus Davey's paintings have an existence and essence of their own quite separate from whatever visual source they may have had in nature. In experiencing his paintings, one is seldom concerned to know who is represented in a portrait or where this or that scene is located. Subject matter has been relegated to a means, and the paintings as a self-contained entity have become the end result. In discussing and evaluating a work of art one may certainly ask for nothing but that the painting will have its own intrinsic existence.

In the paintings of Randall Davey we have a forceful and vigorous statement about the essential spirit and soul of man and his world. This segment of our world has too often been neglected for that which is sordid, or ugly, or painful. Above all, his painterly statements of the joy of love, of life, have rejected the devices of the sentimental and trite which at one time typified many segments of American painting. The statement of optimism in his paintings is conveyed to us by the fine inner convictions of the paintings themselves, for since painting is a mode of human expression it becomes an object of value only when the painter has something worthwhile to say. In the final analysis, this is perhaps the factor which distinguishes great artistic production of any period from its mediocre counterparts. This is the factor which distinguishes and sets off the work of Randall Davey. It will be for future generations to decide on the ultimate contributions in our own period, but one may be quite certain that the artistic contribution and the personality of Randall Davey will be an important factor to be reckoned with.

CONCERNING A
SMALL UNTROUBLED WORLD

BY GUSTAVE BAUMANN

VOLUME 78, NUMBER 1

MARCH, 1972

When I first saw Santa Fe, and not being familiar with adobe architecture, the old part seemed to be like picture book stuff that somebody had dreamed up and then had found it comfortable to live in.

There was little evidence of the occupational therapy that had been applied years earlier other than the ruins of Fort Marcy on a nearby hilltop and some decrepit structures near the river that had probably been dance halls. The town as a whole gave one the feeling of a fairly well adjusted mixture of Spanish and Anglo culture, with the Indians as an uninterrupted civilization still pervading it all. It made for a unique situation not likely to be found anywhere else.

Archeological diggings were going on in what Dr. Hewett had designated as a hundred-mile square using Santa Fe as a basis to work out from. That hundred-mile square contained the entire Pajarito plateau with its Frijoles canyon and Puye ruins along with a number of lesser evidences of prehistoric occupation.

To preserve all this, Dr. Hewett, being a very astute and farsighted gentleman, had brought influence to bear in high places to have set aside the entire region in perpetuity as a national park.

What Dr. Hewett did not foresee, however, was the presence of a private boys' school sitting right in the middle of his national park; and being more interested in the ruins, why should he? The school went about its business quietly. As a pedagog he would see no reason why they shouldn't stay there. Besides that, Los Alamos was a nice name for a boys' school.

What he also could not foresee was that someday history would be rewritten from there on into an unforeseeable future.

The Pajarito plateau was a wonderful out-of-this-world place where you could wander and wonder no end while an occasional bear or deer crossed your tracks.

If you visualize artists and archeologists in two distinct camps, there still were times when the artists forgot their business and went completely archeological. We learned all the familiar terms and became quite expert in identifying potsherds as belonging to this or that period. Since it all dealt with the dim past there was no quarreling with modernity.

We all had a pet ruin somewhere in which to conduct secret diggings unbeknown to Dr. Hewett who, while he liked artists, did not want them messing around in his business. For which I didn't blame him. I never brought home anything in the way of a pot other than dust in my lungs, excepting once.

One nice balmy winter I had as a neighbor a Dr. Sam Guernsey from the Peabody Museum in Boston. Sam was recuperating from digging in Arizona where they, too, have dust. He moved about continuously and rested a lot. Wandering past our driveway one morning he saw me readying my car.

"Where are you going?" he said.

"Digging," I replied.

There was a long silence, then in a quavery Boston voice and with great hesitancy he continued, "You understand, Gus, I can't go with you in a professional capacity, but I'd like to to go with you, but I have to go home first." His home being on our way we stopped for something he said he needed and we were off. I now don't know where the San Marcos ruins are but we found them then.

I can still see Sam with his Boston derby getting out and walking away from the car as I began looking for a likely spot to dig. Alas, all places looked alike to me.

I saw Sam lifting his derby to scratch his head when he suddenly turned. In no time at all he was at my side. "No, no, Gus," he said, "don't dig there. You see this rock sticking up? I'd dig there if I were you; that rock did not come there by itself."

I looked at the rock while Sam walked away again. I gave the rock a push with my shovel and there it was: an intact pot covering a child burial. The morning was still young and the weather balmy. It was too early to go home so I said, "Sam, now let me find another by myself," while Sam walked away again. There is nothing so incongruous as a Peabody archeologist pacing San Marcos ruins in a derby hat.

I whacked away at another rock standing up when Sam returned. "No, no, Gus, not that, see that flat rock here? I'd dig there," and he walked away. I felt a little foolish and mumbled something about history does not repeat itself, at least not twice in one morning, but thought I'd better listen to an expert. The rock came away from a rise of rubble and there was another child burial—just like that. I turned the two pots over to put in some artifacts and bones when Sam returned. "No, no, Gus," he said, "this we have to do professionally." With that he took a rolled cloth from his coat pocket. In it was his pet trowel, a whisk broom and, as I remember, a little notebook to record the find.

He then helped me lay out all the findings professionally. Of the three pots one of them was a very unusual ceremonial piece which I felt should go to the Peabody Museum. The others I still have to remember Sam by. The postscript to the story is, what with a lot of digging on my own, I never have found anything since then other than isolated shards.

To find a common ground for the two professions of artist and archeologist I suppose we can say that one is interested in bones while the other is more interested in the skin of things. Instead of being tied to a musty museum the artist likes to herd in colonies where life and landscape are a source of inspiration. There are many of these all over the United States, some of them have worn themselves out. Of those that persist, Provincetown; Brown County, Indiana; Taos, New Mexico; and Laguna Beach, California are perhaps the best known. While Santa Fe has its quota of artists, it never was a colony in the accepted sense. Its interests are too diversified, which as far as I was concerned was a lucky break. You can lose yourself in it and go about your business quietly.

Be that as it may, after all these years I still have a lingering nostalgia for the old Canyon road and Camino days when I was part of them. The little home I lived in is still there on a little flatiron corner where Garcia joins Canyon Road. It had a white picket fence that enclosed a garden where zinnias and marigolds grew rampant and one lonesome artichoke plant that someone had brought me from California which, not being indigenous, had to be nursed along. It bore two artichokes, one of enormous size. I could hardly wait to make a salad of it. Not knowing that artichokes have to be cooked I dipped the leaves in what I thought could be the proper dressing and bit into them. Not until I was married years later did artichokes again appear on my menu.

The artists then living in studios that meandered up Canyon Road and the Camino were a busy lot. Most of us had arrived as professionals looking for a place in which to work out our problems, to which the big city did not lend itself.

Since this was all before the car era, some of the artists had gone horsey and Stetson hats and cowboy boots were the vogue. Sheldon Parsons with a spanking team of horses had made himself a self-appointed guide for all newcomers, of which I was one. Windy Bill Henderson, whom I had known in Chicago where he had left a highly sophisticated studio, was reborn here with leather chaps and spurs. His house on the Camino was a small one that frequently bulged with guests where Bill did all the talking, so he finally accepted the "windy" with resigned amusement. The Camino was then one isolated string of houses inhabited by the "Cinco Pintores," trying hard to live up to a good name that persists to this day.

We were all young and if in need of diversion we could meander up and down Canyon Road or the Camino and find a party going on somewhere. It did not matter if you were not on speaking terms with the host; a party was always neutral ground. To the east of the Camino there were no houses, the little valley boasted of nothing but a threshing floor. Happening to be up there one summer day I had to take refuge in one of the Cinco Pintores houses because of a thunderstorm.

Threshing had been going on and it was interesting to watch it. Then a sudden flash of lightning hit the threshing floor, following by the usual deluge of rain, killing all the goats. It was one of those major tragedies the native economy was frequently subjected to, and just about equivalent to losing a number of unfinished paintings that you had expected to send to an exhibition.

The Rolshovens to whom I refer again later, had followed me down from Taos and located in a large house now occupied by the "I Ams." Remembering a trip up there she, that is, Tine [Rolshoven], had always looked upon me as an uncouth bachelor in need of training in the social amenities. Also, there was her gentle insistence that tea only must be served at tea parties. In all this her husband, Uncle Julius as I called him, stood aside while she had all her tea ceremonial things moved to my studio tea table—Florentine teacups, silver, and all. Since then nothing like it has been seen on Canyon Road.

Everybody came, including Madame Fenjes, who arrived in a chauffeured car and a super ostrich-feathered hat which fussed me so I forgot her name. I still don't like tea. The party was a grand success and we still have the table to remember it by.

Canyon Road was getting a little hectic, the need of a change becoming apparent, and I began looking about. An abandoned church on lower San Francisco Street came to my notice. Owned by the Kenneth Chapmans, it had been remodeled with a north light, while the two Sunday school rooms under the choir loft had been turned into a bedroom and kitchen respectively. The bell tower had become a nesting place for pigeons that gurgled all night long. To fill the studio I had four hard board settees put in. Set back from the street, the church had a front yard and a picket fence. All the other houses on the street were built right up to the sidewalk.

In those days lower San Francisco Street was a place where nice people did not go. After midnight there was a lot of going-home traffic. Groping hands would feel their way along smooth adobe house fronts until they arrived at my picket fence and there they would stop to rest and recover their voices. Awakened from a deep sleep in my Sunday school bedroom, I learned all the old Spanish songs then the vogue. "Cielito Lindo," "El Rancho Grande"—they all pealed forth while the singers held onto my picket fence. Occasionally this was repeated several times a night. Then they would wend their way to upper San Francisco Street and perhaps to the cathedral to attend early Mass.

I had an old Koshare friend from Santo Domingo. Having once taken him to my doctor for some ailment that troubled him, I seemed to have earned his eternal gratitude. Knocking at my door late at night and after the customary hello, his story was always the same. "Baumann," he'd say, "pretty cold to sleep out, got only one blanket, don't want to go to Indian School; can I stay here?" "Come in, Diego," I'd say, when Diego added, "Can I bring my friend?" His "friend" was always *three* since he knew I had four settees they could sleep on. In the morning I'd go to the Mayflower Cafe for breakfast and when I returned they were gone, to return some other cold night when they were in town.

Years later after Diego had died I happened to be at Santo Domingo. During a rest in the dance an Indian came and stood in front of me and said, "You know me," and then added, "I'm Juan, Diego's brother; he always said you were the best friend he ever had." It is one of the many things that sometimes set me to thinking, especially in these days when old loyalties have a way of dissolving.

It appears that New Mexico came into my life long before I became aware of it during a sort of apprenticeship in the arts—that is, one phase of it. The turn of the century found me employed in the studio of a Curtis Gandy, where art of the marketplace had priority. Taken as schooling in fundamentals it was invaluable. Among Gandy's clients was the Santa Fe Railroad, then in need of means to familiarize the public with travel in the Southwest. Gandy was of sturdy seaboard stock that was practically indestructible, but the health of this family made moving to New Mexico advisable. For a time they lived on First Street in Albuquerque. Working out from there he learned all about New Mexico, judging from the voluminous letters I received. Not paying much attention to them as something too far removed from my immediate needs, I never bothered to keep them. What I recall of them now were meticulous descriptions of Indian life in the Pueblos such as Isleta, San Felipe, Zuni, and the Hopi country.

No wonder that the Santa Fe Railroad had found him an invaluable interpreter of their particular interests. Returning to Chicago a year or so later, and with his family recovered, he went back to the old routine, surrounded by fragile pots, loud-patterned blankets, and even bows and arrows. In need of new stationery, he devised a letterhead with a little Indian boy he called, "Tatta Uh," whom he had known in Isleta.

When work in hand demanded a rest period, he'd light his pipe and begin, "Now Gus, you see this blanket? It isn't Indian, it is what is called a blue Chimayo and it is Mexican," and so on *ad infinitum* while I was struggling with the problem of painting irresistible buying appeal into a fried egg reposing on a slice of a particular kind of ham, that had to be finished to meet a deadline.

The vicissitudes of art begin and lead us to strange places, desirable and otherwise. Before Gandy had become a competent illustrator he had been a Pullman car striper and had used up miles and miles of gold leaf doing so. Having accumulated some grandiose ideas, Gandy went to New York and was finally lost in anonymity. Something had happened that I knew nothing about. When I saw him again he had a large space in a loft on Fifth Avenue near Washington Square, and what was he doing? Painting large signs intended to grace the sides of Brooklyn Bridge with black whales that had a large white spot supposedly cleaned by Sapolio. Now if that sounds at all funny it is unintentionally so. In the meanwhile I had opened a studio of my own, having discovered how to put buying appeal into automobile ads that made the purchase of them irresistible. They were the ultimate in snazziness then. When they turn up in my files now, as they do occasionally, they look so old-fashioned.

While I've never found life to be particularly dull, when it became a little fuzzy on the edges it always indicated a need of change. It would have been so easy then with all the information at hand to have gone to New Mexico, excepting for a strong pull in the other direction. There was a kind of magic adhering to the word *art* as it existed in Europe. If you would just plunge in and bathe in that, you'd come out a perfect specimen. Well, what I found was that going to Europe to study was no subtle labor-saving device; it still left me floundering around in a sea of uncertainty as I reopened my studio. While times had changed in the meanwhile, the same old problems continued. The building I was located in had a select saloon I patronized occasionally, where one day I saw Walter Ufer with his foot on the rail and a sunburn he had brought back with him from New Mexico. He too had been to Europe, but it was all overshadowed by what he had found in Taos. He too had been through the commercial art mill and we had competed with each other at times, which was all in a day's work. Walter was a vehement person and with a nasal accent. He talked through the corner of his mouth to emphasize what he had to say.

At that time the Santa Fe Railroad was making inducements to established artists to bring them to the Southwest, and he had benefitted by it by talking to their advertising department. Not unlike my friend Gandy, he let his enthusiasms run away with him after I had said, "Let's have another drink." On and on it went until the five o'clock rush home. Since he was going home one way and I another, he called me back to tell me, "Don't go on the Santa Fe; I'm just getting a Ford all fixed up as a studio to work in, and you can just come with me"—and as they say, I got sold on the idea.

Considerable time intervened to dream about Taos while completing some work I had obligated myself to do, what with hopping from one place to another, breaking a lease, getting rid of a lot of stuff and packing a lot more to go to Taos. Then, "What do I do after I've seen Taos?" It all came to me in an overly cautious moment. You just can't go on that way indefinitely without endangering your mind. Since misery loves company, I adopted the Walter Ufer manner to tell some of my artist friends who were floundering around in unhappy surroundings to go to Taos where all their troubles would dissolve in the thin summer air.

When the next summer came I was already there to greet Ufer as he arrived in his Ford studio contraption, but not before I had been introduced to the amenities of Harvey House cuisine at Santa Fe stopovers. I still recall a natty waitress with an appealing voice looking over my shoulder and saying, "D'you wish sausage?"

The elaborately carved mahogany paneled sleepers creaked and groaned all night, but then you did not as at present have to call the porter to find out which switch it was that gave you more light, more heat, or more air. You just went to sleep to the bumpety-bump of the wheels on the rails and it was all so pleasantly stuffy. Suddenly the train came to a grinding halt and there it stayed until morning. I could hear voices outside, and footsteps, but this wasn't a Harvey House stop; we were somewhere on the open prairie and most of the passengers were huddling to look under a car, the floor of which had just escaped being ripped open by a turned-up rail. A wrecking crew appeared from somewhere and with some shunting of cars the defective rail was replaced by another. We all found our berths, and the passengers bound for California dreamed of a safe arrival.

There is no mountain so tall as when you see it from level prairie ground: There it is, bathed in inscrutable blue. The train engine gives a whistle as if the engineer saw it too. While it is an old story to him, the passengers feel as if they are getting somewhere different from where they've been and read the railway folder for perhaps the tenth time. They reset their watches from Standard to Mountain time and glue their noses to the windows.

Just what rat it was that Raton Pass is named after, the railway folder doesn't say. But having arrived at its foot, extra engines equipped for the top push and pull us over. As if out of breath they give an occasional whistle that reverberates in the deep cuts where you feel the sides of the cars were being scraped. The train comes to another stop and then you are in New Mexico.

Like throwing your coat and pants away, you've shed old problems to assume fresh ones still to be learned about.

New Mexico is an easy place to call home. It was to me, although I was still to learn about it. While its long stretches of grama grass mean more to ranchers, you can say it is good for the eyes, especially when you see a herd of cattle or sheep grazing it. Seemingly to avoid running over them the train rolls along in endless curves. The next stop is Las Vegas with its Harvey House, but a saloon across the street looks more inviting, especially after the past night's experience. With a stomach that is going to growl before arriving at the Harvey House stop, you reboard the train. It is all completely unfamiliar country that you somehow can't identify as being in this United States.

The train toots its way seemingly to avoid a bare spot that the railway folder says are the Pecos Ruins and begins to climb again to Glorieta Pass, where another family of engines awaits to push and pull us over. If your ticket reads "Lamy," as mine did, the conductor takes it away from you and tells you too look after your luggage, leaving you a stub that says "Santa Fe."

At Lamy we passed a little Harvey House that was the gem of the entire system, until changing circumstances in mode of travel made its continued existence a dream and had become uneconomical. A friendly conductor waved us goodby and what had been home to us for the last thirty-six hours started rolling towards Albuquerque. Awaiting us at Lamy the little narrow gauge train of two cars certainly looked diminutive, but it pushed up a long mesa to what was another version of New Mexico landscape in which it rolled along as if time was no object.

There was no heavy cloud of smoke overhanging Santa Fe to indicate its presence when there it was, as if hiding in piñons and cedar bushes. What I saw of Santa Fe at the time did not impress me much other than its unpolluted air that invited taking deep breaths.

Adjoining the Santa Fe tracks, a Denver and Rio Grande train, also a narrow gauge, showed evidence of life. There is always a lot of puffing and snorting; the smaller the train the more snorting. Taxis bustled people into town. Others, including myself, boarded the little snorter that would eventually arrive somewhere in Colorado after having deposited me at Taos Junction. It rolled along slowly as if it were exploring a new continent that had to be investigated. Passing an Indian pueblo, it stopped at Española. Almost all the residents of this village were there to greet us as if it were the important event of the day. Cowhands and ranchers went this way and that, as if on important business, or rested themselves in a waiting buggy. Whatever was happening was all picture stuff if you chose to see it that way. There were no jittery taxi drivers ready to bite your head off if asked a civil question. I remember reboarding the train with considerable regret.

With train toots at cattle crossings we entered the canyon of the Rio Grande, to stop at Embudo for lunch. We had been all morning going some forty miles, while now you can go all the way to Taos and back in less time. At Embudo mutton stew was the entire bill of fare and you could hear much slurping of it along the counter. Among the diners there was a spotlessly dressed, distinguished-looking couple who had been fussing about soot. They held forth about it in loud terms, as spoiling their clothes, while I had found the rear platform of the car to be a nice place to dangle my feet. The track was close to the river bed; in fact, the track followed it all the way until it began to climb out of the canyon. Jutting out of the water here and there were black rocks with strange pictographs on them that puzzled me then, but would at a later time have ultramodern value that no one had even thought of before. While the roadbed had obliterated all evidence, this must have been a trail that ultimately led to Taos when walking and fording rivers were the only means to get there. For the little train the terrain became impassable, so it puffed and snorted its way out of the canyon, sometimes almost meeting itself on curves, until it found itself on reasonably level sagebrush country. By that time evening was approaching. Thinking that we might forget it, the conductor opened the door and announced that Taos Junction was the next stop. A porter to brush us off couldn't have helped, we were too messed up by soot from New Mexico coal. What we needed most was a bath in a nice clean bathtub.

The train gave a farewell toot when what I learned later was Long John Dunne made a belated appearance in weathered blue overalls and a tattered Stetson. A cud of tobacco gave his walrus mustache great mobility as he surveyed the scene, looking us over and then scratching his head as he counted the baggage, most of which was labeled "Rolshoven, Florence, Italy." Then, in a voice accustomed to speaking to servants, one heard, "I want all that baggage brought over with us because I have to dress for dinner tonight."

"Sorry," said Long John, "It will be brought over in the morning."

(Before I go any further, this is perhaps the place to mention that Julius Rolshoven, a very prominent portrait painter of the period, had long resided in the medieval splendor of an old Florentine castello. The war had brought him home with Madame Rolshoven, who had been accustomed to ordering lesser folk about. It really took her a long time to become adjusted to New Mexico folkways, or for that matter to Gus Baumann's bad manners.)

Having been on the road for a while, Long John stopped the car, unfastened some planks on the side and laid them across a ditch; that done, we crossed over them. Then picking them up again, he remarked that he did not leave them there just so some damn lazy paisano could cross on them. Giving the planks a parting kick, we spluttered along in the approaching dusk, until we came to what looked like a deep hole.

"What's that?" said Mrs. Rolshoven.

"The Rio Grande Gorge," replied Long John.

"Have you ever driven it before?"

"No ma'am," said Long John, "this is the very first time." Whereupon Mrs. Rolshoven in a commanding voice said, "Then let me out."

John put on the brakes and helped her down. Waiting for her to get ahead, he followed. High-heeled shoes are not so good in the Rio Grande Gorge and soon Mrs. Rolshoven began to hobble.

What with her losing the second heel, John obligingly stopped the car, opened the door, and Mrs. Rolshoven took her seat. As he had told her when we crossed the bridge, we'd go up the other side. The lights of Taos began blinking in the distance, to come nearer and nearer without a peep out of Mrs. Rolshoven. We arrived at the Columbian Hotel where Mrs. Rolshoven hobbled in to the desk clerk.

"What do you mean," she said, "sending a man to drive over that terrible road who had never driven it before?"

The clerk, fumbling around with some papers, asked her politely, "Who was it brought you over, Madam?"

Pointing, she said, "That man."

"Oh," replied the clerk, "that is Long John Dunne, he's driven that road for 25 years."

The day had been an eyeful for me along with an excursion into nice people's behavior and we all went to bed, I presume.

To have dreamed about Taos for years and then one fine day actually waking up in it made me wonder. The sounds of voices that came over the transom were strange; even the silence was of a different sort. Much of the gabble-gabble during breakfast was in Spanish. There seemed to be a lot of time to chat. What you heard was a mixture of Anglo, Spanish, and Indian. One of the Indians had walked in from the pueblo to have his breakfast. Maybe he didn't like home cooking, or he hadn't been home, although as a rule Pueblo Indians are homebodies.

I suppose we all have a certain routine of living. The last few days had completely upset mine. What the tourist sees is one thing, what registers with the artist is another. Every once in a while you throw away impressions as obsolete and start all over. For this, Taos is as good a place as any.

As I prepared to pay for my meal, the motherly sort of waitress informed me that getting a meal ticket made it much cheaper. It was part of the mores of Taos I had yet to learn about.

Instead of being a landmark that could be seen from miles away, the Columbian Hotel's floor was below ground. Looking out of the windows you could see the feet of passersby in cowboy boots, fancy pants, slippers or blue overalls. The blue overalls proved to belong to John Dunne returning from Taos Junction to deposit Mrs. Rolshoven's luggage. I thought, "Heavens, do you suppose she sat up all night waiting for her nightie?"

Venturing out, I had my first look at the plaza in the daytime. There was no mad street traffic, or trains rumbling overhead. Horses and wagons were moving at a slow pace when not standing still. I spoke to a mocassined Indian. Sizing me up as not knowing Spanish, he replied in fairly good English when I wanted to know where Walter Ufer lived.

"Oh, I know Ufer," he said, "I pose for him. He has a studio that says 'Dynamite' on the door." Pointing to the far end of the plaza he added, "You go around corner and there is Ufer Street." So they name their streets after artists, I thought.

Ufer had not as yet arrived with his Ford studio. I suppose he was still somewhere on the plain, and I wandered about.

There was something about Taos streets and alleyways that was more felt than seen. The houses looked as if they had been pushed up out of the ground to have a roof clapped on them, that is, the older ones before Taos became architecturally conscious. I recall seeing Taos later from the Ranchos side in the evening light as a thin line of houses that seemed to be of one piece. It looked like something out of biblical history that had been preserved all these years. Aside from a few clumps of trees, there was nothing but sagebrush, broken here and there by little fields of alfalfa.

If you were in a mood to stop you could hear the burble of meadowlarks, now completely out of time with the present hubbub of traffic that overrides everything. It was a time when sentimentality was permissible as a quiet enjoyment, and good for the soul, whatever that is.

Having seen something of sketching grounds in the East, wandering about in Taos streets and alleyways almost drove me frantic. There just was no limit and there was no need for imaginative interpretations or of giving your versions of it; it was all there as is, with some leeway for your personal interpretations. Overriding it all, there was Taos Mountain with its eternal presence. No wonder Blumenschein and Phillips, bound for Texas, decided to stay here to break the ground, as we say, for the rest of us.

Living in Taos wasn't easy. The water problem made it necessary to get your supply from above the Pueblo. There was a tremendous demand for milk cans to bring it down in. Oil lamps were not unknown since a wheezy power plant, casually installed, had a way of going out for the evening. All of which didn't matter—you adjusted yourself to it and that was that. While I did not have a car to make its presence vitally important, there was one lonely gas station at the open end of the plaza, while wagons with horses tethered to hitching rails still preempted space set aside for them.

There may have been some gravel on the adobe roads and streets, but when a gentle summer rain turned into a downpour of some duration, Taos mud, unlike any other, made the possession of rubber boots a valuable asset. I had brought these with me as routine equipment seldom used but just in case they might help in stalking a particularly interesting subject or, as they say, get me out of a hole.

That Taos was a small town or perhaps just a village would seem to be indicated by its telephone directory, which just about filled the inside cover, much to the surprise of a New York lady who had asked for it to put on a chair for her small daughter to sit on. Having once been a part of it, there is great temptation to recount facts and foibles of a very active artists' and writers' group to annotate what they themselves have said.

Seeing a long mountain range from the distance always makes me wonder what is back of it. This particular range had a road through it that led to Santa Fe, if you were in no hurry to get there. Long John had been over it; it left him in no mood to recommend it. Since we always think we know better, I found someone of the same opinion as mine. If you have been used to flat country all your life, the rough stuff that is a part of city life prepares you for anything, even without John Dunne's recommendations.

In those days there were three cars that stood up to the problem. One was that funny old Ford, then the Dodge and the Cadillac. We made it in a Ford after throwing a ceremonial kiss to Taos. The Ford rattled its way over roads and ditches, past little ranches with cows stopping their cud to see who was going by. The ranch looked as if the owners had left it to go away somewhere. It all took longer than it does to tell it.

When the Rio Grande appeared then we knew for certain the Denver and Rio Grande tracks were on the opposite shore. When the railroad was built they must have thrown all the rocks they did not need over on our side to discourage competing traffic. (Since then the rocks have been removed.) What took us over eight hours now can, if you are so minded, be done in one hour. It isn't the big rocks you see that make trouble, it's the little rocks you don't see.

When bang went another tire; you stopped, jacked up the old Ford and smeared a patch on the tire, all of which takes much longer than it does to tell. It made you wish you had taken the advice of Long John Dunne; who at that very moment might be thinking of those blankety-blank fools going over that blankety-blank road.

In due time the mountains lose their grip on us. You cross a ditch and a rocky arroyo bed and there you are in Velarde with a sign saying "Apples for sale." Since sandwiches have given out long ago we munch apples the rest of the way. It is no wonder that the Ford legends consist of a lot of funny stories that persist to this day. We were thinking that we could add one or two when we passed Alcalde with its trees and acequia madre wandering through it. We did not know then that years later it would be the place where we would spend many happy summers at Florence Dibell Bartlett's ranch, El Mirador, that eventually gave root to the Museum of International Folk Art.

Compared to what we had to scramble over, the road from then on was reasonably negotiable, excepting for rivers that had to be forded, where a nearby rancher always made his appearance to pull you over with a sturdy team of horses. The flat rate was two dollars. If you took a chance and got stuck it was five.

Camel Rock appeared and then the turn-in to Tesuque Pueblo. Having passed through a rain the river there was up, too; besides that we had had all the fording we wanted. What I learned later was an old oxcart trail meandered over some piñon-covered hills destined to be topped by the Santa Fe Opera complex at some still later date. While I didn't know it then, we were within the city limits of Santa Fe, which had yet to learn about four-lane highways. We bumped through a long, sandy arroyo and there it was.

What with a casual and not overly impressive entrance, I had seen Santa Fe from the other side only, and I still haven't learned all there is to know about it. All I know is that it merits delving into, or as we say, "doing a little snooping." Unconsciously I gravitated to the plaza. It was a happy mixture of past and present with an incongruous obelisk sitting in the middle that made you wonder who it was that was buried there. You could sit on comfortable benches shaded by a roof of trees and look around. While three sides of the plaza were preempted by stores the other side was occupied by a low building extending the entire length with a portal, that somehow overshadowed the three commercial sides and looked as if our Indians from Taos Pueblo might have had something to do with it. Could it be the art museum I had heard so much about? Since I had expected to leave in the morning, I thought I'd better take a look, as my Taos friends had advised.

Directly across the street where it faced the museum was an old dilapidated ruin that was a jumble of beams, door frames and mud bricks. A coyote, of which I had first learned about in Taos, came slinking out of the dark interior looking furtively this way and that; it went slinking and loping down the street to find another hiding place I presume, or perhaps to find an ashcan and a suitable breakfast. That particular corner is now occupied by the First National Bank, which replaced a defunct movie house of the silent movie days, but not however until we had seen "The Cabinet of Dr. Caligari" on its screen. The art museum was unlike what I had been accustomed to in the east, where the mausoleum pattern was the proper and accepted style. Seeing it for the first time was quite a revelation. It did not seem possible in what I had known in my earlier years as the Southwest, which was entirely filled with just Rocky Mountains and a town in the middle of them with a name that had two Qs in it; and now, of all things, to find a town named after a railroad with a full-fledged art museum. Accustomed as I was to having art housed in those completely foreign Greek temples invariably alien to the surroundings, here was one equally strange, but somehow there was a certain feeling of rightness about it and I learned the meaning of the word indigenous, but it took considerable readjusting to see it that way.

Here on these walls were all my friends represented by pictures, some of which I had seen in progress. Representational material of a novel kind that stood for Taos filled the alcoves. The time to quarrel with it had not yet arrived from Europe. So befeathered chiefs and Indians drilling beads before a fireplace were informative material for people living beyond the borders of New Mexico, or the occasional tourist, if he did not buy a picture, could talk about it when he arrived home. I, too, had gotten the "Indian fever" and its glamour had not yet worn off. It gives me something to think about. Maybe we should leave it to a new generation of Indians that have "art in the blood" to interpret.

I wandered about and came to a hall with a carved beam ceiling, that platform of which I am sitting on now. Little did I know then that it would make for an entirely new activity later, and wandered into the lobby or whatever you call it in an art museum. Paul Walter was then the curator. Being of German ancestry we had something in common, although we said nothing about it, being just at the end of the first World War. It was a time when you had to be very careful. We exchanged notes and talked about the Taos artists' exhibitions and I divulged that I'd like to locate somewhere in New Mexico after straightening out my affairs in Chicago, adding that what I had seen of New Mexico made it a likely place to live and work out one's problems.

"So, I'll return as soon as I can, maybe next summer."

I still recall Paul saying, "Why don't you stay now?"

"I can't, Mr. Walter, I'm broke."

Then in his slight German accent he said, "Why don't you stay?" for the second time. "If you need the wherewithal, tell me how much and we'll go to the bank and get it." And so help me—we did.

I revised my schedule, was provided with working space in the basement of the museum and from there on looked at life as worth living. Paul Walter has been gone these many years, but I still have reason to remember him kindly.

What we see of the museum now did not just happen as something that popped up out of the ground to say "Here I am." Santa Fe in the formative period following the occupation was in the process of finding itself in an atmosphere overshadowed by economies. What we term culture was knocking on its doors, but few had time to say "Come in."

Among those more or less familiar with Santa Fe's cultural needs, and we can say it with a certain pride, were three men we have reason to remember who had somehow made common cause. They were Frank Springer, Edgar L. Hewett, and Colonel Twitchell. Frank Springer was also identified with the Smithsonian Institution through his interest in crinoids found in rock formation of long-forgotten days. Dr. Hewett, while head of the Las Vegas Normal School, was absorbed in archeology, which finally brought him to Santa Fe.

As a lawyer and historian of considerable reputation, Colonel Twitchell was a fire-eating gentleman who completed this trio. I have reason to believe that Colonel Twitchell was not too fond of artists when they became involved in Indian affairs they had yet to learn about. However, we got along famously until the Colonel was reviving the annual Santa Fe Fiesta about 1919. Being a stickler for historical exactitude, he had talked the Indians into consenting to be shot at—with blank cartridges, of course, but forgetting that the paper wad in a cartridge does not always burn up. So it made for considerable friction between art in fact and art in theory. It is a painful interlude to the Re-entry of De Vargas that the Colonel was very sensitive about.

As an otherwise grand success it would all be witnessed from a grandstand built into the plaza trees where they faced the portal of the old museum as a background. It made a perfect stage for the large number of participants that were required in this revival of an old custom. While it is a long time since, I can still see this effective trio wandering about the art museum with a well-deserved this-is-our-baby look. It is not often that things come out just right; what makes it all the more remarkable was their quiet way of bringing about something in a field they were not overly familiar with.

What with vitally interesting facts eluding me, that ends the "How come the art museum?" and brings us to what to do with the auditorium. For music it is almost ideal. One winter, at Dr. Hewett's invitation, we had the eminent Russian composer Ernest Bloch working there after closing hours. He was that vital, robust type we've learned to know as being Russian. As a man with a large family he liked to have people around when composing. Impatient to get going, he was already there when we arrived to settle down in the benches. He was working on a piece that since then had been incorporated in the musical repertory of many orchestras. What with a piano to tinkle on and a tootling organ he felt right at home. While several of us did not know what it was all about, we kept him company or stretching out on hard benches, went to sleep.

We all have reason to remember Aaron Copeland [*sic*], now one of the outstanding modern composers. While to my knowledge he did not make extensive use of museum facilities, we used to see him wandering about town in a kind of trance, which indicated that he was getting something. Sometime after this we happened to be at the Metropolitan Museum where a composers' conference was in session. Having greeted us, he spoke warmly of his stay in Santa Fe with considerable feeling.

It appears that the understanding of music is not an essential requirement for the artist that is a painter. Some, like B.J.O. Nordfeldt, who lived up our street, were tone deaf. Musical sounds gave him the fidgets, while the scratching of the etching needle was music to his ears.

It was the era of the silent movies, with tinkling piano accompaniment. Well, if that did not fill your needs there was always the St. Francis Auditorium in which to provide something better.

Will Shuster and I went about concocting something with educational value, and I went about writing the script or scenario. Since it had to have informative value we called it "How to Draw an Egg." It required about one hundred slides for which we had found an obsolete projector, and we had somebody tinkle the piano while you were learning. It disturbed the cultured mood a little, but it went over. But somebody not so impressed said, "Let's do a play, but no funny stuff, let's do something serious." When it arrived, Mary Austin became the interpreter. Mary had had some experience while with the Golden Bough players in Carmel and she was bursting to share it. She was an energetic soul and before we knew it we were voting after somebody had said, "All in favor please say 'Aye'." The play nearest Mary's heart was "The Man That Married a Dumb Wife," by Anatole France. Then a Mrs. Asplund, who was a great woman's clubber with organizational ability, interrupted.

"Mrs. Austin," she said, "here we are obligated to do a play and we don't even have a name."

By that time it was well beyond twelve o'clock and enthusiasm for doing anything was wearing down and I thought it time to go to my room, when somebody piped up, "Why not call it 'Community Theatre'?"

This having been duly approved, the meeting was adjourned, but not before my being appointed stage manager and scenic artist.

This auditorium platform, as you see, is hardly a stage. It requires all manner of improving. I forgot my own work and dreamed up something that would not fall down, and rehearsals began under the guidance of Mary's all-pervading presence. Not content with the problem of directing, she also yearned to appear in it incognito—that is, unknown to both audience and players, which meant that she had to have a stand-in for her part. I thought, "Mary, you are crazy, but let us see where it gets us."

It was difficult to convince the stand-in to forego the glamour of appearing in the play after all that rehearsing, but we did it. The admission charge was twenty-five cents, thereby breaking the rule against charging any admission, but we had a full house. Backstage the mood was anything but what it should have been and I overheard Mrs. Asplund, I think it was, saying, "If that woman says another word to me, I'll scratch her eyes out." Mary escaped this by making her entrance "incognito" but, of course, was recognized immediately, which pleased her greatly.

Having recovered from this doubly dramatic venture the Community Theatre took a rest which gave us time to think of something else, especially as Mary's time, she found, was needed to finish her book, which we found later was dedicated to our daughter Ann.

The St. Francis Auditorium stage was dark for a long time after that.

Heaving a sigh of relief and yearning for unrehearsed activity, we remembered that the Camino and Canyon Road was always the place where you could find it.

If you feel that a story requires a happy ending, then this is as good as any.

And now you can all go home and I'll follow you.

FOLK ART

The article on Todos Santos by Bertha E. Dutton which opens this section is a model of field work and reporting. The reader sympathizes with the saddle-soreness and obvious hardships Dutton experiences on the trail in the western highlands of Guatemala, shares her wonder at the magnificence of the region traversed, and is transfixed by the minute details of the ceremonies accompanying the celebration of All Saints Day in the remote community of Todos Santos. The dances, rituals, sounds, and smells are all there, seen and heard through the eyes and ears of the experienced ethnographer. Dutton reports that the dance masks are hand-carved in various villages but it comes as a surprise to learn that the Indians, instead of owning their costumes and paraphernalia, travel many miles over difficult trails to hire them from a man who has inherited the business from his father and grandfather! Reports like Dutton's are a rich lode to be mined by curators when searching for ethnographic information needed to document objects or to describe the social context in which they are used.

Florence C. and Robert H. Lister, a husband-and-wife team of anthropologist and archeologist, can be aptly described as cultural detectives. Their aim is not only to inform the reader of the historical background of majolica but also to demonstrate how the study of museum collections can help clarify enigmas concerning trade exchanges and cultural contacts in the Americas in post-Discovery times. The Listers have not lost sight of their purpose, and the results of their more recent research is embodied in their new book, *Andalusian Ceramics in Spain and New Spain*, published in 1988. Their study, however, stops at 1700. It is logical to expect that the next phase of their work will be to document trade patterns and their impact on cultural change from 1700 to modern times. The fifty-four characteristic majolica pieces they acquired in the 1970s for the International Folk Art Foundation from Portugal, Spain, Mallorca, and Morocco, as well as the Mexican Talavera ware housed at the Folk Art Museum, should be of significant assistance to them in achieving their purpose.

From "Mexican Folk Costumes as Stitches in Time" by Nora Fisher, the reader gains an insight into the manner in which museum holdings evolve from modest beginnings into diversified and important collections. Fisher's descriptive approach is a broad and thorough one. She progresses from materials basic to the creation of Mexican Indian costumes, retention of natural dyes or their replacement by synthetic pigments, and methods of weaving and constructing garments for male and female wear to comparisons within specific tribes, between tribal groups, and from one area to another. Fisher stresses the importance of tools, photographs, and monographs by specialists as a means of documenting techniques and social use. Nor does she fail to explain the historical pressures that underlie change in Mexican Indian costume. The Folk Art Museum is well served by the publicity its very fine collection receives with a reprint of Fisher's excellent article.

Systematic fieldwork as a method of documenting living cultures is an innovation of the great pioneering anthropologists of the second half of the nineteenth century. Art historians have been much slower in adopting the technique. Accordingly, the firsthand observations by Gloria Fraser Giffords on "Mexico's Last Saint Makers" are all the more significant because they apply to a disappearing class of artisans whose working methods would have gone unrecorded otherwise. Giffords' investigation is also extremely valuable for the scholar interested in cross-cultural comparisons of the *santo* phenomenon that occurs in several former colonies of Spain and Portugal such as Puerto Rico and Goa on the western coast of India.

—YVONNE LANGE

ALL SAINTS' DAY CEREMONIES
IN TODOS SANTOS, GUATEMALA

BY BERTHA P. DUTTON

VOLUME 46, NUMBER 8

AUGUST, 1939

Attracted to the western highlands of Guatemala by the paucity of archaeological and ethnological records of that region, in October-November of 1937, Miss Hulda R. Hobbs[1] and the writer spent a few weeks in the departments of Huehuetenango and San Marcos. These departments[2] constitute the major territory occupied by the Mam-speaking Indians.[3] The people, Indians and Ladinos (all people of relatively Spanish culture and speech, as opposed to the Indians)[4] alike, were found to be friendly, courteous, most cooperative, and helpful. This condition made possible our investigation of a number of archaeologic sites and visits to several villages not commonly seen by outsiders. Our headquarters for about three weeks was in Huehuetenango, chief city of the department of that name. There we learned that an important ceremony would be held at Todos Santos on All Saints' Day. Consequently, arrangements were made with Mr. Raymond Stadelman, representative of Carnegie Institution then located in that village, to go to Todos Santos at that time.

It is possible to go from Huehuetenango as far as El Rosario by automobile, but we made the entire trip on horseback. The distance by horse trail is about thirty miles. On October 29, directed by an efficient Indian guide, Alfonso Hernández, the rocky climb was accomplished in eight and a half hours. For miles, every step of the trail led over large and small cobblestones which had broken from the great rocky crags of the mountains.[5] Back and forth, ever up and up we plodded.[6] All along the way a great deal of traffic was met—mule and human packs; people carrying charcoal, wood, flowers, wool, hides, corn, etc.

At an altitude of 11,682 feet, we reached the summit, La Ventosa, marked by a small but important cross. At that particular time, dried turkey blood could be seen on the rocks at the base of the cross, for the Indians, as part of their ceremonies at Todos Santos, brought their offerings here and performed rites.[7] From there our descent began. The Todos Santos river has its source in the arroyo which starts at La Ventosa and this, in fact, is the beginning of the Chiapas river.[8] Our trail ·

crossed and recrossed the river, which gradually grew in size. Recinos says, "The usual trail crosses the arroyo innumerable times by 47 *copantes* (narrow little wooden bridges)."[9]

Nearing the village of Todos Santos, the strains of a marimba came to us with the tinkling of bells and the rattle of gourds, and we came upon a home where a dance was in progress. We stopped only a few minutes, but noted that the costumes appeared similar to those seen in a ceremony at Tecpán Guatemala,[10] and that the masks were those of Spanish conquerors. In a short time we entered the village, where we were welcomed by Mr. Stadelman and established in his home.

The house itself was an experience to us. It was constructed of adobe, whitewashed like the rest of the Todos Santos structures, and surmounted by a thatched roof. It had an ordinary earth floor. "Don Raimundo" had built in certain partitions and added a small room to serve as kitchen, thus achieving a few features not found in the Indian homes. There were no windows, the only light being admitted through the doorways, which stood open during the daylight hours.

Gathering clouds and showers, which herald the approaching end of the rainy season in that region, kept us indoors the remainder of the day; and we were willing to rest after our long journey.

Early the following morning church bells began to ring. Later we found that three old bells were suspended from the beams of a "belfry" which stands some distance in front of the church. It is elevated on four sturdy poles, about eight feet above the ground, and is covered with a thatched roof. A single notched-pole ladder, like that used by the Pueblo Indians in days past, gives ascent to the campanile.

The village is orthodoxly built around a plaza. Along the northeastern side of the square were a few booths,[11] and two or three others were located at the north end of the *cabildo* or municipal building on the west side. In these, colorful bandannas, cheap novelties, and odds and ends were sold. In the center of the plaza Indians were standing, strolling about, or sitting with their wares—mostly black *chamarras* (blankets), although they also had a few white ones with gray stripes; black *sacos* (coats) for the men, and long over-garments called *capisayos* that have open sleeves; palm leaf ponchos or *zuyacales;* well plaited baskets, *canastas;* and crude spindles, *malacates*—slender sticks about fifteen inches long, with whorl of hardened clay. Indians from the lower regions had brought up oranges to trade or sell. Usually, although there is no set rule, the market is held here on Saturday, but during *fiestas* there is a market each day. The Indian officials were pleasant and cordial; and we found it not difficult to converse with them in Spanish.

While we talked, a marimba was carried in and set up in the church plaza which joins the main plaza on its north side, on a level about four feet lower than the latter. At 11:40 two young men began ringing the two larger church bells, pulling each by a short rope tied to its clapper, and ringing them in unison—almost. Shortly, a procession of men appeared from the southeast, marching in double file. Carried in the train was one large, double-headed drum and a wooden flute; several men had bundles of skyrockets[12] upon their backs; and upon the shoulders of one was a black wooden box, about twelve by forty inches in diameter and ten inches high. Within the latter, we were told, were the papers pertaining to the town's foundation.[13] None of the individuals were particularly garbed, but our conversationalists informed us that they were the dancers of tomorrow. As the procession appeared, the marimba and its players moved into the church. Those making up the procession then entered the sanctuary and the marimbists commenced playing. At 12:00 o'clock the music ceased.

An Indian man approached us and inquired if we wanted to buy *huipiles* (women's blouses). He and his wife, whom he called from aside, led us up a stony trail to a typical Todos Santos household. From rafters of the ceiling hung jerked meat, hides, bags of various articles, *machetes,* etc. The dwelling was very dark, the only light entering through one small window and the door. Over a small fire, built on the floor toward one end of the room, an older woman was roasting coffee on a *comal,* large earthenware "griddle" which is seen in every native home. The *huipiles* were very characteristic—red stripes on a white background, with embroidered yoke—the same material from which the men's shirts and trousers are made. One of them, with a dark blue skirt which completes the larger items of a Todos Santos woman's costume, was priced at sixteen dollars. The woman of Todos Santos also wears a *tzut* of the blue or striped material, either on her head or about her shoulders, and secures her skirt with a red *faja* or belt. We bargained a few minutes and got the price down to eight dollars, but that was still too expensive. Although we did not buy their garments, the Indians remained gracious and pleasant. Returning down the trail, we stopped at yet another house to watch two young women weaving the white, red-striped cotton material. They weave it on waist looms, making a strip of cloth about twelve inches wide, and from this the garments are fashioned. On the portico of the *cabildo* several men sat embroidering and sewing small pieces of cotton material. One was making a small bag.

During the remainder of the day, the Indians carried on their market and visiting; one noted various acts of preparation for the following day. Marimbas were played from time to time, and occasionally two or three men practiced their dancing. A number of men were busy erecting a new house, closed on three sides, at the southeast corner of the plaza. It was built of fresh-cut saplings and green boughs, and reminded one of the *hogans* which the Navajos build for some of their ceremonies. This, however, was not seen to be of ceremonial nature but, rather, was used for social dancing.

After nightfall we saw a fascinating sight from outside our abode. At first, it seemed as though some of the multitudinous bright stars of the crisp, silent October

night were moving, far and near, down the valley to the west and to the very mountain top at the south. The countryside appeared alive with lights, which proved to
be *ocote* (pitch pine) torches that the Indians carried to light their way over uncer-
tain trails as they came toward the village. One got an idea of the great numbers
of people who were congregating for the ceremonies of the following day, for each
torch indicated a group of several persons.

The next morning, Sunday, the church bells were rung very early[14] and people passed back and forth, with some of the men making a very poor attempt at
singing. Later, but still quite early, a marimba was played, and we immediately
noted that they were playing the same tune that we had heard so frequently at Tecpán, Guatemala.[15] Now and then, as during the past days and nights, fireworks
were set off. When we arrived at the plaza, two boys were ringing the larger bells.
We watched them, speculating as to how they would descend the notched ladder.
Sure enough, when their task was finished, they came running down the log, face
forward, as any Indian might be expected to do.

The Catholic church, which dates from the sixteenth century, is built along the
east side of the church plaza. Its main entrance is in the west end, but there is a
more frequently used door along the south side. Directly in front of the main doorway, toward the west side of the church plaza and north of the campanile, two tall
wooden crosses stand. These pertain entirely to the Indian religion. At their bases
rocks and earth have been worked into an altar. Most of the time during these days,
when no particular ceremony was going on, Indians could be seen standing or
kneeling at this altar, or on the church steps, with small fires and waving censers
of smoking *copal*.[16] There were splotches of dried blood on the rocks, evidencing
the sacrifice of turkeys, an important rite in the life of these Indians.[17] At times the
worshipers chanted most unmusically.

One of the customs at this time is to place offerings of food and *aguardiente* for
the deceased.[18] At the cemetery, down the valley a short way from the village, these
items in small quantities could be seen on the graves. Indians were going to and
from the *campo santo* early and late. It is believed that the spirits of the dead come
out of their graves; they are hungry, and partake of the food and drink. They also
listen to the music of the bells, marimba, drum, and flute.

At each of the four corners of the church plaza are small thatched-roof structures, open on the sides toward the plaza, the other two sides closed by whitewashed adobe walls. These are the *capillitas*. The church is crude and very plain.
It consists of a long, narrow, rectangular chamber, with no transept. There is no
priest at Todos Santos, but the church is under the direction of the *padre* of
Chiantla, about three miles from Huehuetenango. In the church, a few Indians
were kneeling before the main altar and one of the four side altars. Flower petals
were strewn about the front doorway, others lay on the altars, and some were scat-

tered about a few candles which had been set on the floor. On the first altar to the right, a row of brawny, brown cherubs carved of wood supported an upper panel.

The day's excitement commenced with a favorite sport, the rooster pull races.[19] Leading east from the plaza is the only section of street which can boast of being anywhere near straight, and even that is not level. But there the activities of the morning centered. A number of small, thin, and bony horses were mounted by gaily bedecked Indians. Over their red and white trousers (the stripes of which have caused them to be known as Uncle Sams)—made more conspicuous in some instances by reason of the *pantalónes rejados* (split trousers) being tucked up behind—and their *camisas* (shirts) or, in a very few cases, black wool *sacos,* they were adorned with bands, usually of bright red—two crossing sashes secured under the arms, passing across the chest and back; colorful sashes around the waist; wrist cuffs of red bandannas or cerise colored cloth; red or blue bandannas or cerise squares, *tzutes,* about the neck as 'kerchiefs; and other *tzutes* on each man's head, surmounted by a straw hat from which streamed long, bright colored ribbons. The hats were fastened by a throat strap so they could slip off, as they did with the first jump of a horse, but not to be lost. One man wore a purple kilt, decorated with yellow and cerise ribbons and adorned with small mirrors. The hats of many, including those not participating in the races, were trimmed with feathers of yellow, purple, wine, green, and a few of blue color.

These Todos Santos hats demand special attention. They are woven of two thicknesses of fine fiber braid, closely stitched, which makes them heavy, exceedingly stiff, and practically waterproof. The crowns, tapering in slightly, rise about four inches above the perfectly straight brims which are a little under four inches wide. They are flat, or nearly so, across the top. A coarsely woven braid of the same material forms the basic head band. With age, the hats become darkened in color, usually turning to a deep brown. Like the remainder of the Todos Santos costume, they are particularly striking and can be identified at a glance. Women as well as men may frequently be seen wearing them.

Three ropes had been stretched, six or eight feet apart, from one side of the street to the other, and from these were suspended six live roosters, two on each line, tied securely by their feet with heads dangling downward. At 9:15 the races began. The riders, twenty-eight in number, all gathered at the east end and, when the signal was given, came riding pell-mell under the roosters, *gallos.* Of course, the idea was to pull off the cocks' heads, but the riders, hanging onto their saddles with both hands—grim determination written all over their serious faces—or at best hanging on dearly with left hand while beating the bony little horse wildly with a quirt held in the right, had very small opportunity to even touch the fowls. More often than not, they rode under the suspended birds without making a single grab. At the most, a few feathers were plucked and allowed to scatter in the wind.

Shortly after the race began, one chap had his stirrup strap break, letting him fall from his steed, and thus eliminating him from the contest. Back and forth they urged their ponies, some of which balked frequently. Then another rider fell off, just as his horse stopped after a mad dash. At the end of the first hour the *gallos* were removed, all somewhat the worse for wear and tear, but all possessing their heads. Nine other fowls were strung up in their places, four on the east line, three in the middle, and two on the west. About this time, a group of officials marched up to the east end of the street and then retraced their steps. Again the contest was resumed.

At 10:35 the first, and only, head was pulled—a great triumph for that rider. About that time, a marimba was carried to the north side of the street, close by the suspended roosters. From then on it was played at intervals during the remainder of the afternoon. Again they played the piece we had heard early in the morning— the tune of Tecpán. At 10:45 one of the horses went lame, eliminating him and his rider from further participation. The officials, carrying their staffs, clubs, and canes, marched to the east and back again.

The second installment of *gallos* was taken down at 11:05 and a third group put up in their place—five, three, and two from east to west. The fruitless (or fowl-less) chase went on until 11:27, then the riders dispersed and the crowd broke up. Near the vegetable vendors who had lined up from east to west on the terrace between the church and main plazas, we found two *monos* (men dressed as mon-keys) attracting attention. The one who later proved to be dance director was bark-ing, talking, and acting funny—earning fruits, vegetables, and other rewards from the people. At that time he wore a wooden monkey mask.

The church bells began to ring at 2:40, and the tinkling of small bells was heard as a group of dancers came up the main street and entered the church plaza. The elevation north of the two tall crosses afforded a commanding view of the succeed-ing ceremonies. Within five minutes the dancing began. There were twenty-eight dancers, fourteen on opposing sides, lined up from east to west. Ten were wear-ing deer masks; two, who carried *mono* masks[20] and later put them on, and one other man wore high crowned "soldier" caps of black velvet, with short stiff bills, and trimmed with gold braid. Another man was dressed as a woman; he and the fourteen other dancers wore masks of the Spanish conquerors;[21] the latter wore tricorn hats. The smaller of the two *monos* was head director of the dance; he called out the change of movements and gave signals. The other *mono* was assistant direc-tor. Both carried leather quirts and policed the crowd from the dance plaza.

The first movement of the dance was very simple, the two lines of participants advancing toward each other a few steps, dancing backward to original position, and then couples (in each line independently) dancing around each other. The two lines next met, crossed, and then resumed their positions again. This continued for five minutes, after which there was a five-minute intermission before they resumed the same steps. Again they danced for five minutes, then to enjoy a ten-minute recess.

These intermissions allowed for inspection of the costumes worn by the dancers. The *monos* were dressed in black velvet—straight-legged trousers, with long slender tails appended, and waist-length jumpers, around the bottom of which were suspended two V-shaped panels. Both trousers and jumper were embellished with gold braid and touches of red. On the head was worn a red bandanna and over this the "soldier" cap. The caps were further adorned with feather pompoms— one standing erect in front, another at the back. The front of the crown was about six inches high, the back about four inches. Most of the time while the dances were in progress, these two leaders kept their positions at the west end of the lines, one on each side.

Next to the leader danced the "woman" (in the south line). She had long, reddish-blond curls falling below her shoulders. Her costume consisted of green velvet skirt and red jumper of like material. Both were richly decorated with festoons of beads, gold and silver braid and fringe, medallions, and mirrors. On her head she wore a straw hat with three-inch brim and crown of the same elevation. The brim was turned down all around. About the crown was a colorful ribbon, and bright streamers trailed behind; further embellishment consisted of feather and ribbon pompoms. The "woman's" legs were clad in long cotton stockings, and on her feet were leather items that appeared to be a cross between shoes and sandals.[22]

Beside the assistant director danced the "woman's" partner. He was the third one wearing a "soldier" cap. He carried a brass-topped cane around which heavy silk cord was wrapped and from which hung colored tassels. His attire consisted of gorgeously decorated knee-length breeches and jumper of velvet. His legs were also covered by long cotton hose. On his back was a highly ornamented cape of velvet. Later in the ceremony, he added to his costume by putting on a short-headed dog mask.

In each line, the next figures toward the east were those of five deer, four of which had small China silk or thin cotton handkerchiefs, each with a purple or yellow border about one inch wide around it, secured in the mouth of the wooden deer masks which the dancers wore on top of their bandanna-swathed heads. These were kept in place by stout strings which came down the sides of the masks and were held, one in each hand. The heads of the masks were painted tan, with eyes painted realistically; the short antlers were silver colored. On some of them small bells were hung; usually there were further decorations of colored ribbon streamers. Each deer wore knee-length breeches and jumper of contrasting colors of velvet, richly decorated with braid, beads, small bells (on the breeches), mirrors, variously shaped medallions above the knees, etc. And each wore purple puttees fashioned from some shiny cloth and decorated with white strips and small mirrors. They were tied across the back of the calf. Colored scarfs or bandannas covered the rear of the head and were secured to rectangular, round-cornered mantles of velvet which hung on the board across the shoulders. The mantles were highly decorated with contrasting border bands of silk material, gold braid, mirrors, etc.

To the east of the deer, likewise in each of the lines, were seven Spanish grandees with costumes similar to those of the deer, excepting that they wore the tricorn hats, richly decorated and frequently surmounted by several clusters of colorful bird feathers. Tassels of small beads hung from each corner and brilliant streamers of ribbon about two inches wide flowed behind. The hat of one dancer on each side was further adorned with a tin crown of royal shape.[23] Their breeches were royal blue. They also wore velvet mantles and gauntlets profusely embellished. Each carried a brass-topped, cord-wrapped cane. These two men appeared to lead the dance movements in the general dances. A few of the grandees, including the "crowns," had on dark-haired masks with corresponding dark mustaches, but most of them had curls like those of the "woman." All of these wore long cotton stockings of gray, pink, tan, blue, or indistinguishable tints.

Practically every dancer wore heavy, exceedingly misshapen shoes which were very ill fitting. A few wore heavy sandals. The faces of all, from their noses down, were covered with red bandannas. Several carried masks tied in a bandanna which was held in the left hand. All but the deer carried small bells on a thong about the right wrist and held in the right hand, with which they made an attempt to keep time with the music. Throughout the ceremony it was to be noted how few really kept time to the melody of the marimba, and none of the onlookers or children (with one exception, later noted) standing about seemed to "feel" the time and desire to move thereto, as so frequently observed among the Indians of the American Southwest. A few of the dancers did very well. All the time, the same simple step, similar to that of the Circle Dance of some of our Southwestern Indians, was danced, but instead of the toes receiving first contact with the ground, the heels seemed to figure more prominently.

The wooden masks are hand-carved in various villages, such as Chichicastenango, San Cristóbal, and Comalapa. The costumes are rented from dealers in San Cristóbal and Totonicapán.[24] Speaking of this traffic, Mrs. Osborne says: "Indians will travel many miles over difficult trails to obtain something that they wish as when they celebrate religious feasts in their villages, and they come into Totonicapán from all over the country, and even Mexico, to hire costumes, for their ceremonial dances, from a man called Miguel Chuj (El Moreno), who has a large store crammed full of all sorts of paraphernalia for that business that he has inherited from his father and grandfather, who in their time carried on the same trade. The shop is stocked with masks of all kinds; clothes of every variety that are used in the dances, with especially gorgeous velvet suits and wigs for personages representing Don Pedro de Alvarado and his principal aides, about whom some of the dances are performed. The dance costumes rent anywhere from a dollar a set to perhaps as high as one hundred dollars for a complete outfit; it depends upon whether the costumes are much ornamented or not, or if the dance consists of many performers or few."[25]

During the intermission everyone had dispersed, most of the crowd going down the street to the scene of the rooster pull. At 3:40 the cocks were cut down for the day. Dancing began again at 3:45. The "crowns" led, and following them were the "tricorns," deer, etc., with the *monos* last. One line went to the northeast and the other to the southeast corner and, in diagonal lines, crossed in the center of the plaza, turned back and repeated the figure. This movement lasted for thirteen minutes and was followed by a five-minute recess. Then the participants lined up along the west side of the church plaza and stood for five minutes facing the two tall crosses. They stopped dancing, all was quiet, and then one after another the "crowns" and two of the "ricorns" addressed prayers toward the crosses, while lifting the right hand in a gesture of throwing something toward them.

NOTES

1. Curator of Archives, School of American Research, Santa Fe, N.M.

2. Comparable in organization with our states.

3. Mam is a member of the Mayance linguistic family. See: Stoll, 1938, pp. 184-185, 193-196.

4. La Farge and Byers, 1931, p. 7.

5. See: Recinos, 1913, pp. 7-13, for an account of the orography of the Cuchumatanes.

6. Cf. Stephens, 1854, pp. 368-370; La Farge and Byers, 1931, pp. 9-12.

7. Cf. La Farge and Byers, 1931, p. 178.

8. Cf. Recinos, 1913, p. 185.

9. Recinos, 1913, p. 185

10. Dutton, 1939, pp. 73-78.

11. Cf. Stephens, 1843 (I), p. 191.

12. See: Stephens, 1843 (I), pp. 207, 378; *Ibid.*, (II), p. 99; 1854, pp. 128, 133, 155; Dutton, 1939, p. 77.

13. Cf. La Farge and Byers, 1931, p. 14.

14. Cf. Stephens, 1843 (II), p. 99.

15. Hobbs, Ms.—for early publication in *El Palacio*.

16. Resin of the copal (*Hymenoea verrucosa* L.) is used extensively by Central American Indians in their

religious rites.

17. Cf. Brasseur de Bourbourg, 1861 (?), p. 253; Brine, 1894, p. 246; Tozzer, 1913, pp. 504-505; Gann, 1917, p. 414; Sapper, 1925, p. 392; La Farge and Byers, 1931, pp. 114, 178, 182; Osborne, 1935, p. 64.

18. Cf. Stephens, 1843 (I), p. 45; La Farge and Byers, 1931, p. 89.

19. Cf. Stephens, 1854, p. 364; La Farge and Byers, 1931, p. 95.

20. See illustrations, Lothrop, 1927, p. 73.

21. See illustration, Dutton, 1939, front cover.

22. Osborne, 1935, p. 25, says, "Peculiar sandals which have a heel-cup are worn by the Indians in many villages of the Cuchumatanes mountains [Todos Santos]."

23. Cf. Starr, 1904, p. 81.

24. La Farge and Byers, 1931, p. 100.

25. Osborne, 1935, p. 85.

MAJOLICA: CERAMIC LINK BETWEEN OLD WORLD AND NEW

BY FLORENCE C. AND ROBERT H. LISTER

VOLUME 76, NUMBER 2
SUMMER, 1964

Few kinds of pottery can boast the very long history of perhaps a thousand years' duration and the widespread distribution over parts of at least five continents that distinguish majolica. This colorful low-fired earthenware with a hard surface covering of vitreous material has been formed into unusual pieces restricted to special occasions and into common tableware. Still produced in considerable quantity as "peasant" pottery in many European and some Latin American countries, majolica is of local importance to art historians and archaeologists because fragments frequently come from excavations of places in the New World occupied during the period of early Spanish or Portuguese contact.

There is no evidence that majolica ever was made in America north of central Mexico where the Catholic priesthood established workshops shortly after the Conquest. Thus fragments of majolica recovered in California, Arizona, New Mexico, Texas, Florida, and at scattered points up the Atlantic coast represent imported vessels. They were frequently part of mission furnishings but occasionally, especially in Florida, cargo from sunken ships wrecked off the coast.

The principal historical ties of majolica lead from the southwestern regions of the United States, where Spanish settlers, missionaries, travelers, or traders penetrated in the sixteenth century, back to the heart of Mexico, the Caribbean, or directly to Spain. In the case of Brazil, the link is to Portugal.

The majolica tradition does not have its origin in Iberia. As is the case of many other crafts, the Islamic invaders who occupied the peninsula for seven to eight centuries were responsible for its early evolution. The Umayyad caliphate in Spain had learned of majolica from fellow Muslims farther east. They, in turn, had been inspired by the world's greatest potters, the Chinese.

Chinese pottery, still in a porcelaneous stage of development, is known to have reached the area of ancient Mesopotamia as early as the ninth century A.D. It was so admired by the Muslims of the area that they immediately set about to try to duplicate it. Craftsmen in that region probably had been among the first peoples in the world to discover the secret of ceramic glazes formed by certain metallic oxides, fluxed by lead, and pacified by tin oxide to create a permanent opaque lustrous surface finish on the vessel. Examples of this glaze from excavations at Susa and Babylon date in the fifth century B.C.

Peoples in that part of the world probably were among the first to use potter's wheels and true kilns. Glazes there generally had been used sparingly on pots because of the difficulties of keeping designs sharp. In their attempts to duplicate Chinese pottery the Muslims were unable to produce porcelain because they had neither the proper ingredients nor kilns which would reach sufficiently high temperatures, although they did copy three-color T'ang pottery with remarkable skill. But by the addition of tin oxide to their familiar transparent lead glazes, they reachieved an opaque white glaze over which, in the dry unfired state, they could paint patterns in oxides that fused in firing into the glaze body. Motifs were not obliterated by an overglaze. Thus majolica was developed—wheel-turned earthenware covered with an opaque light-colored glaze or enamel which provided a smooth background for the decorative painted representations of which the Arabs were fond.

During much of the time when Islam held southern Spain (eighth to fifteenth centuries) there was a ban upon the use of gold and silver vessels in the palaces. Consequently, the potters turned to a ware made originally by the Persians, essentially a majolica, but decorated in gold or copper oxides after the glaze firing and refired in a muffle kiln with a reducing atmosphere at a very low temperature to set the metallic design. This is termed lusterware, of Hispano-Moresque. It was expensive, not only because of the precious metals used but because the rate of successful firing has been estimated at less than ten percent. Naturally this kind of pottery was restricted in its use, and more serviceable majolica continued to be produced simultaneously. Although of artistic merit, this lusterware is not of particular interest to New World archaeologists. Only very rarely did any pieces arrive overseas, probably because their manufacture had almost ceased by the end of the fifteenth century when the Nasrid caliphs were driven from their last stronghold at Granada. One can still find old specimens for sale in Spain, but they are very costly. Small modern copies of lusterware using copper oxides are made today in the Valencia area. Modern Muslim potters of North Africa, descendants of those who once lived in Spain, still make beautifully decorated majolica, mostly platters for wall display, but lacking the ancient luster overglaze.

The first major tradition of Spanish majolica was evolved by the thirteenth and fourteenth centuries, when the Moors were the Muslims in control. Majolica production was largely confined to regions under Islamic domination—Andalusía, the Spanish Levant, and Aragón—but neighboring Catalonia, with its ties to Gothic Europe rather than to the Arab world, also began to develop a low-fired glaze tradition. The earliest design colors used on a thin cream-to-tan body glaze, often covering only a portion of the vessel, were green (copper) and dark mulberry (manganese). Granada in Andalusía, and Teruel, Manises, and Paterna in Aragón and the Levant were the leading centers of this pottery. The body glaze developed in the Granada area, particularly in the barrio called Fajalauza, was more lustrous, and the designs were more the all-over Arabesque tradition rather than the depictions of medieval castles, courtesans, and distorted flora and fauna which give Teruel-Paterna pottery such charm. The latter must reflect a stronger northern influence. In both the Andalusían and the Levantine industries the decorative workmanship displayed on domestic majolica was poor when compared to that on the lusterware.

Gradually the green-mulberry on cream tradition gave way to types decorated in blue (derived from cobalt) on a white stanniferous glaze. A variety of forms were thrown and molded, but the decorative treatment remained of low caliber with a characteristic lack of control of pigments and brush. There was a notable increase of Christian motifs, heraldic emblems and Gothic script as Islam retreated.

The secret of majolica manufacture did not remain confined to southern Spain. Fifteenth-century Italians imported the pottery from the Mediterranean coast of Spain by way of Mallorca (from which locality the Italians derived the corruption "majolica"). Soon the Italians had refined the decorative style into what is now known as "faience" for Faenza, one of the leading centers of production in Italy. They developed an elaborate polychrome style which reflected their Renaissance concern with landscape, portrait, and allegorical painting.

During the next century itinerant Italian craftsmen stimulated the establishment of a majolica industry in Castile. Thus, the second Spanish majolica tradition was born, one which paralleled some of the southern styling but very strongly reflected its Italian heritage and the Christian religious affiliations of its makers. The village of Talavera de la Reina, together with neighboring towns of Toledo and Puente de Arzobispo, assumed great importance for their output of pottery. Much of it was sent south to Sevilla. There, throughout the sixteenth and seventeenth centuries, it is presumed to have been included in cargoes headed for the New World.

Sevilla also gradually lost its concern with Arab ceramic design. Along with much of southern Spain, it came under Italianate influence, both directly from Italy and indirectly from Castile. Sevilla became the center for the manufacture of tile compositions in the Italian manner. Potters at Sevilla and Talavera adopted the strong colors of Italian polychromes, adding yellow, orange, green, and mauve to the palette. They made extensive use of *montería* motifs, based upon the hunt, bull-fight scenes, copies of engravings, and luxuriant vegetation. In decoration and form these displayed the excesses and garishness of all seventeenth-century Spanish art. The factory at Triana, a suburb of Sevilla, still turns out a great deal of majolica of this sort.

At the time Spain and Portugal were making secure their holdings in the New World and concentrating upon building churches and fine homes, the China trade was opening up. With that development came a flood of Chinese porcelain into Europe, mostly of the blue and white Ming type. Portugal was the first country with an East Indies Company and a trading post on the Chinese mainland (Macau). She remained a leading importer of Chinese porcelain during the seventeenth century, holding huge trading fairs in Lisbon where thousands of pieces were sold at high prices.

With this stimulus, Portuguese potters quickly adopted the majolica glaze tradition. They had not had the benefit of Islamic technology and consequently were late in flowering in ceramics. With the advent of the China trade era, workshops or true factories sprang up in Lisbon on the coast and later at Oporto to the north and Estremoz, a castle-dominated outpost on the Spanish Estremadura border.

Judging from museum collections such as that at the Museum of Ancient Arts in Lisbon, the Portuguese development was in no way a weak echo of Spanish work. Portuguese majolica was a superior product. Probably because of the Oriental influence, Lisbon pottery was predominantly blue on white with a Chinese repertoire of form and decoration. Its formal layout of design was more rigid than anything Spanish.

In the 1700s, one feels a whisper of French influence can be seen in Spain where, in the early part of the eighteenth century, a pottery was established at Alcora near Valencia and workmen were imported from Moustiers. A few years later, a porcelain factory at Madrid brought more French inspiration.

At a later date a yellow-green-brown on cream mode of decoration arose in north central Portugal, quite reminiscent of some work done in Castile. In time, potters in Portugal, as well as in Spain, resorted to the use of stencils for some of their elements, particularly center medallions. Colors became harsher, the use of molds increased, and much of the vitality, expertise, and spontaneity displayed in seventeenth- and eighteenth-century works declined.

Majolica was made in Mexico perhaps as early as the end of the sixteenth century. It was the same blue and white tradition as in contemporary Castile. The quality of the cobalt pigment differed, and the style of decoration varied. Furthermore, during the middle 1660s Mexican majolica being made at Puebla, Guanajuato, and Mexico City was directly influenced by Chinese pottery. In taking cargoes of Chinese porcelain across central Mexico from Acapulco to Vera Cruz for reshipment to Spain, some pieces found their way into private hands and were copied by local potters. Perhaps some Oriental influence also came into Mexico by way of Europe, where slavish copies of Chinese motifs were common.

A great deal of Chinese porcelain made its way from Macau to Brazil, where early colonists had become wealthy plantation owners. It was accompanied there by Portuguese majolica copies—some of the finest examples produced in Europe.

Majolica of the Colonial period is reported also from Peru, Ecuador, Venezuela, some of the Caribbean islands, and Central America. How much of all this pottery was imported from the Old World or is of New World origin is unknown at present.

As already indicated, the Majolica tradition still flourishes in Spain, Portugal, north Africa, and much of Latin America. Even though many of the designs today are lifeless copies taken from the past, and workmanship tends to be careless and gaudy, these qualities have always been present in these ceramics. The fact that the ware is still being produced is important to both archaeologist and art historian because of the insight it provides into old techniques and for its implications about cultural processes.

Despite a considerable amount of literature on the subject of majolica in both the Old and New Worlds, recently admirably summarized and expanded by the work of the late John M. Goggin (1968), there are many aspects of the manufacture and distribution of this type of pottery, especially in the Western Hemisphere, that require clarification. The present authors, interested both in archaeology and art history, have initiated a program of research upon majolica particularly focused upon its production in western Europe and northern Africa during and subsequent to the sixteenth century, and its diffusion to and manufacture in the New World.

Initially, collections of majolica in the Metropolitan Museum of Art and the Hispanic Society of America, both in New York, and the Museum of International Folk Art in Santa Fe were examined. Then, during the summer of 1968, majolica vessels were studied in the Museum of Ancient Art in Lisbon, the Museo Cerámica González Martí in Valencia, the Museo de Bellas Artes in Barcelona, the Museo Ruíz de Luna in Talavera de la Reina, the Museo Arqueológico Nacional in Madrid, and the Sultan's Palace in Tangier. Centers of the present-day manufacture of the ware in Talavera de la Reina, Puente de Arzobispo, Triana, and Manises, Spain and Estremoz, Portugal were visited, and modern, locally produced specimens were observed in northern Morocco and on the island of Mallorca. An assortment of fifty-four characteristic majolica pieces from Portugal, Spain, Morocco, and Mallorca, ranging in age from the sixteenth century to the present, was obtained for the International Folk Art Foundation. Samples of clays, materials used in glazes, and potsherds from various localities also were secured.

The date obtained and the specimens collected on the trip will allow us to recognize specimens of Spanish majolica imported into the New World and, as we become more familiar with majolica made in the Americas, to identify the place of manufacture of vessels or fragments of vessels found here in archaeological or early historical contexts. Chemical and other analyses of clays and glazes will assist in distinguishing between majolica of diverse origins.

In the future, considerable research upon majolica in Mexico is anticipated. It will focus upon determining the date of the first manufacture of the ware in that area, relocating the early centers of such craftsmanship, and attempting to learn by a series of test excavations in old potters' refuse dumps whether each place of manufacture had distinctive traits and styles. Areas where majolica is still being made, such as Puebla and Guanajuato, also will be studied. In addition, it would be of value to the investigation to become familiar with majolica in the Caribbean area.

Once an historical background of majolica is obtained and the physical and chemical characteristics of various forms of the ware from different centers of manufacture are recognized, an examination of majolica specimens from New World archaeological sites occupied at the time of the Conquest or during the Colonial period may allow better interpretation of the cultural history of those sites and also contribute to our knowledge of the origin, development, and distribution of majolica in the Western Hemisphere. The latter aspect of the research will focus first upon the greater American Southwest and be extended across the southern United States and Mexico.

SELECTED REFERENCES

Angulo Iñiguez, Diego
1946 *La Cerámica de Puebla* (Méjico). Publicaciones de la Escuela de Artes y Oficios Artsticos de Madrid, No. 24. Madrid.

Barber, Edwin Atlee
1915a *Mexican Maiolica in the Collection of the Hispanic Society of America*, Publication No. 92. New York.
1915b *Spanish Maiolica in the Collection of the Hispanic Society of America*, Publication No. 91. New York.

Frothingham, Alice W.
1944 *Talavera Pottery with a Catalogue of the Collection of the Hispanic Society of America*. New York.

Goggin, John M.
1968 *Spanish Majolica in the New World*. New Haven: Yale University.

González, Martí Manuel
1933 *Ceramica Española*. Barcelona.

Peñafiel, Antonio
1910 *Cerámica Mexicana y Loza de Talavera de Puebla*. Mexico City.

Subias Galter, Juan
1948 *El Arte Popular en España*. Barcelona.

Toussaint, Manuel
1948 *Arte Colonial en México*. Mexico City.

Vaca Gonzáles, Diodoro and Juan de Luna Rojas
1943 *Historia de la Cerámica de Talavera de la Reina*. Madrid.

MEXICAN FOLK COSTUMES
ARE STITCHES IN TIME

BY NORA FISHER

VOLUME 81, NUMBER 4
WINTER, 1975

At the Museum of International Folk Art is a Mexican Indian costume collection that ranks as one of the largest and finest in the United States. Representing 24 separate tribal groups, it consists of 116 complete costumes and over 300 costume parts—some 750 garments all together. The vast majority of these is part of the International Folk Art Foundation collection at the Museum of International Folk Art, while fifty or so pieces belong to the Museum of New Mexico, Museum of International Folk Art unit.

These garments have been acquired through both gift and purchase since the Museum's beginning in 1950. The base of the collection is the bequest of 22 pieces from Florence Dibell Bartlett, founder of the Museum of International Folk Art and the International Folk Art Foundation, but the majority of the pieces has come from the collections of Donald and Dorothy Cordry. The Cordrys have traveled throughout Mexico for many years, visiting almost inaccessible villages to photograph and study tribal costumes, and their book, *Mexican Indian Costumes* (University of Texas Press, 1968), is by far the most complete reference on the subject. One group of costumes which they collected between 1937 and 1943 came to the International Folk Art Foundation as a gift in memory of Elizabeth Norman. Comprising over 300 garments, this is the largest group of Mexican Indian costumes within the International Folk Art Foundation collection. In 1974 the Foundation purchased an additional fifty costumes from the Cordrys, an acquisition which almost doubled the number of complete costumes within the collections. Supplementing both the Norman and Cordry collections were a number of weaving and spinning tools as well as 150 photographs which provide valuable documentation for the entire collection. Finally, over 200 other pieces coming from donors, dealers, and collectors have significantly enriched this unusual collection over the past 25 years.

Within the collection are a number of very strong areas which make it possible to pinpoint certain villages and make comparisons among certain tribal groups.

Particularly impressive is a group of Mixtec garments, consisting of 23 complete costumes from various villages and towns. And from Oaxaca, a state in which at least nine tribal groups continue a very rich textile and costume tradition, the Museum has about 300 garments, comprising over sixty complete costumes.

Despite its extraordinary ethnographic scope and depth, however, the collection cannot be divorced from some of the ingredients basic to the creation of Mexican Indian costumes: prepared fibers, the loom, both natural and synthetic colors, commercial cloths, laces and ribbons, and a needle and thread or sewing machine.

The preparation of fibers is a laborious process involving a number of very simple tools. Cotton is first cleaned and picked over by hand to pull out seeds and other impurities. It is then fluffed out and laid on a mat or some other clean surface to be beaten with sticks or cotton beaters. This prepares the cotton for spinning, the process of simultaneously twisting and pulling out the fiber. The Mexican spindle or *malacate* is simply a stick with a weight on it; these vary in size and shape according to the type of fiber and desired thickness of yarn. Generally the spinner rests the weighted end of the spindle in a container. The two-pronged beaters and a spindle similar to those from Oaxaca are used to prepare fine white cotton for textiles.

The backstrap loom, a pre-Columbian device, is the most common weaving instrument. This is simply an arrangement of sticks which can hold the warp yarns and control them so as to facilitate the interlacing of the weft. In fashioning such a loom, a warp is made up, yarn being carefully wound to desired length in figure-eight fashion. The cross of the figure-eight keeps the yarns in order and prevents tangling. Next, the warp is attached with a cord to both the warp and cloth beams, ultimately creating a fabric with four selvedges or finished edges. The weaver weaves a narrow band or heading at one end and then turns the loom around. The weaving progresses toward the heading and finally the fabric is finished off in the area of terminal weaving with a needle. The top side of the loom is attached to a post or tree, the lower side to a backstrap which encircles the wearer's waist. This is such an extremely simple tool that it is more flexible than any of the more highly mechanized looms. Tension of the warp, for example, is automatic, since it is controlled by slight movements of the weaver. . . .

Mexican Indian costumes, for the most part, are strikingly colorful. Dazzling hues result from numerous dyes, both natural and synthetic. Two of the natural dyes of animal origin are especially important; cochineal and shellfish. In pre-Columbian times both of these dyes were much in demand and played a large role in trade and tribute; even today they are prized.

Cochineal is made from the dried bodies of the female cochineal insect that lives on the nopal or prickly pear cactus—a behavior trait that makes the dye extremely hard to collect. The color it produces is reported to range from pink to dark red, always a little on the bluish side. When used on silk, as it often is in southern Mexico, the color appears as a purple or reddish-purple. . . .

Shellfish dyeing has been practiced for many centuries in several areas of the Western Hemisphere. The dye has been positively identified on Paracas textiles from the South Coast of Peru dating from c. 300-400 B.C. The laborious and complicated process of extracting the dye from the shellfish has also long been practiced on the southern coast of the state of Oaxaca. Thus, it is used mainly by the Indians in the proximity: the Mixtec, Zapotec, Huave, and Chinantec. Most frequently it produced a light purple shade. . . .

In the late 19th century synthetic dyes became popular, obviously because they are easy to use, but more importantly because they can imitate the colors produced by natural dyes. Certainly the reds and purples echo the shellfish and cochineal in the Zapotec and Mixtec pieces. And *fuchina*, a synthetic dye named for a natural dye of similar tone extracted from the fushia plant, has been used as a paint on the Chinantec huipil from Usila. This same synthetic dye may also be used to approximate shellfish dye.

Love of brilliant coloring brought not only synthetic dyes but also commercial yarns, fabrics, and trims into wide use. . . .Just as the Mexican Indians now use both commercial and natural dyes, so there has been a merging of indigenous and contemporary in both use of materials and form of costume in almost every part of Mexico. From the western and northwestern parts of that country, an area inhabited by five tribal groups, the collection includes two women's costumes typical of the Seri, a small group living mainly on the Sonoran coast opposite Baja California. . . .The Huichols are noted for their prayer plumes and other ceremonial paraphernalia, their elaborate finely-woven double cloths, and colorful tourist-inspired variations of their religious *god's eyes* and yarn paintings—all found in either the Museum of International Folk Art collections or the Robert Zingg collection of ceremonial objects at the Laboratory of Anthropology. The Huichols are also one of the few groups that excel in embroidery, employing a fine cross-stitch on almost all their costume parts. Their men's costume, though often fashioned of commercial fabrics, is unusual for both its elaborateness and its adherence to pre-Columbian form.

The costumes of the Tarascans of Michoacán [include] the Tarascan hand-woven, high-backed pleated skirt. This garment is certainly not European in inspiration, but rather, like its relative, the more common wrap-around skirt, is pre-Conquest in origin. The Museum has five complete Tarascan costumes, including even a child's garment of this type.

From farther south, the central Mexican highlands, a large area that encompasses parts of the states of Hidalgo, Querétaro, Michoacán, Vera Cruz, San Luis

Potosi, and the Distrito Federal, there is a group of about eighty pieces, primarily Nahua and Otomí.

The Nahua, or Nahuatl-speaking people, are the largest indigenous group in Mexico. Over a million of them live in the above-mentioned states as well as in adjacent areas. They have no easily recognizable costume, for Nahua dress not only varies widely from town to town and state to state, but also carries on several pre-Columbian traditions.

There are two principal women's upper garments that are pre-Columbian in origin: the huipil and the *quechquemitl*. These, like almost all true indigenous Mexican garments, are untailored; that is, they are fashioned of uncut, four-selvedged fabrics woven on a backstrap loom. The huipil is a garment made out of a simple rectangle of cloth, folded at the top and seamed down the sides, with holes left for the arms and the neck. The quechquemitl, now frequently made and sold for tourist use, can simply be made of two rectangles sewn together at right angles, producing a triangular garment with a neck hole. Both of these garments are made and worn in a variety of ways. And, though this may not always have been the case, the quechquemitl is generally worn in the north and northwestern areas of Mexico, while the huipil is found in the south.

Nahua people, depending upon the village and the area in which they dwell, wear either garment. The Museum owns a very fine old huipil from the Nahua town of San Sebastián Zinacatepec, Puebla, of a sort, the Cordrys maintain, that has not been woven since at least 1935. This rare garment is made of three seamed, backstrap-woven loom widths of extremely fine hand-spun cotton. All three widths exhibit narrow weft bands of reddish-pink unspun silk, and this same material, reminiscent of cochineal-dyed silk, has been used around the neck-yoke for embroidery. Embroidered decoration itself is unusual, for the Mexican Indian weaver is generally attuned to embellishing a piece of cloth only during the weaving process, as for example, with brocading or supplementary weft patterning. . . . Embroidery, used in pre-Columbian times, is rare even today, and when it does occur, it is usually far less accomplished than that found on the San Sebastián Zinacatepec huipil, Huichol cross-stitch, or the Mixtec man's costume of Santa María Zacatepec. It is interesting to note that while embroidery itself has a pre-Columbian heritage, the satin stitch used in the San Sebastián Zinacatepec huipil is European inspired. The form of the garment, however, as well as the method of spinning and weaving, and possibly also the color combinations, are still pre-Columbian. . . .

Like the Nahua, the Otomí of the central Mexican highlands of Hidalgo, Querétaro, and Michoacán have a wide geographic distribution. Some of the Otomí villages are situated in warm climates, and there the costumes are rather lightweight. The highland village women of Santa Ana Hueytlalpan, Hidalgo, on the other hand, wear a heavy wool belt, the traditional wrap-around wool skirt, and a wool and cotton quechquemitl. The quechquemitl, as we have mentioned, is made and worn in a variety of ways, and in Santa Ana its two pieces are shaped during weaving on a backstrap loom to have rounded corners that will fit tightly over the wearer's shoulders. Here part of the warp, the other border, turns the corner and becomes used as the weft. This practice of shaping a fabric to a given need is found in indigenous textiles throughout the Western Hemisphere; indeed, the shaping of quechquemitls constitutes one of the most innovative types of shaped weaving practiced in the 20th century.

The majority of the Mexican Indian costumes in the Museum's collections comes from the southern Mexican highlands and adjacent coastal regions, principally the states of Oaxaca, Guerrero, and Puebla. This area also includes the largest ethnic range of peoples in Mexico. Ten tribes are represented at the Museum, but the finest collections are Mixtec, Zapotec, Chinantec, Trique, and Amusgo. Of particular interest are the costumes of the Mixtec, Zapotec, and Chinantec, all from the states of Oaxaca.

Within collections there is a large group of Mixtec garments from nineteen separate villages of the *Mixteca Alta*, the majority comes from the warm Pacific coastal region, sometimes known as the *Mixteca Baja*. Probably the best-known garment of the latter area is the woman's *posahuanca,* or wrap-around skirt. One example of this is. . .a wedding skirt from Huazolotitlán. Pinotepa de Don Luis is the main center for the weaving of skirts such as this one, and commercial dyes and fibers are coming into use there. Yet, this very special wedding skirt from Huazolotitlán carries on indigenous traditions in all respects: the spinning of the yarn, the weaving and structure of the fabric, the style of the garment, and the manner in which it is worn. It is made up of three four-selvedged pieces, woven on a backstrap loom and then seamed side by side to make a rectangular garment about 50 inches wide and 65 inches long. This is worn wrapped lengthwise around the body without any pleats of fullness. The dyes used are all natural: the purple-red is cochineal-dyed silk; the light purple is shellfish-dyed cotton, and the blue is cotton, dyed with anil or indigo. The yarns are all handspun. The heading and the small area of terminal weaving are plain-woven, while the remainder of the garment is an irregular twill which makes possible the patterning of the stripes.

After the Conquest, Mexican Indian men had much more contact with the Spanish than did the women. As a consequence, men's costumes changed radically, so that there is often very little of the indigenous left. In fact, most men's garments are woven on the treadle loom, the type of loom brought by the Spanish to the Western Hemisphere. Although the most famous of the garments woven on this loom is the serape, the commonly used plain white *manta* shirts and trousers are also most often woven as yardage on this loom. Thus, throughout Mexico there remain few distinctive men's costumes.

The Museum has ten Mixtec men's costumes, and among these, despite European influences, can be found many interesting details. A shirt from the village of Santa María Yosocani in the vicinity of Jamiltepec for example, seems at first to be a rather simple sleeved garment. With all loom ends hidden, there is no evidence of the type of loom used. And it sports a breast pocket, clearly a European element. Still, this shirt is worthy of notice. All of the yarns used in it appear to be hand processed, and it exhibits natural-dye warp stripes. The tan stripes are *coyuche,* or coyote-colored cotton; the reddish-purple stripes are *hiladillo,* or cochineal-dyed silk, and the light purple is shellfish-dyed cotton. This use of natural dyes seems to be common among Mixtec men's costumes, as is use of the backstrap loom for their weaving.

Most spectacular of the Mixtec men's costumes, however, is that of the town of Santa María Zacatepec. The shirt of this costume is formed from one very long four-selvedged textile, to which rectangular sleeves have been added. It has no side seams. For wearing, the long tails are pulled up, arranged, and secured with a belt. As has been mentioned, this Mixtec shirt and the related trousers are among those decorated with colorful, elaborately embroidered motifs.

Though men's costumes are relatively rare, there is yet another distinctive man's costume in the collection that deserves mention. This is the Zapotec costume from San Bartolo Yautepec, which consists of three pieces: scarf, sleeved shirt, and trousers. . . .Cochineal has been used on what is probably handspun silk to produce the reddish-purple hue of the animals [on the trousers], while the smaller yellow-orange and blue-purple accents have been accomplished with yarn that is synthetic-dyed and perhaps also commercially prepared. Extremely fine handspun cotton fabric constitutes the white background. This fabric is of such quality that it was undoubtedly woven on a backstrap loom, although no loom ends are in evidence, all selvedges being hidden beneath hand-sewn hems. The garment, as one might already have guessed, is tailored, styled in a European manner.

Very little information is available on the costumes of this village, whether men's or women's. We know that the Museum's example was collected in 1950 but all indications are that no costumes have been woven in San Bartolo Yautepec for well over thirty years. Nor does there seem to exist any photograph showing this sort of costume in use. A clue, perhaps, is found in Irmgard Johnson's writings; that is, she notes that the huipil of this village was not worn, but rather saved for use in burial, and that a similar fabric was woven specifically as a burial shroud. The costume in the Museum's collection has never been worn. Furthermore, it can be conjectured that it was never meant to be worn, for the fabric is so transparent and fragile that it would hold up to only a very few wearings. There are also no ties; in fact, there is no evidence of any type of fastening at the waist of the pants. Was this very special costume indeed intended only for burial? Might similar garments of non-European cut have been woven for this purpose in former times?

The Zapotec people not only occupy the southern edge of the Valley of Oaxaca, where San Bartolo Yautepec is situated, but also extend throughout the valley, eastward into the Isthmus of Tehuantepec and northward into the highlands....

In the northern part of the Chinantla, an area famed for its colorful women's costumes, lies the village of San Felipe Usila. Particularly interesting is the fiesta huipil traditionally worn there....This huipil is made up of three four-selvedged backstrap loom-woven pieces and exhibits several types of decoration. The patterned bands are embellished not only with loom-woven brocading but also with embroidery—two types of decoration that are often practically indistinguishable in Mexican Indian costume. Embroidery is counted to the thread in the weft direction, and only embroidery needle holes can prove that the decoration is added rather than loom-woven. Such a close resemblance between these two techniques is even more amazing when one considers that the embroiderer is frequently not also the wearer. Some huipil strips are produced in the weaving center of Analco and sold throughout the Chinantla, specifically to be embroidered and decorated by the wearers. It may be that this practice has furthered the use of embroidery by the Chinantec, but, in any case, most Chinantec huipils combine the two types of decoration....

After the huipil strips are embroidered, they are next seamed by hand, and the huipil is stretched on a frame. Now it is ready for yet another type of decoration—painting with the synthetic dye, fuchina, and natural indigo. This is the only place in Mexico where painting of this exact type occurs. No reason for painting the huipil has been given, except perhaps fashion-consciousness, for which the Usila women are known. As the Cordrys put it, many Mexican Indian towns and areas are conservative. The people are satisfied with their traditional costume and don't want to change it in any way. Other areas and villages, however, are style conscious. Usila is a prime example; its indigenous huipil has changed in dimension, and the accompanying skirt worn has come to be generally a machine-sewn garment of flamboyant, flowered commercial cloth.

After the huipil is painted, finishing touches of brilliantly colored commercial trims are attached by machine stitching, and the garment is finally donned by the wearer.

The southernmost part of Mexico is represented in the Museum's collections by about 175 pieces. Seven tribal groups are included, but among these by far the largest number of pieces comes from the Tzotzil. little studied or recognized until the 1930s, the Tzotzil are one of the Maya-speaking groups that occupy not only Chiapas, Mexico, but also Guatemala and British Honduras. The Tzotzil have tenaciously clung to indigenous religious and material traditions. Their costumes, everywhere, are elaborate. These, however, reflecting the Tzotzil people's strong attachment to their individual communities, vary from place to place.

For the most part, the Tzotzil are a highland people who wear heavy wool garments. Some, however, live in warm, almost tropical lowlands, such as the town of San Bartolomé de Los Llanos, or Venustiano Carranza. These lowland Tzotzils have long been famed for both their spinning and weaving, which has little in common with that of the highland Tzotzils but is related instead to the costumes and textiles of the neighboring Zoque Indians of Tuxtla Gutiérrez and the Maya-speaking peoples of Guatemala. Just as the Chinantecs of Usila are noted for their flamboyantly colored costume, the Tzotzils of San Bartolomé de los Llanos are well-known for their intricately worked white-on-white brocading. Their work, highly esteemed because of the skill required in weaving, finds a ready market among the neighboring Zoque women of Tuxtla Gutirrez, who, having long ago ceased to weave such fabrics themselves, buy San Bartolomé de Los Llanos fabric to use for their own huipils. This white-on-white work, furthermore, is related to the well-known white gauze weaving and brocading of Coban, Guatemala.

The Museum's costumes from San Bartolomé de Los Llanos are represented by four: a little girl's costume, that of a small boy, and those of a man and a woman. But not only is the whole family included; there are additional garments as well: men's shirts, women's huipils, and hair ribbons. Finally, there are implements: cotton beaters and two looms, one for weaving a woman's *servilleta* and the other for weaving a man's brocaded belt.

Despite its renown for white-on-white brocaded textiles, San Bartolomé de Los Llanos also uses color. . . .This [can be seen in a man's] headcloth, aniline dyed to imitate natural-dyed fabrics, [which] is made of three four-selvedged pieces seamed side to side. On its panels are both warp and weft stripes, which create a bold red-and-white plaid background, and multi-colored brocading, which is looped as well as wrapped to give an effect of depth. The most elegant and elaborate of Mexican Indian men's headcloths, this particular cloth is quite closely related to those worn by nearby Guatemalan Indians. Its elaborateness, furthermore, is carried over into the rest of the typical man's costume: ballooning pants with small, colorful brocaded motifs, a bright red sash with multicolored brocading at either end, and a white-on-white brocaded shirt which may have a band of multicolored decoration across the chest.

The woman's costume of this town is equally impressive. First, there is the fancy white huipil, brocaded in white and sometimes also in colors. . . .These huipils, as one may gather from the fact that the collection's example is only 14 inches in length, are extremely small and light in weight. At times the women of this warm climate even go without this fragile garment and wear only the elaborate traditional skirt, the *costal*. Yet another variant of the indigenous wrap-around skirt, this costal is tubular in shape, generally being made of two backstrap-woven indigo-dyed fabrics joined together on both sides. All seams are then covered with a *randa,* a band of complicated satin stitch embroidery. The lower hems of skirts display embroidered fanciful animals and floral and geometric designs. . . .The randa is most certainly indigenous to the Western Hemisphere, and apparently the designs at the hem have Tzotzil names, a fact that may indicate that they, too, are traditional. This unusual skirt is worn with a *bolsa;* that is, the garment is tied so that a bolsa, or bag of fabric, is formed at the right front of the waist of the wearer. Another costume part is the traditional hair ribbon. One continuous piece, its brilliant multicolored center section spans the back of the head, and each end is worked into a braid. And finally, the women of San Bartolomé de Los Llanos wear a servilleta, or tortilla cloth, which fulfills many purposes: food cloth, carrying cloth, and headpiece.

San Bartolomé de Los Llanos' men and women, however, are not the only ones who wear elaborate traditional costumes. Girls and boys, even babies, wear miniature handmade duplicates of their parents' clothing. . . .For example. . .a little girl's servilleta. . .is a four-selvedged textile [of] a mere 12 by 14 inches. . . .The entire piece is brocaded in brilliant color; dominating are two large pink rectangles at the center, themselves surrounded by smaller checks, zigzags, and stripes in dazzling yellow, orange, blue, green, purple, pink, and red. The elaborately embroidered handmade skirt which matches this servilleta is only 21 inches long, the little brocaded huipil measures 11 inches long by 13 inches wide. How strong the traditions of this town must be that the people take time to hand-fashion miniature costumes for their children!

Over the past four centuries, the demands and techniques of European civilization have had a strong impact upon Mexican Indian costume. The Seri, as we have seen, wear Victorian style blouses of brightly colored commercial fabric, while the Huichols have adopted white commercial fabric for most of their traditional costumes. Many women, such as those of the Mixteca Baja, have had to don blouses for the sake of propriety, and the Tzotzil of San Bartolomé de Los Llanos now use commercially prepared and dyed yarns for their brilliant brocading. Nor are these pressures diminishing. The people of Usila, having to relocate their village for the sake of a new dam, may prove unable to carry on many aspects of their old life. Yet, traditions and the ability to focus upon the smallest details still remain and make possible the continuing existence of indigenous Mexican Indian costumes.

BIBLIOGRAPHY

Christensen, Bodil, "Otomi Looms and *Quechquemitls* from San Pablito, State of Puebla, and from Santa Ana Hueytlalpan, State of Hidalgo, Mexico," in *Notes on Middle American Archaeology and Ethnology*, Vol. 3 (Cambridge, Massachusetts: Carnegie Institution of Washington, 1947).

Cordry, Donald Bush and Dorothy M., *Costumes and Textiles of the Aztec Indians of the Cuetzalan Region, Puebla, Mexico*, Southwest Museum Papers 14 (Los Angeles: The Southwest Museum, 1940).

Costumes and Weaving of the Zoque Indians of Chiapas, Mexico, Southwest Museum Papers 15 (Los Angeles: The Southwest Museum, 1941).

Mexican Indian Costumes (Austin: University of Texas Press, 1968).

Emery, Irene, *The Primary Structures of Fabrics* (Washington, D.C.: The Textile Museum, 1966).

Johnson, Irmgard W., "Dress and Adornment," in the *Ephemeral and the Eternal of Mexican Folk Art*, Vol. 1 (Mexico, D.F.: Fondo Editorial de la Plastica Mexicana, 1971).

Vogt, Evon D., ed., *Handbook of Middle American Indians*, Vols. 7 and 8 (Austin: University of Texas Press, 1969).

MEXICO'S LAST SAINT MAKERS

BY GLORIA FRASER GIFFORDS

VOLUME 83, NUMBER 3
FALL 1977

In parts of modern Mexico old customs, similar to those of Spanish Colonial times, continue for many people. Yet, because of increasing education, improved transportation, and better communications, the style of life is finally becoming more up-to-date, even for these people. The generation gap between parents and their children in these remote areas is not yet extreme, but with the death of the parents many folk traditions, including those concerning the reverence for and manufacture of items for religious worship, will certainly cease and be forgotten.

The individual production of religious figures, both sculpted and painted, has practically disappeared during this century. There were probably hundreds of artists throughout Mexico, even as late as the middle of this century, carving and painting small, usually inexpensive, religious figures for household shrines. With the availability and popularity of the highly realistic, brightly colored and gilded plaster of paris statues during recent times, this tradition is possibly finished.

The following information on Mexican saint makers was accumulated while I was engaged in iconographical research for a master's thesis at the University of Arizona.

The closeness that Mexico and her old territory of New Mexico share greatly helped my efforts during the beginning of my research. The identification of *santos,* iconography, and reasons for beseeching various saints had been explored in a number of publications about the New Mexico *santo* and *santero* (Wilder and Breitenback 1943, Boyd 1946, Espinoza 1960). Because of the paucity of similar material available about *santos* popular in Mexico, I used the New Mexican material to provide some beginning reference points in my research concerning the Mexican tin *retablo.* However, the bulk of the material about Mexican *santos, retablos,* and *ex-votos* was gathered in the field during a ten-year period. The lack of secondary material provided the opportunity to explore new sources, make personal contacts with the people, and absorb the atmosphere and feelings surrounding religious folk art.

RETABLOS, EX-VOTOS, AND SANTOS BULTOS

In the past century and a half there has been a flourishing religious folk art in Mexico. This has taken the forms of three separate expressions: the *retablo,* a small painting on wood, canvas, but mostly tin, of a holy personage; the *ex-voto,* a small painting on the same material as the retablo depicting a miracle or blessing received; and the *santo bulto*, a figure carved in the round of a particular saint or the Holy Family. Of these three types of religious folk art only two are still being made in Mexico today; the santo bulto fabricator may be extinct soon but the ex-votos can be still found in abundance in some places. The paintings of the saints, once so plentifully painted on tin, rapidly diminished at the end of the last century with the availability of inexpensive lithographs. The retablo aspect of saint making has virtually disappeared (Giffords 1974).

The term *santero* is used in New Mexico to designate an individual who creates santos, either in two or three dimensions. In Mexico this term is not used in that context. It might refer to some individual in the church who is the caretaker for the religious figures, but the artist or craftsman responsible for their creation is simply a *pintor* or *esculptor.*

A santo, generally speaking, is a saint or a holy personage. When applied to a work of art in Mexico or New Mexico it most generally means a carved or molded statue (bulto) or a painted image (retablo). The word "retablo" properly applies to the area behind the main altar of a church that was devoted to the displaying of images. In colonial times in Mexico and other Spanish territories this area was developed into an elaborate spectacle of paintings, statuary, and architectural members, highly painted and dazzlingly gilded. However, at an individual's level, a retablo was a small religious painting. These small retablos can be divided into two types: a painting of a saint or saints, or a small painting depicting a miracle. Because the former can also be referred to as a santo or *imagen pintada* and the latter as a *milagro* or ex-voto, I have in this article simplified the nomenclature by referring to the miracle paintings as ex-votos, the saint painting as retablos, and the sculptured figures as santos bultos.

THE EX-VOTO: MIRACLE TESTIMONY

In Mexico the most plentiful of the remaining two expressions is the ex-voto. The custom of dedicating something to an image as a token of gratitude for blessings received is a very old one, a rich legacy. The tradition is at least as old as the Greeks of early fifth century B.C. whose votive offerings of silver and gold were accumulated in the temple of Athene on the Acropolis of Athens (Wittlin 1970:5). Votive offerings have been made in Spain since the earliest days of Christianity and even before. Excavation of the pre-Roman city of Numancia (Soria) turned up tiny clay feet presumed to be votive offerings, now displayed in the Soria museum. The tablet type of ex-voto dates at least from the fifteenth century, and during the nineteenth century they were plentifully done in Canada, France, Spain, Italy, and Portugal. Mexican ex-voto paintings continue to be produced today, although the tradition is waning.

Briefly, the ex-voto is a visual testimony of a miracle that has occurred or the commemoration of a blessing received. At some moment of great need or distress an individual asks some holy personage for help, and upon receiving it, in gratitude will commission a painting illustrating and describing the incident. It will then be placed in the church or sanctuary close to the image besought. This might even entail a long pilgrimage to the site miles away. The painting will usually include a scene of the principal character(s) at the moment of need either praying or involved in the incident, the personage from which help is requested, and a written script at the bottom explaining the episode. These paintings were extremely popular during the nineteenth century in Mexico and in some sections of the country their popularity continues into this century. There are several churches and shrines in Mexico which are festooned with thousands of them, many quite recent. San Juan de los Lagos, Jalisco, and Plateros, near Fresnillo, Zacatecas, contain thousands.

There weren't many incidents, no matter how trivial, that escaped being recorded. In these we see plagues, wars, revolutions, false imprisonments, accidents, illnesses, costume changes—civil and military, varieties in styles of furniture and architecture, and aspects of political social history. In the words of Brenner (1929:164-65):

From place to place and period to period, significantly, occupations, situations, official clothings, progress in caravan against a changeless endless background, vibrant of human trouble and of racial agonies throughout. Plagues, droughts, conflicts, are dated and described. The very emotion concurrent is charted, in kind and quality. In the quiet of miracles some years, the violence others: in the faith that makes them numberless [the ex-voto] . . . is a moving record of a nation, a stethoscopic measure of its heart.

Not to be disregarded is the fact that often a genius of color, design or abstraction appears and creates a delightful work of art.

Several contemporary ex-voto painters were traced and interviewed. They worked in a variety of styles and methods. They all felt, however, that they were fulfilling a very necessary function within their community. The following is a brief description of one ex-voto painter's background and work.

A MAKER OF EX-VOTOS

José Francisco Hernandez Rodríguez lives in Rincon de Romas, Aguas Calientes. He has been painting for about thirty years; however, he has worked at a variety of jobs: farm laborer, shoe factory employee, welder, and baker. He started painting ex-votos when he married because he needed steady employment. He has no formal training, but had demonstrated an interest and inclination toward art as a child. Since he began he estimates that he has painted 2,000 ex-votos in about fifteen years, depicting a variety of episodes and saints. His starting price was 35 pesos (then $2.80 U.S.) and up, depending on the amount and detail and characters depicted. At the time he was interviewed he was teaching art in the local elementary school.

. . . [In] a typical ex-voto of Sr. Hernandez, he attempts a realistic rendition with the inclusion of many details. His foreshortening and shadows are incorrect, but the drama in this painting and others is convincing. Cartoon-like, the characters act out their roles. This impression is further heightened by the bubble apparatus emerging from the main character's mouth with his plea: "*Santo Niño de Atocha ten piedad de me.*" The legend accompanying the painting gives thanks for the life of a man's son "*de los duros combates en la GUERRA del Ano 45. en una parte de Europa nombrado OKENOUA* [*sic*]." It is interesting to note the date of the presentation or painting of this blessing is at least twelve years after the incident happened. A dedication years after the event is not an uncommon feature. There are several ex-votos by this artist in the church at Rincon de Romas and at the sanctuary at Plateros, Zacatecas. His name appears on the face of the painting, a recent occurrence within the last twenty years. Reasons for this could reflect the increased awareness on the part of the artist of his identity as such, or perhaps simply the advertising of his services.

Sr. Hernandez described his method of working. Someone wishing to have an ex-voto painted will come to his home and describe the scene or the incident. The size of the panel, how many images were invoked or which one, and the number of people involved to be included in the painting will determine the cost. After a week or so, the client will return and if the work satisfies him, will pay the painter. The accompanying text, which had been decided upon by the client at the time the painting was contracted, is usually placed in a plain section reserved for it at the bottom of the painting. Sr. Hernandez, however, sometimes places the letters over the painting and above the figures in the painting. . . . [In] a typical work from another painter who lives in the village of Villanueva, Zacatecas, the ex-votos are prepared ahead of time with the figure of the saint and the areas for text included. Then upon demand, the appropriate number of people are included, with perhaps some element of the miraculous act. . . and the personalized inscription. Sometimes on these prepared-in-advance pieces the inscription is scratched through the paint; at other times the message is painted on. This type of ex-voto is not in the majority. It is. . . [mentioned] here to show a different approach.

In comparing the pieces by these two men it is obvious that Sr. Hernandez considers the entire format and regards these creations as artistic expressions as well as a marketable commodity. The impression received from a wall of identically prepared ex-votos such as those by the painter in Villanueva is one of a strictly functional product—and they are a lot less interesting. However, Sr. Hernandez and other painters working as he does, as well as the mass producers of ex-votos, commonly share the feature of portraying non-individualized persons. While the people represented would be sexually correct, and the men clean-shaven or bearded, it is extremely rare to see an attempt at a portrait. The characters represent the *idea* of a person seeking aid and become a symbol of any and everyone who might have asked for divine intervention.

The custom of presenting a painted ex-voto is disappearing. A tradition associated with pilgrimages and shrines, the miracle is now commonly being commemorated by the donated small, silverplated replicas of body parts or figures (popularly called *milagros)* to attest to the miraculousness of a particular image. While there are priests in some churches that preserve and encourage the painted ex-voto, there are many churches that have sold or thrown away thousands, encouraging the people to make gifts of money or donate the silver milagros which are easier to display and can be resold. Crutches, photographs, X-ray plates, braids, braces, and hospital identification bands are also given and displayed. They, too, are graphic testimony of grace—and equally a graphic testimony to the replacement of individual expression with something mechanically produced and less artistic.

SANTOS BULTOS OF CARLOS BAZAN

The modern, individually created santo bulto is much rarer, and in fact their creators are becoming extinct. In 1970 and again in 1972 I visited Carlos Bazan Guerrero in his home and workshop in Quetzalan, Puebla. During these visits information was collected on his work as a sculptor of religious images. In December 1974, I made another trip to Quetzalan to speak with him and to collect additional samples of his work. Sadly, Sr. Bazan had died about eighteen months before. Among the very few remaining sculptors of saints in Mexico, his passing threatens another folk art in the face of Mexico's shiny new modernity.

Carlos Bazan was a slightly built man in his sixties, a native of the town of Quetzalan in the state of Puebla. The village he lived in is a fairly large one. With its outlying populations, many of Aztec descent, the region numbers about 25,000. The area is mountainous and the town itself is built on a slope. The climate is tropical and there is much coffee growing, as well as timber cutting. Sr. Bazan's mother and father were born here as well.

Sr. Bazan had been a carpenter all his life, having been instructed by his father who in turn had been a trained sculptor. The father, Ysauro Bazan, had received his training in the city of Puebla in a school for sculptors. He died about forty years ago at the age of seventy. There are still examples of his work in churches in the village of Huehuetla and Reyes de Vallarta, Puebla. There are also cement busts of important political figures in the square of Quetzalan and in the nearby towns of San Miguel and La Colinia made by the elder Bazan. Luis Bazan, brother of Carlos, had a small head the father had carved from an extremely heavy, dense black wood. It was finely modeled with realistic attempts at veining and hair. In addition to larger figures done for the community and church, the father had made small figures of saints and sold them in the surrounding *ranchos*.

Carlos seems to have followed his father's occupation. He referred to himself as a sculptor; his main source of income was the carving, painting, and assembling of small wooden saints bought and used by the people in the town and surrounding areas. He also carved items other than religious figures, including rocking horses and animals whose forms he saw in odd pieces of wood, shaping the wood into more realistic forms and then applying paint. The whimsical pieces seemed to be for his pleasure only, the rocking horses for clients. In addition to these, he produced a great many masks that were used by the Indians in their dances during fiestas and feast days.

His workshop was at the rear of his home. It was a small shed attached to the house, about 15 feet long by 10 feet wide. There was a workbench near the opening that led out to a tangled backyard with some small animal pens and a couple of smaller one-room storage buildings. The construction of houses in this area is of stone or cinder block. His home was made of roughly cut stone, with a plaster interior finish and with large flat stones for flooring. His work area, however, was a wooden addition with an earthen floor. There were shelves on the stone wall of the workroom filled with small cans of enamel, which he used to paint his figures. A soft covering of wood shavings over the floor near his work area produced a pleasant aroma, combining with the smell of fresh paint.

MAKING AND SELLING THE SANTOS

Sr. Bazan's day began around 6:30 a.m. and he worked until about 3 p.m. He averaged about two saints a day, a deceptive figure in that his operation included the cutting of the wood, shaping, finishing and painting that was done in an assembly line manner. I found boxes of figures in various stages of completion and refinement sitting around his shop, and bits and pieces of limbs and attributes lying around waiting their assignment. His materials consisted of cedar which he bought from a local woodcutter and a variety of tools ranging from machetes to chisels. He bought the steel pieces and fitted them to wooden handles. The crude lumber was bought in large pieces, about 4 feet long and 18 inches wide. He carved the pieces wet and allowed them to season. He described his technique by demonstrating the use of the larger tools to rough out the shapes and the smaller knives to finish the forms. He estimated that he made about 100 pesos (at the time $8 U.S.) a week, and his prices ranged from $2 to $8 per santo bulto—depending on the size of the piece and work involved. There was little effort to cover nail heads except with the bright house enamel which he applied over the figures.

His figures ranged from approximately 10 inches to 24 inches high. They are stocky, carved in the round, and have very little detail or distinguishing facial features. The figures have a strong family resemblance, and are distinguished by the attributes he included or by the colors they were painted. The head, body, and feet were carved in one piece, sometimes including the base. The arms were then attached, as well as the halo, by nails into the body of the figure. Attributes were either nailed into the hands of the figures or pushed through the openings carved in the hands. They were carved for frontal presentation. Like their maker, they are uncomplicated, honest, and have an attitude of practicality and purpose. They are dignified and substantial, reflecting perhaps Sr. Bazan's sincere conviction as a carver of a necessary household object.

Sr. Bazan would produce a number of the same subject, then set them aside while going on to another saintly theme until he had accumulated thirty or forty. He then would hire a boy to carry them and the pair would go into the surrounding settlements for a three- or four-day selling trip. There are trails to many of the ranchos, but one must go by foot or beast because of the grade or lack of a passable road. The destination determined the subject he took with him, as he was of course aware of who the patron saints were in the various churches around the countryside. His door-to-door sales volume varied with the success of the latest coffee crop.

"Do people buy smooth, plaster of paris statues now instead of your hand-carved ones?," I asked him. "No," smiled Sr. Bazan, "they prefer mine. If they fall, they don't break!"

While he generally was paid cash for his santos, Carlos sometimes traded them for goods or even for an old carving he would later resell. Regardless of the outcome of the trip, however, his carrier was always paid, even if it meant no profit for the sculptor.

He had certain favorites: San Miguel, la Guadalupana, Santiago, San Isidro, San Antonio, and La Sagrada Familia; but he would carve any figure requested. When questioned about Santa Librada and San Acacio, mythological saints, two of the Fourteen Holy Helpers that enjoyed popularity in the nineteenth century, he described them perfectly.

"I once had a book with pictures of the different saints," he said, "but some time ago the government sent men to spray my house against malaria and the book became lost." Although he did not have a particularly reverent attitude toward the figures or saints *per se*, he was impressive with his sincerity, industry, and willingness to discuss his trade and techniques of manufacture and merchandising.

The wooden masks used in Lenten carnivals and local festivals were carved from the same wood, and had the same rough quality and bright paint . . . . During my second visit in early December 1972, at a fiesta for San Andres in the nearby village of San Andres Tzicuilan, the atrium of the church and surrounding churchyard were filled with hundreds of Indians of Aztec descent, dancing and performing in costumes and masks. Dozens of the masks had been made by Sr. Bazan.

THE LAST GENERATION

He had trained no one to follow him; he had no children to imitate him as he had done with his own father. When asked if he had considered training someone he explained, "The boys are too clumsy. They just cut themselves. Besides, when they become young men they leave here and go to the cities to work in the factories."

Carlos Bazan's brother Luis still lives in the village of Quetzalan. He, too, is a carver of religious figures; however, for him it is more of a hobby than a profession. His style of work more closely resembles that of their father. The figures are very smooth and refined . . . . He had been working on some unfinished pieces that had been commissioned by the Director of the National Museum of Popular Arts in Mexico City for three months in his spare time, but could not find enough time to finish them because of his profession as a village official. The figures are well modeled, have articulated limbs, but are not in proportion to one another. The two figures represent the scene, "Flight to Egypt." The female figure, Mary, will have limbs that will allow her to be seated on a donkey. However, in comparing the size of the figures, she is a little larger than the Joseph now, and will be considerably taller than him when her legs are connected. They are of the type of religious figure that will be finished in natural flesh colors on the face, hands, and feet. The torso and limbs, however, will likely be modestly painted a light blue to the wrist and ankles—almost like longjohns. This area will never be publicly seen because the figures will be dressed in miniature clothing.

Luis has also carved masks for the dances as well as small wooden "shields" with the image of the sun carved on them, also used by dancers.

In contrast to the quantity of production and the number of tools in Carlos' workshop, Luis' had only a few tools on the work bench and not many pieces of unfinished saints. Although he carved santos and masks for clients he seemed not very interested in the craft. He worked in a room adjoining his second-story bedroom in the same house where Carlos had lived. Both the bedroom and work area were large but poorly lighted.

The two brothers were as different in their attitudes and personalities as they were in their work. Carlos was married and had a quiet, dignified quality about him. His open workshop, more than likely by necessity, was in the yard near the large kitchen. The smell of his workshop mingled agreeably with the smell of burning wood, cooking food, and of the penned animals. When asked to pose for a picture, he disappeared into the house and returned minus his work apron and wearing another shirt. He laughed easily and was very hospitable. Luis, about 60, is brusque, robust, and has an impatient, curt manner in responding to questions. A sister of the two men is a painter, the only other member of the family to continue the artistic tradition of the Bazans. She lives in Mexico City but was not contacted.

During the 1972 visit a number of pieces were bought from Carlos. There were also two unfinished hobby horses in the studio. He agreed to finish them and deliver them and the other pieces to a hotel in Mexico City before the week was out. On the specified day he arrived by bus with the seven santos and two hobby horses, which weigh about 25 pounds each, packing them on his back in a huge carton from the bus depot to the hotel.

Carlos Bazan was perhaps the last full-time sculptor of religious images in Mexico. Another one has yet to be found, although there are many dirt trails not explored, and many ranchos accessible only by truck or foot. It is hard to believe that there are no longer people supplying their neighbors with such essential commodities as santos, handcrafted in the old tradition. The search for others, however, continues.

BIBLIOGRAPHY

Boyd, E. *Saints and Saint Makers of New Mexico* (1946: Laboratory of Anthropology, Santa Fe).

Brenner, Anita. *Idols Behind Altars* (1929: Payson and Clarke, Ltd., New York).

Briggs, Charles L. "What is a Modern Santo?," *El Palacio* 79, no. 4 (1974) 40-49.

Charlot, Jean. "Mexican Ex-Votos," *Magazine of Art* 42, no. 4 (1949) 138-42.

Espinoza, José Edmundo. *Saints in the Valley* (1960: University of New Mexico Press, Albuquerque).

Giffords, Gloria Kay Fraser. *Mexican Folk Retablos* (1974: University of Arizona Press, Tucson).

Montenegro, Roberto. *Retablos de Mexico* (1950: Ediciones Mexicanas, Mexico, D.F.).

Wilder, Mitchell A., with Edgar Breitenback. *Santos: The Religious Folk Art of New Mexico* (1943: Taylor Museum of the Colorado Springs Fine Art Center, Colorado Springs).

Wittlin, Alma S. *Museums: In Search of a Usable Future* (1970: The MIT Press, Cambridge, Mass).

Videl, Teodoro. *Los Milagros en Metal y en Cera de Puerto Rico* (1974: Ediciones Alba, San Juan, Puerto Rico).

MONUMENTS

Lincoln Town, in spite of its scant population and ten-mile distance from the nearest trunk highway (Roswell to El Paso), is among the best-known communities in the history of the frontier West. Not an "ancient" town in comparison with some others in New Mexico, it dates to the middle 1850s but is old enough to have known years that were rampant with valor and greed, the dreams of people who were building an empire, and the tragedies thereof—and the brutal feud between rival factions known throughout the world as the Lincoln County War. The leaders cast in the drama were surnamed Murphy, McSween, Tunstall, Riley, Fritz, Garrett, and, above all, the swashbuckling tramp-cowboy nicknamed Billy the Kid.

Billy the Kid! The story of Lincoln is centered around this young horseman, outlawed by society from his earliest years and presented first by the popular novelist, Walter Noble Burns. His book, *The Saga of Billy the Kid*, which first appeared in 1925, has gone through many editions, making known the existence of Lincoln Town and its heroes and villains. *The Authentic Life of Billy the Kid* was published in 1967, reprinted from the book written by Maurice G. Fulton of Roswell in 1927 and signatured by ex-sheriff Pat Garrett. Since then hundreds of articles, stories, books, and radio and television productions have been written around Billy the Kid, even including a ballet. In 1956 Frazier Hunt (with much help from Maurice G. Fulton) published the first thoroughly researched book, *The Tragic Days of Billy the Kid*, which broke the back of the long-standing myth.

The exploits of Billy the Kid and the tragedy of the Lincoln County War were staged in and around the town's most prominent edifice, now called the Old Lincoln County Courthouse. First built as a place of business and home for the merchant-czar of the county, it later served as the political hub for the largest county in the United States, which covered all of southeastern New Mexico— seventeen million acres as large as Connecticut, Delaware, Massachusetts, Rhode Island, and Vermont combined. After "The War" it continued as a courthouse until, in 1913, the seat was moved to Carrizozo. For a time it was used as a schoolhouse.

I remember Lincoln as it was in the years before J.W. Hendron and the Museum of New Mexico began renovating the town and making it into the historic monument it deserved to be. Year after year in the late 1920s and early 1930s I rode down the street—the only street—by saddle-horse, bed-horse, and packhorse from my cabin on the north side of the Capitan Mountains to sundry jobs amid the sheep hills south of the Hondo Valley or on cattle ranches along Salt Creek. And what a serene little town it was then, only fifty years after the sounds and havoc of 1878, when hard-riding and gunfire cut into any peace the village possessed. As I passed the Old Courthouse I saw a forlorn building, seemingly weather-beaten and good for nothing but to serve as a sad memorial to the wild events that had happened within and around its walls. Few outside New Mexico had ever heard of Lincoln, unless they had read the *Saga* by Walter Noble Burns. But there were historians in Roswell and Santa Fe, and families long resident in Lincoln County, who were conscious of the treasure that dozed in the green valley of the Rio Bonito.

In April 1938, the Old Courthouse site was acquired by the Museum of New Mexico to be restored as a museum and preserved as a state monument. J.W. Hendron of the museum staff was assigned the task of reconstruction, as he describes in the following article. The work continued until April 1940, when the building was opened to the public—not as a museum concerned only with the Lincoln County War, but with emphasis also on pioneers and frontier settlement of the region.

Sent down from Santa Fe, I took residence in the museum as the first curator and, with the generous help of long-established families of the area, filled the museum with the truckloads of exhibit cases that came down from Santa Fe. On loan were archaeological artifacts and items of historic interest and the art of local painters such as Dan Kusianovitch and Peter Hurd. Dioramas and printed labels explained various points of interest throughout the building. I led tourist excursions, acting as host to groups whose sole interest seemed to be the hero himself—Billy the Kid. The museum was completely installed by May 1940, when the first Billy the Kid pageant was performed along the street, the outlaw impersonated by Peter Hurd.

The monument continued under the Museum of New Mexico until 1949, when the Old Lincoln County Memorial Commission took over the site. Operations included acquisition of several historic buildings throughout the town—the Tunstall Store, the site of the burned-down McSween house, the Fresquez house, Dr. Watson's house, the Sheriff Bent house, and the San Juan church and convento. The commission was abolished in 1978 by legislative action, and the Museum of New Mexico again began operation of the Courthouse and historic sites throughout the town. The Lincoln County Heritage Trust—a nonprofit organization dedicated to defending Lincoln Town from ever-threatening commercialism and preserving its historic wealth—operates a summer visitor center. The Trust and the Museum work together to maintain the town as one of New Mexico's leading monuments, for the pleasure of generations to come.

—JOHN L. SINCLAIR

THE OLD LINCOLN COURTHOUSE

BY J.W. HENDRON

VOLUME 46, NUMBER 1

JANUARY, 1939

In April, 1938, the Museum of New Mexico and the School of American Research sponsored a project for the restoration of the famous old Lincoln County Courthouse at Lincoln, New Mexico, sixty miles west of the city of Roswell. The work was done by the Works Progress Administration and supervised by the Museum staff. I was appointed to do the historic research and actual reconstruction, but little realized the complications that would be encountered for I felt that I had a fine knowledge of the history of Lincoln County, the Lincoln County War of 1878 and the courthouse building.

When I arrived upon the scene and viewed the problem first-hand, an entirely different picture quickly appeared. A gentleman from Lincoln County who accompanied me to Lincoln Town said, after going through the old building, "I don't believe I would know where to begin, do you?" I hardly knew, myself, but felt that I would find a starting point sooner or later, and I did—the cleaning of the building. This in itself brought to light many features of a puzzling nature, which could only be worked out by gathering historic data from the few old timers still alive and by comparing these data to various construction problems encountered.

A considerable amount of history had to be studied and untangled in order to solve these few problems which seem so simple now, and at this point I wish to express my most sincere appreciation to Mrs. Amelia Church and her sister, Mrs. Davidson, now residents of Roswell, who as children played in old Lincoln. Their father was postmaster at the courthouse some years before the Lincoln County War, and the family lived in the historic little town for many years, knew Billy the Kid and saw him ride by many times. To Mr. George Coe, early frontiersman of Lincoln County and companion of Billy the Kid. He played an important role in the war and attended many Courthouse sessions at Lincoln. He now resides on the Ruidoso at Glencoe. To Mrs. Lily Klasner who knew the Kid, and whose father was one of the victims of a murderous gang during the early days of Lincoln County. She now lives at Picacho, New Mexico. To Mrs. Ruth T. Penfield, long-time resident of Lincoln Town, who owns and operates the McSween-Tunstall store which was established in 1877. To Señor Francisco Gomez, who as a boy saw the Kid as he made his escape from the courthouse, and who was probate judge there some years later. To Señor Daniel Carbajal, who knows much of Lincoln County history and of native building construction; and to all others who so willingly and unselfishly furnished me with the desired information.

It is impossible to accept as conclusive all of the stories extant regarding Lincoln County because of the inconsistency of statements from various sources and the manner in which they are told, and it is high time someone did a thorough job of historical research, as the time is growing short. A few more years and there will be little left but indirect information and that very poor. For my purpose that is more or less beside the point, but I do feel the necessity of discussing briefly the history of Lincoln County in order to bring the subject of the Lincoln County Courthouse and its importance to a convenient starting place.

Major Lawrence G. Murphy and Colonel Emil Fritz were post traders at Ft. Stanton, then a military base eight miles southwest of Lincoln Town. They had come to Lincoln County about 1868 with the California Column, a group of military volunteers following the Civil War. Numerous bands of Apache Indians had been corralled and were then being held at Ft. Stanton until their transfer to Southfork, now the Mescalero Indian reservation, and until that time Murphy and Fritz carried on a very profitable business among the soldiers and Indians, but the moving of the Apaches prompted the moving of the business to Lincoln Town in 1872.

At first they were forced to use as a store and office several small rooms, the store in time to become the residence of Alexander McSween, the burning of which terminated the Lincoln County War. It was decided that a new store building and quarters combined was in order and so construction was begun on what was to later become the Lincoln County Courthouse. About a year later, in 1873, Murphy and Fritz began business at the new post and it was known as Lawrence G. Murphy & Co.

The building was a two-story structure, conveniently built so that the business could be operated downstairs and the proprietors could use the upstairs for living quarters, there being approximately 2,800 square feet of space on each floor. The downstairs consisted of a post office and business office on the east end, two large rooms in the middle, the front one being used for the store and the back one for storage, and a single long room in a narrow west wing which was called the billiard room. However, I have been told that this was the loafer's room, where the riffraff gathered. Leading from the storage room was a narrow staircase and it was here that Bell tried to outwit Billy the Kid and met his end. The steps led up to a central hallway running north and south through the center of the building. The upstairs consisted of two small centrally located rooms which were used for living quarters and a long narrow room on the west, about which we have little information since it was supposedly Major Murphy's Masonic room, Major Murphy being a thirty-second-degree Mason. This room had no entrance from any of the other rooms, so I am told, and this seems logical, since the vestige of a doorway can still be seen in the south wall at the west end where the opening has been filled in with adobes and a window of very late construction has been placed. In former times a narrow staircase or ladder led down from this point to the ground. The east end of the upstairs was made of four moderately sized rooms; the two on the north side were used for living quarters by Major Murphy and Colonel Fritz, Murphy occupying the corner or northeast exposure and Col. Fritz the other. Major Murphy's room, incidentally, was the one in which Billy the Kid was held prisoner eight years later. The two rooms on the south were used for storage.

All of the woodwork was painted a dead white, the floors of six-inch planks were all carpeted upstairs, it is said, and the rooms were beautifully furnished. Each room except the Masonic room had an adobe fireplace lined with an iron sheeting and a beautiful wooden mantel of white pine enameled black. The ceilings were covered with unbleached muslin tacked first to the corners, then around the edges until fairly tight; then they were painted with gaspe to shrink the cloth, making it tight and giving the appearance of plaster. Gaspe is a white finish discovered and developed by the Spanish-Americans.

The billiard room had a fireplace in the west end but it is said that in the winter the store proper was very cold since no provision had been made for heating. Deep shelves covered the long south wall. Massive counters were built in front of them and at the west end of the room was a huge bar to quench the many thirsts in Lincoln County. Whiskey was brought down in barrels from Speigelburg & Co. in Santa Fe and was sold in bulk instead of in bottles, and the thirsty ones paid dearly for their enjoyment. At the east end of the south wall was a doorway leading back into the storeroom and even today a close examination will reveal a path worn in the floor by the thousands of feet which have passed across the room from the big double doors in front, around the counter and into the storeroom.

This was the hanging-out place in Lincoln, comparable to the corner drugstore of modern times, and when the building was completed people for miles around came to see it, as it was the pride and joy of Lincoln County and nothing of its kind had every been known there before. The opening might have been compared with an important hanging which residents of the whole surrounding countryside would come to see.

Murphy and Fritz carried on a most profitable business until the outbreak of the Lincoln County War in 1878. Col. Fritz took care of most of the customers while Murphy, who was the brains of the organization and more of a polished gentleman, would sit in the sun on the porch of the store which was built up to the second floor. At that time there were no steps leading up to it and there was no roof over it and it was probably built according to the taste of the Major himself. Lincoln County then included all of the southeastern part of New Mexico and business was drawn from as far east as the Texas line. The great difficulty was that the greater portion of the county was made up of farmers and cattlemen whose accounts were carried on the books from year to year, in the hope that during the next year they might be able to pay, but to some of them that time never came and the business ethics of L.G. Murphy & Co. have been questioned from time to time.

Colonel Fritz made a trip to Germany, his former home, to visit his father and died of pneumonia. James J. Dolan, a bookkeeper for L.G. Murphy & Co., was then taken in as a partner, the circumstances of the partnership not being known. John H. Riley was also taken in to handle the active end of the cattle business. The firm was then called Murphy, Dolan & Co. Murphy and Dolan were favored with all of the government contracts from Ft. Stanton without any trouble, which is understandable since their connections there were very close, a number of the officers being personal friends.

In a short time a new personality appeared on the scene. It was Alexander McSween, a shrewd young lawyer, and before long he was in the employ of Murphy and Dolan to attend to legal matters which they encountered. It so happened that Col. Fritz had taken out an insurance policy made payable to his sister for $10,000, and upon his death McSween was hired to collect the money, since the insurance company would not pay, using the excuse that Col. Fritz had died of tuberculosis which was not covered by the policy. McSween collected and then quit the firm of Murphy and Dolan, it is reported because of their shady deals. On the other hand, it has been claimed that the insurance money was never turned over to the proper parties, but was retained by McSween. In partnership with a a young Englishman by the name of John Tunstall, McSween opened a store in 1877, almost within calling distance of Murphy and Dolan and Co., and immediately a great deal of jealousy manifested itself.

The business of Murphy and Dolan began to slump. Then, in the interest of Col. Fritz, inasmuch as he had been their close friend and business associate, Murphy and Dolan took it upon themselves to demand the insurance collected by McSween. Upon his failure to pay, the Sheriff of Lincoln County, Major Wm. Brady, undertook to attach McSween's interest in the cattle at the Feliz Ranch, which was owned by John Tunstall, business partner of McSween and financier of the McSween-Tunstall properties and employer of Billy the Kid.

On February 28, 1878, Major Brady and his posse rode toward the Feliz Ranch to serve their warrant but on the way they met Tunstall, Billy the Kid, and Dick Brewer, friend of the Kid. At some distance the party was ordered to halt, but instead, the Kid gave an order to scatter and Tunstall was shot, while the Kid and Brewer fled to the hills. Other stories have it that Brewer and the Kid had strayed off the beaten path to chase some wild turkeys when they heard the shot. Just who else was in the party is not known, but at any rate Tunstall was not armed. When the news reached Lincoln it created a great deal of excitement, for Tunstall had no enemies. Everyone grieved over his death, for he was an innocent bystander so far as the Lincoln County War was concerned, and it is said that even Murphy and Dolan felt badly about it. His death created little ill feeling on the part of the friends of the Murphy-Dolan firm, but literally speaking they were now broken financially.

Much has been said of the friendship which existed between Tunstall and Billy the Kid, and then again its sincerity has been doubted. At any rate Tunstall's death was avenged on April 1, 1878, when Sheriff Brady and one of his deputies were killed from behind a wall running parallel with the McSween store. Brady and his party were going east in front of the store when they were fired upon by the Kid and his gang of four. It was not known at the time who comprised the murdering party, but the next day the Kid was seen angling across the fields on the off side of his white horse, shooting from under the horse's neck just to create excitement as he made his getaway. The Murphy-Dolan crowd then fired at him from their store without success. When the Kid reached a safe distance from their shots he stopped, turned around, and waved his hat as he led his horse over the steep hill.

The attention of everyone was now focused on all of the trouble and business dropped to nothing. James Riley quit the Murphy-Dolan firm and Major Murphy went to Santa Fe to live, but Dolan remained in the country and led his faction through the war, retiring from business altogether. Neither the McSween faction nor the Murphy-Dolan faction remained in Lincoln Town proper, but often they would arrive at about the same time. Whoever arrived first would occupy the Torreon, an old stone fortification built by the early Spanish-American settlers in 1852 to ward off attacks made by plundering, nomadic bands of roving Indians.

This sort of thing continued with an occasional killing in different parts of the County until the termination of the war on July 22, 1878, with the burning of the McSween home to the ground. It was in this skirmish that Alexander McSween met his death from one of the Murphy guns. During the fight the Murphy faction sent Deputies Robert Beckwith and Jake Owens to ask the McSween crowd if they were ready to surrender; instead they shot Beckwith down, while Owens escaped. The Kid and his friends inside the burning house tried to persuade McSween to fight for his life, but he refused and walked outside unarmed only to receive a fatal bullet. I have heard indirectly that in later years when Mrs. McSween was asked if her husband came out of the burning house that night with a Bible in his hands, she replied, "Well, he was a religious man but he wasn't a damn fool." Many men on both sides were wounded, but the Kid escaped over the back wall amid a shower of lead. He had timed his escape well; after seeing McSween fall the Kid waited his chance until the clouds of smoke were to his advantage, ran out the door and around the house, leaped the wall without a scratch and made his getaway into the hills.

Both the McSween and Murphy-Dolan factions were powerful but this question still remains unanswered: Would the Murphy-Dolan faction have been victorious had it not been that a company of negro [*sic*] soldiers from Ft. Stanton had picketed the town?

The burning of the McSween home practically ended the Lincoln County War, and little of the population remained except the riffraff who were generally regarded as rustlers. Billy the Kid was a convict at large in the eyes of the law and he was constantly on the alert while he his out with many friends. It was during this period that he did most of his cattle stealing.

Thomas B. Catron from Santa Fe by that time had taken over the interests of Murphy-Dolan and Co., later selling the merchandise on hand to J.C. Delaney, who was then running the post trader's store formerly operated by Murphy and Fritz at Ft. Stanton. Delaney ran the business at Lincoln until the old store was sold to Lincoln County in 1880.

The building was immediately set up as the Lincoln County Courthouse, having offices for the Sheriff, County Clerk, and Probate Judge. One of the smaller rooms was used as an armory. Pat Garrett was made Sheriff in 1880 and he set out to get Billy the Kid, even though they had been friends several years previous. With much difficulty the Kid was captured and tried at Las Cruces, sentenced, and then brought to the Lincoln County Courthouse to be held prisoner until his execution in the summer. Garrett brought the Kid from Las Cruces to San Antonio on the train and then took the coach from there to White Oaks, a little mining town a few miles north of Carrizozo. When the coach left the halfway station between the two towns, the Kid said to a group of bystanders to whom he had been talking, "Goodbye fellas, you had better come over to Lincoln on the nineteenth, we're going to have a necktie festival."

The Kid arrived at the Courthouse safely, but at that time there was no jail. The one hitherto used was at the other end of the town and was no more than a two room dungeon, so arranged that the muddy water from the acequia could be turned into the cells to drown out the prisoners. The Kid had been imprisoned here in 1877 but managed to escape. Whether or not anyone was ever actually drowned here I cannot say, but it might have been one of those rare incidents never publicized. Such things did happen in Lincoln County.

No one will every know exactly what happened inside the courthouse on April 28, 1881. The time was drawing near for the necktie festival the Kid had joked about. His guards were James Bell of whom we know very little, and Bob Ollinger, to some a coward, sneaking and jealous; to others, a deputy in good standing, courageous and brave, and honest as the day was long. But whichever description fitted Ollinger, he hated the Kid and the Kid hated him. Ollinger was awaiting his chance for the Kid to make a false move so he would have the opportunity of saying, "I killed the Kid," but Billy was too smart for him. He knew that he would have to wait his time, though undoubtedly escape was ever paramount in his thoughts. It is said that Bell was a more kind-hearted soul than Ollinger. He would frequently play cards with the Kid and apparently it was during one of these games that the Kid relieved him of his revolver and proceeded to lock him in the armory. With his ankles still shackled the Kid marched Bell through Garrett's office, Garrett being away at the time, and upon reaching the hallway, which ran north and south, they walked northward toward the armory. Evidently Bell was thinking fast; the embarrassment of letting the Kid escape would be a blot on his record as a deputy. The narrow staircase to the right which they were nearing was the only means of escape for him; seventeen steps to the bottom, a lunge to the left, out the door and he would be free. The deputy touched no more than four or five of the steps when a shot rang out and he fell to the bottom. Perhaps he never attempted to escape; it is quite likely the Kid deliberately shoved him down the steps and then shot him.

The noise caused much excitement among the Lincoln people and immediately all eyes were on the courthouse. Everyone thought the Kid had been shot. Bob Ollinger rushed over from Wortley's Hotel across the street where he had been having lunch. As he passed the corner of the courthouse to go around back to the stairway he suddenly stopped and looked up; at the window was the Kid with Ollinger's own double barrel shotgun aimed straight at the deputy. Again there was a shot and Ollinger fell. In a few seconds the Kid appeared on the balcony in front of the Courthouse and when he saw Ollinger still squirming, kicking and groaning, he raised the gun and fired the other barrel of buckshot into his body.

How the Kid left the Courthouse remains a question. Some say he came down one of the pillars supporting the balcony and others say he left by the back stairs, but regardless of the way, one of the County employees was forced to break his shackle chains. The Kid then borrowed a horse belonging to the County Clerk and made off while the people of Lincoln Town looked on. This was probably the boldest deed their eyes had ever witnessed. Even the horrors of the war itself were not as penetrating as this and not a soul dared to stop him.

When Pat Garrett returned the townspeople were in an uproar and not a word about the Kid could be heard anywhere. A few weeks later news came that the Kid was in Ft. Sumner. This seemed to Garrett an impossibility, the Kid was in Mexico, and thinking it a wild goose chase, he made ready and led his posse in the direction of Ft. Sumner.

Peter Maxwell was a friend of the Kid and Garrett knew that he would know the whereabouts of the escaped prisoner if anyone did. Garrett kept quiet and out of sight because of the great number of friends Billy had in Ft. Sumner, but he appeared at Pete Maxwell's house, leaving two deputies outside. He was inside for only a few moments when a door opened and in walked a small, slim figure. He shut the door behind him, Pete Maxwell was in bed, and on a cot in the corner lay Pat Garrett on his left side, with his shooting arm free for action. "Quien es?" was the question directed to Maxwell. Maxwell did not answer, it was almost dark in the room and Garrett knew it was the Kid's voice. Two shots rang out and Billy slumped to the floor. Thus ended the life of William Bonney, the most notorious killer and outlaw of the time.

Pat Garrett served his term as Sheriff of Lincoln County and was re-elected for a second term to rid the County of its bad men and trouble makers, retiring in 1884. Jim Brent, one of his deputies, succeeded him. It was about this time that the County undertook the remodeling of the Courthouse, building a narrow staircase from the east end of the balcony, installing two vaults downstairs, sealing up windows and breaking up the large rooms into offices. A chimney was built in the east end to supply heat to the offices downstairs, and Major Murphy's Masonic Room was changed. A door was cut through the east wall in the southwest corner to replace the outside entrance, which was put downstairs in the west end of the front wall in the billiard room. A few years later, two full-width staircases were built on both sides of the balcony in front and a roof was built over Major Murphy's sun porch. A jail was erected in the rear of the building by the Paulley Cell Co. after the removal of the outbuildings of the Murphy, Fritz and Dolan regime. These consisted of stables, grain rooms, mess hall and cookhouse, and all were enclosed by a high adobe wall which joined the courthouse at both ends. Near the building on both sides were gates so that the people from the County could drive their teams and wagons inside the compound to carry on business.

By 1910 an old timer who had not seen the Murphy-Dolan Store since the days of the Lincoln County War would not have recognized it. In the downstairs had been installed the County Clerk's office and vault, the County Treasurer's office and vault, a store room, the Probate Judge's office, Surveyor's office, the office of the Justice of the Peace, and the District Attorney's office. Some new work had been done on the front porch. Even a windmill and well had been installed in the back. The entire east end of the building was converted into a courtroom and the rest of the upstairs rooms were used for the Sheriff's office, waiting room, Petit Jury room, and Grand Jury room. Even the original adobe chimneys were tapped so that stoves could be placed in each room. All of this remodelling and converting certainly did the old building no good, in fact it was weakened considerably, and it is no wonder it needed reconstructing.

In April, 1913, the County Seat was moved to Carrizozo and the courthouse was deeded to the schoolboard and used as a school building until 1936. In 1937 the building was deeded to the State of New Mexico for use as a museum. . . .

In repairing the building it was our intention to restore it as nearly as possible to the time when Billy the Kid made his escape, in 1881.

The east wall, like the two west walls, had developed a huge crack from the top to the bottom when the chimney was installed, and more than that, it had bulged at least three inches in the middle, and was expected to fall at any minute. It was pulled down from corner to corner and successfully restored. Adobes were made that duplicated the original ones, but only heavy steel rods could be used to strengthen the walls at the other end without tearing down the building completely. Many of the later partitions built by the county were removed, and old vaults were left intact.

The courtroom on the second floor was merely repaired, since it is to be used for a community hall. This is the only part of the building which has not been restored to some extent.

The staircase could be entered only from the back storeroom, and so a door has been cut through the opposite wall leading into the old Murphy-Dolan store so that access to the second floor would not be so inconvenient. While setting in this new door, it was found that the county had torn away one or two of the bottom steps and had built in a landing eighteen inches above the old floor.

The original roof was of shingles of yellow pine. A second shingling was done with wire nails, and some evidence of a red paper sheeting was found which might have been laid under the shingles as insulation. In 1920, a corrugated galvanized iron roof was put on, but, in time, spring windstorms ripped the sheets loose. In the restoration, red cedar shingles were put on with an exposure of four and one-half inches.

Our plan was to restore the Lincoln County Courthouse, for use as a museum and as an architectural monument, and to preserve as much of the original structure as possible. With this idea in mind the entire program was carried out. Even the old cut nails that were not broken were used again in places where the strain was not too great. Most of the old wood trim was preserved, though some had to be duplicated. The adobes were made exactly the same size as the old original ones.

A caretaker is to be assigned to look after the display and exhibits, to explain to visitors the significance of the Lincoln County Courthouse in the history of the region, the gaiety and splendor that Lincoln Town once enjoyed, and the state of quietude into which it has descended through time and events.

THROUGH THE YEARS WITH ''EL PAL''

In the early years *El Palacio* kept its readers up to date on social and cultural happenings in Santa Fe and further afield. We think the following excerpts demonstrate that "mumble jumble of chumminess" once attributed by writer Witter Bynner to the Santa Fe of years gone by.

JANUARY 1916

The Museum has during the past year fitted up several more studios for artists and has placed a new roof on the rear tier of buildings of the Palace of the Governors. It has made other necessary repairs and paid off the $1,000 which was still owing on the reconstruction of the portal, doing this with current funds. . . .The patio of the Old Palace was planted to lawn and flowers and otherwise beautified.

APRIL 1916

What could be more delightful than an outing in the Pajarito Park amidst these surroundings and under such auspices [with the Museum's Puye field school]? The glorious New Mexico skies, the cool breezes laden with perfume from pine and cedar, the air of romance that hallows every step of the way from Santa Fe to Taos, from Española to Jemez—where in the world is their superior? To know one's own country is a satisfaction that no man or woman of culture can afford to neglect. "See America" has become a patriotic slogan, any many who have followed it from a sense of duty find that it leads them into experiences unexpected and delightful. Here in the Southwest is the real America!

From "The Santa Fe of the Future" by Wm. Templeton Johnson:

It would seem that Santa Fe can make the greatest progress as a tourist resort and as a pleasant place of residence for cultivated and intellectual people. If this is true what should the city do to make people want to go to Santa Fe in increasing numbers?

The average tourist is no more nor less than the average human being. He wants to be comfortable, to have good service and better meals, he wants to be amused, to improve mildly his stock of knowledge, but above all he wants to see something new and strange that he has never seen before.

. . .the brick blocks and modern store fronts with plate glass windows have crept into Santa Fe and the problem now is to gradually restore the town as nearly as possible to its original aspect, for only in this aspect will it appeal to the traveling public. . . .

JULY 1917

E.L. Blumenschein spent several days in Santa Fe before going to Taos to resume his summer's work. Mrs. Blumenschein remains at home in New York City, the altitude of Taos being too high for her.

Sheldon Parsons and daughter Sara are back in Santa Fe after several weeks spent in the La Joya valley and at Truchas, where they obtained many sketches of the beautiful landscapes in that practically unknown region. . . .

The Santa Fe Art Colony produced the posters—and they were striking—for the Cowboys' Ball given in the National Guard Armory on Thursday, July 26. Miss Grace Ravlin was chairman of the Poster Committee, and W.P. Henderson of the Decoration Committee.

NOVEMBER 1917

Robert Henri, the noted artist, who left for his studio and home in New York City after his second summer in Santa Fe, writes Henry Lovink, a fellow artist, as follows:

"Things are very interesting here. The new museum is a wonder. . . .The painters are all happy. The climate seems to suit well both temperaments—to work or not to work—and here painters are treated with that welcome and appreciation that is supposed to exist only in certain places in Europe. Being of the 'to work' temperament myself I am having a fine time."

JULY 1918

True to its character as a community center, the Museum has become a center for the community war work. In addition to the Red Cross activities, all centered there, the various war work bodies, councils of defense, war savings associations, both for state and county, have been meeting there and planning their campaigns. War speakers have used the auditorium again and again and spoken to audiences that ran up to over a thousand in several instances.

On the theory that the Indian war songs that put "pep" into the Red Man in ancient days should be "good medicine" for the troops in the army camps today, Charles Wakefield Cadman, who gave a concert in Santa Fe last November, is devoting his time to visiting army cantonments in the West and lecturing on Indian music, as well as performing martial compositions based on the Indian melodies. Tsianina, who sang with Cadman while here, expected to go to France on a similar mission.

AUGUST 1918

The gathering about the fireplace in the reading room of the New Museum on

Tuesday evening, Museum Night, this week was a distinguished and notable one. Artists, writers, preachers, teachers, and visitors from afar were among the audience. The closest attention was paid to Dr. E.L. Hewett's analysis and critical review of the Santo Domingo Corn Dance of the Sunday before, which many had seen and studied. Notebooks were in evidence and there was a rapid fire bombardment of questions and observations which went to the very heart of Pueblo culture and archaeology.

MARCH 1919

Thursday evening the Cave Dwellers [an informal discussion group that met at the Museum] will have another one of their interesting seances around the Museum fireplace. This time, the theme for discussion takes on a decidedly artistic cast, for Edgar L. Street will present his views on "The Essential Nature of Art and the Significance of Beauty," and the members will discuss the points he raises.

The Cave Dwellers as usual greatly enjoyed their meeting around the fireplace of the New Museum on Thursday evening. There is a comraderie [sic] about these juntas that seems to hit the right spot. Cacique Asplund called the men to order and turned over the session to Edgar L. Street. The theme "Psycho-Therapy" was presented graphically by Dr. Walter Trowbridge. The discussion that followed was as animated as it was illumining.

MAY 1919

For two Museum Nights in succession, Mary Austin greatly pleased the large and thoughtful audiences that gathered at the Museum with continuation of her series of lectures on "Literature as a Craft." The one on April 19 was "Literature in the Common Life," and that on May 6 on "The Promise of the American Drama." The lecturer spoke incisively on the modern trend in literature and drama and laid down the fundamentals from which successful literary craftsmanship cannot depart. Her talks opened new vistas and inspired deeper thought on problems that are vital and that affect life on every side.

JUNE 1919

MORE STUDIOS FOR ARTISTS

K.M. Chapman of the Museum staff has purchased the Spanish Methodist church and parsonage on San Francisco street to be used as studios for the many artists who are coming this summer. The church will be occupied during the summer by Albin Polasek, the Chicago sculptor, as a studio, while artists John Sloan and Davey will probably occupy the studios to be fitted out in the parsonage.

OLD TREASURE CHEST

In sending a photograph of an old leather treasure chest resembling those in the Historical Society collection in the Museum, Professor Edgar J. Goodspeed of the University of Chicago, writes: "Will you let me have your impressions of this old strong box which is said to have been found in the Ladrone mountains in a cave, and to have contained six 16th-century books (now in my hands) mostly religious? I suppose it was some personage's strong box and I have a fancy the books may possibly have been intended for that college that was planned in 1777 and 1779 and for which Pino says a convent was built about that time. (I suppose it was to have been at Santa Fe, was it not?) My surmise (a wild one, I admit) is that this chest may have been on its way to the college when it was captured or stolen by the Apaches, hustled into the nearest safe cave and there opened, the valuables taken, and the old books left behind."

A BRILLIANT AFFAIR

Covers for 52 were laid Museum Night, Tuesday, January 20, in the banquet and reception room of the Woman's Museum Board at the new Museum. It proved to be the most brilliant of a series of brilliant social gatherings held each week on Tuesday evening during the winter. Mrs. H.S. Kaune and Miss Manderfield, representing the Woman's Board, were the hostesses and Mrs. M.B. Smith the caterer. The artists had a table to themselves while at the other tables distinguished visitors from far and near were scattered among the local guests. Dr. Arthur Upham Pope, for ten years teacher of art criticism and professor of philosophy at the University of California, in a ten-minute talk paid eloquent tribute to Santa Fe as the "most civilized spot" he had found on 5,500 miles of travel in the United States, referring especially to the community and civic work by the Museum and the School of American Research, their influence on town planning and public affairs, on art, architecture, literature, and life. He referred to the spirit of Santa Fe as manifested at the Museum supper as "Greek" in its passion for beauty and democracy. . . .

WHY BOTHER ABOUT ART?

Because a knowledge of art can give you more pleasure than anything else. It can make you rich. It can give you a vista—and a vision. It reveals hidden beauty. It is like the window in the workshop that lets in the sunshine and gives a beautiful outlook—it makes life worthwhile. It makes common things more valua-

ble. . . .The difference between a kitchen chair and a Chippendale chair is a matter
not of materials but of Art. . . .The artistic home is the one everyone would choose.
The difference is a matter of choice—taste. If you want to know how, you must
know about Art. —*American Magazine of Art*

INDIAN ARTISTS IN NEW YORK

For the first time, Pueblo Indians will break into one of the big art exhibits of
New York City. At the Waldorf-Astoria, the Independents [an informal group of
artists who worked and exhibited outside traditional academic circles in the first
two decades of this century] will have their annual exhibit in March and among the
pictures to be hung are a series of Indian figures and dances by the late Cresencio
Martinez of San Ildefonso as well as several paintings by pupils of the U.S. Indian
School. New York artists who were shown the pictures privately praised them
enthusiastically and insisted that they be given space at the Independent exhibit,
which annually includes that which is most virile and original in American art.

JULY 1920

BAUMANN HAS RUNAWAY

Gustave Baumann of the art colony had another runaway with his new Chevrolet. Just after the DeVargas procession had returned to the Cathedral from Rosario
Cemetery, he turned down San Francisco street and lost control of the car at the
southeast corner of the Plaza. The Chevrolet jumped the curb and dashed into a
tree, scattering in flight quite a number of people who were sitting or standing in
that part of the Plaza. Fortunately no one was injured. —*New Mexican*

SLOAN BUYS HIMSELF A STUDIO

Santa Feans will rejoice to learn that John Sloan, the noted New York artist,
following the example of his younger compere, Randall Davey, has purchased himself a home in Santa Fe. The property bought is the Martin house and orchard on
Garcia street not far from the Baumann, Nordfeldt, Parsons, and Cassidy studios
on Cañon Road. Mr. and Mrs. Sloan expect to move in at once and to make extensive improvements.

SEPTEMBER 1926

IMPRESSIONS OF THE MOMENT

Everybody dresses up [at the Santa Fe Fiesta]: urchin, banker, society dame
. . .nursemaid, taxi driver, boy scout, stalking Indian; cowboys real, New York,
and artist; cowgirls likewise three varieties; even the aloofish New Yorkers and
primmish New Englanders toss on sombreros, wind up in turquoises, and clasp
silver belts about their conventionalities. . . .

Men otherwise very conventionally clothed will enjoy folding a serape narrowly and swinging it on the last possible sixteenth of an inch of their shoulder bones. It means nonchalance and swagger. Man may be a preacher, archaeologist, artist, or hardware man, but that serape swinging on to the last minute of his shoulder blade is telling the world . . . .

A doorway marked "police headquarters" steps down into a cool, dusky shadow filled with guitar music. It seems to be the office of the extra street marshals, mostly Mexican, but it seems gaily characteristic to have police headquarters all in tinkle and hum and strum with Mexican folk music. . . .

They have puppies for sale at the drug stores.

When you get a punched quarter you just pass it on. Everybody knows the Indians use them for buttons and when they need money twist one off.

Anyone who goes to Santa Fe wishing to see Indian dances and to get into the dashing and picturesque story of our Southwest, finds it. Those who go disbelieving, hunting the untrue, jibing, contribute exactly that—they carry it there with them. It is their own stuff. . . .

On the street corners and in the shadow of doorways stand silent Indians holding out turquoises set in silver, wares of extraordinary beauty and temptation.

DECEMBER 1926

SENTIMENT A SANTA FE ASSET

Interview with Dr. Lummis

". . . It's what people go to Europe to see—sentiment. Santa Fe would be as foolish to lose it as a baker would be to give up a monopoly on bread and go to cobbling shoes. . . ." I [the interviewer] asked him what changes he noticed most. . . . "The noise," he said promptly. . . . "After the noise, I'd say that the thing that has impressed me most about Santa Fe this time is the fact that the town seems to be pulling together. You seem to have come to a realization of keeping Santa Fe not 'Different,' but itself. . . ." "Restore the portales around the plaza," I suggested. "No—restore the original wall around the town. 'The Only Walled City in America'—that phrase in itself would be worth a million dollars a year."

AUGUST 1928

RECITAL BY TSIANINA

A concert that was unique and enchanting was given at the Los Alamos Ranch School by Tsianina, assisted by Mrs. Adamson from Raton. The boys listened, spellbound, to the music, and all who were fortunate enough to be Mr. Connell's guests were thrilled with Tsianina's glorious voice. Her repertoire is as extensive as that of any singer, but because of what it means to her people and because of her ability to make it live as no white singer could, she is devoting her programs solely to the music of the Indian. Everything connected with Tsianina is interesting—

her magnetic personality, her physical beauty—but not the least interesting is the fact that she is the only Indian woman invited by the Secretary of the Interior to serve on an advisory council investigating Indian affairs.

NOVEMBER 1930

NAVAJOS AT PLYMOUTH

Pray for Rain Near Site of Pilgrim Landing to Keep Pledge to Tribe

The *Boston Evening Transcript* of November 1 carried the following item of interest:

An impressive ceremony, never before enacted here, the sprinkling of corn pollen upon the waves, will take place Sunday afternoon in Plymouth, when the three Navajo Indians, who are attending the fifth exhibition of Craftsmen-at-Work, will be taken to the landing place of the Pilgrims by Cyrus Dallin, the sculptor, to carry out a pledge given to their tribe when the three craftsmen left Coolidge, New Mexico, a week ago.

On the shore, near Plymouth Rock, Deni Chili Bitsui, medicine man of his tribe, whose religious "sand painting" at the exhibition is one of the principal features of this year's show, will pronounce the incantation, while he and Kinnie Bogay Dadoni, worker in silver, and Yeil Habah, the weaver, stretch their hands toward the sky and let the pollen trickle through their fingers to the surface of the tide.

This ceremony, as explained by Berton I. Staples, patron of Navajo arts and crafts who accompanied the Indians here as interpreter, for they speak no English, is one reserved only for such rare excursions as the desert dwellers make to the unfamiliar sea coast. Mr. Staples, after nineteen years' residence among the Navajos, like the Indians themselves, carries a small prayer bag or leather pouch containing the bright yellow dust held sacred to the Great Spirit.

For the group planning to make the trip to Plymouth by automobile, Mr. and Mrs. Dallin will meet these guests at the sculptor's Arlington studio Sunday morning. From there the party will go to Plymouth, to the Harlow House, where refreshments will be served. Then the Indians and other guests, including many of the craftsmen who are exhibiting at the Hotel Statler show, will go to see the Dallin Massasoit. Following this, the party will go to the beach, where the Navajos will sprinkle the pollen on the waves.

APRIL 1937

BEAUTIFUL CONCERT FEATURES ORGAN DEDICATION

Nearly a thousand people filled the St. Francis Auditorium Sunday afternoon, April 5, to hear Bernard Helfrich demonstrate the range and beauty of tone of the great $35,000 pipe organ given the School of American Research by Mr. and Mrs.

James Graham NcNary. . . .

Director Edgar L. Hewett of the school briefly and happily expressed the gratitude of the institution and community to the NcNarys for this princely gift. The
museum, from the Greek derivation of a temple of the muses, sought to be, he said,
a real shrine of the fine arts, the architecture of the past, painting, and scripture;
and now music, hitherto somewhat neglected. "Our plan," said Dr. Hewett, "is
to have regular Sunday concerts, which will be enjoyed by those visiting the building; not necessarily seated in the auditorium, as this noble instrument will be heard
equally well all through the building."

SEPTEMBER 1941

INDIAN LANGUAGES BECOME "CODE"

The classic World War I trick of using Indians speaking their own language as
"code" transmitters is again being used in the Army, this time during the great
summer maneuvers in the south, says *Science Service*. Three units of the 32nd
Division have small groups of Indians from Wisconsin and Michigan tribes, who
receive instructions in English [and] put them on the air in a tongue intelligible only
to their listening fellow-tribesmen, who in turn retranslate the message into English at the receiving end.

The Indians themselves have had to overcome certain language difficulties, for
there are no words in their primitive language for many of the necessary military
terms. In one of the groups, ingenious use was made of the fact that infantry,
cavalry, and artillery wear hat cords and other insignia of blue, yellow, and red
respectively. The Indian word for "blue" thus comes to mean infantry, "yellow"
means cavalry, and "red" means artillery. The Indian word for "turtle" signifies
a tank. . . .

JUNE 1944

LAGUNA ENTERTAINS CHINESE FLYERS

The Pueblo of Laguna, fifty miles west of Albuquerque, with a population of
2,686, has over two hundred of its young men fighting in various branches of the
armed services in all parts of the world. Much thought is being given to these men,
comprising nearly ten per cent of the population, now so far away from home.

Recently, the pueblo officials considered a similar situation. They knew that
many young men from far-off China were stationed at Kirtland Field in Albuquerque. . . .They expressed a desire to entertain the Chinese army flyers in their
pueblo, and asked permission to put on a program in their behalf. For several days,
the wires were hot between Albuquerque and Washington. Finally, approval was
received, and the Indians began preparations for their "open house" on Sunday,
May 21. . . .

The Indians performed a number of ceremonial dances. Among these was a beautiful Eagle Dance, a colorful Butterfly Dance, and a sacred old War Dance seldom seen by the public. The Indians felt that the latter was particularly significant, now that so many of their men are again engaged in war.

At noon, the visitors were given a delicious dinner which the pueblo women had prepared and which they served, cafeteria fashion, in the council hall. There were many traditional foods of the Lagunas, including corn-on-the-cob, meat stew, fried bread and bread baked in the conical out-door ovens, beans, chile, salmon, macaroni, fresh vegetable salad, rice—a gesture to the Chinese—and dessert.

About two o'clock, a formation of ten four-motored Liberator bombers flew over the pueblo and saluted the gathered throng. . . .

SEPTEMBER 1944

FIESTA COSTUME TEA AT ART MUSEUM

One of the most attractive events of the year in the art gallery was the Fiesta Costume Tea, an official event of the Santa Fe Fiesta, regularly held two weeks before the main program. . . . At the tea, authenticity of costumes is stressed; particularly featured were native costumes of Latin-American countries most closely associated with the traditions of fiesta. Other native costumes as well as old-time Western attire were modeled, including the showing of Chinese costumes by the well-known Chinese family, the Parks, of Santa Fe. . . .

The patio was especially well-adapted to a charming effect as the models paraded across the grass before the audience seated under the surrounding portal. Music was furnished by La Fonda orchestra. Jacques Cartier staged the procession and planned the various dance groups in costume to be interspersed through the parade of 100 models. He himself gave solo dances during the serving of the tea preceding the modeling.

AUTUMN 1962

From "1910 in El Rito De Frijoles" by Neil M. Judd:

. . . Beauregard and I occupied a suite of half a dozen such lodges or rooms in Snake House, highest of all, thinking we would be safe from interruptions. But, to our surprise, when Charles F. Lummis and his son arrived . . . , they took up residence in a suite just around the corner from our retreat. At that time Lummis was convinced, along with Thomas A. Edison, that no man needed more than three hours' sleep a night, so he built a small fire outside his cavate room at eleven o'clock and played his guitar until four when he retired, unmindful of the fact we working men had to be at a 7:00 o'clock breakfast and ready for work at 7:30. . . .

The Director [Dr. Edgar L. Hewett], never one to give free rein to young appetites, had driven a tight bargain in contracting meals for the summer camp. As I recall, each of us was allowed three thin pancakes and ham gravy for breakfast. We never did learn who got the ham. All we got was the gravy, and it was thin too. If those pancakes had been square-cut they could have served as cigarette papers.